GLASNOST

Gateway to World Revival

Ralph
Mann

Glasnost: Gateway to World Revival

Ralph Mann
Mission Possible Foundation
P.O. Box 2014
Denton, TX 76202

Copyright © 1989 by Ralph Mann
Printed in the United States of America
ISBN: 0-88368-212-5

Unless otherwise noted Scripture quotations are taken from the *New International Version* copyright © 1973, 1978, 1984, International Bible Society and used by permission. Scripture quotation marked *TLB* are taken from *The Living Bible*, copyright © 1971 by Tyndale House Publishers, Wheaton, Illinois, and are used by permission.

Contents

Preface

The problems in attempting such a book as *Glasnost: Gateway to World Revival* are obvious:

1. The figures and data listed become obsolete almost the moment they're written.
2. One can be overwhelmed by the details and miss the emphasis of the subject.
3. With such broad based subject areas, the author is forced to rely heavily on indirect sources of information rather than personal knowledge.
4. Although I've tried to emphasize the consistency of principles and issues, it's easy for the reader to become caught up in specific details and figures that are subject to change.

Finally, I am indebted to a number of people who provided me valuable time and resources through research, typing, and commentary. One worthy of special mention is Henry Kurth of Lebanon, Missiouri, who rendered keen insights and credible counsel in difficult areas.

Ralph Mann
Denton, Texas

Part One
Gateway to Change

1

The Decade of the 90s

On October 1, 1988, General Secretary Mikhail Gorbachev assumed the role of President of the U.S.S.R.

At approximately the same time, one hundred Soviet Pentecostals from around the Soviet Union suddenly began appearing in Vienna, Austria, enroute to refugee camps in Italy—there to await political asylum in western countries. By December 1988, the average exodus was 150 per week—the direct result of Gorbachev's new policy of glasnost.

Immigration officers in the United States predict 6,000 Soviet Pentecostals alone will be processed during 1989. Some 50,000 more are said to await processing. Baptist and other evangelicals, along with increased quotas of Jews, Armenians (also Christian), and Germans (mostly Lutheran and Mennonite), are expected to follow.

For these and other humanitarian efforts, Gorbachev now faces the world as a hero of human rights. In addition, he is considered the architect of world peace for his arms control proposals and the signing of the INF Treaty.

As Western Europe and the United States relax in an atmosphere of reduced nuclear tension, one nation, however, remains skeptical—*Israel.* In fact, the Jewish people consider Gorbachev and his new policies their greatest threat to national security. As other nations applaud the Soviet leader for his peace and human rights initiatives, this tiny Mid-East nation prepares for war.

What do Israel's leaders know that the Church hasn't yet discovered? Don't Christians, as well as Jews, read the Old Testament prophecies? If so, why isn't the Church reacting with the same degree of alarm and preparedness?

Are Gorbachev's accomplished diplomatic overtures so deceptively effective that political and spiritual leaders alike cannot see the handwriting on the wall? Do only an enlightened few recognize glasnost as satanic in origin, supernatural in character, and catastrophic in conclusion?

What will happen if the world wakes up too late?

Events Set in Motion

What is Gorbachev's true objective? Is he a man of peace? Or does he seek to gain world trust to bolster the purposes of a faltering Communist Party?

If so, what would be Gorbachev's next step? Let me suggest a possible scenario for the next few years.

—After gaining worldwide acclaim for allowing Christians and Jews to leave the Soviet Union, Gorbachev turns his attention to the Republic of South Africa. To bolster his world image as a man of peace, he moves to correct the appalling wrongs in that racially-torn country. Led by U.S. liberals and Soviet peaceniks, who are supported by the "religious" structures of the world, this civil rights movement brings tremendous worldwide pressure to bear. As a result, the South African government falls.

—Although a respected world leader outside the Soviet Union, Gorbachev's domestic and economic reforms fail miserably. As a result, the Soviet masses rise up against him in vicious backlashes. Because of these domestic crises

and certain outside influences, Gorbachev is forced to make drastic foreign policy decisions. In an effort to stabilize his position at home and to maintain favor with allies around the world, he makes desperate economic/military commitments with Islamic oil kingdoms—specifically Iran.

Gorbachev's worldwide support and image, however, carry him through the domestic crises that continue to develop within the Soviet Union. His new alliances provide the Soviets with the necessary hard currency to implement feeding programs, provide housing, and upgrade medical care in order for Gorbachev to stay in power.

At the same time, the Soviets' new economic partners— the militant Shiite Moslems coupled with an anti-Semitic Europe—begin to dominate the policies of Gorbachev both at home and abroad. As a result, the Soviet Christian and Jewish communities bear the brunt of criticism for the domestic chaos. A new, more severe wave of religious persecution sweeps over the communist world.

—In Central America and Mexico, Marxist inspired rebellions to ''right civil wrongs of oppressive societies'' become more active. The United States is forced to take defensive action against these forces and their bases in Cuba. Such military action stretches the U.S. defense budget to the limit and eventually affects military commitments to our allies in Europe. As a result, Western European nations are left vulnerable to Soviet attack.

At the same time, violent anti-Semitism spreads throughout the world, and Israel is made the scapegoat for the world's economic and political problems. The Jewish nation, constantly the primary enemy of the Soviet-Islam coalition, is invaded again. This attack triggers the biggest conflict yet—World War III.

This devastating war brings severe, but limited, destruction around the world. Finally, God supernaturally intervenes to deliver the nation of Israel. The Soviets, in spite of their sophisticated weaponry, are defeated.

After the war, the United States struggles to recover from the financial and physical destruction. Now with limited resources, her weakened condition results in diminished status as a world power.

—Gorbachev's renown as a peace proponent and spiritual leader dominates the decimated world. His world Jewish conspiracy is seen by New Agers, Moslems, peace proponents, and Asiatics—now in a world majority—as a justifiable attempt to rectify spiritual wrongs.

Now with a weakened U.S. church and an American government of limited political influence, world power alignments shift. The United Nations moves to Europe, and Jerusalem becomes a U.N. city where world religions are headquartered.

Out of fear, peace becomes the priority issue. To preclude total nuclear destruction between the superpowers, new compromises and international agreements are made among nations. A coalition is formed between the People's Republic of China and Japan, along with an amalgamation of other nations including a united Korea, India, Indonesia, and the Soviet Union. As a result of the economic strength and vast population of the Asiatic nations, the Far East becomes the center of global power.

—Into this world of a devastated church and immense satanic activity, God pours out His Holy Spirit. A tirade of miracles, signs, wonders, and spiritual happenings results in mass conversions around the world. Believers rise up with renewed boldness and commitment to witness and evangelize all nations before Jesus' return.

Is It Too Late?

Where are we today in this scenario? Will tomorrow's headlines read, "Gorbachev Wins Nobel Peace Prize"? or "South Africa Collapses?" It makes little difference.

The crucial question now is: *Can the scenario be changed?* Is there any hope? Can the forces already set in motion be stopped and reversed? By a political entity? Or an economic movement? Will an ideological consensus help?

Is it too late? If glasnost and perestroika fail, will the slide become irreversible, making global disaster imminent?

Most Americans have never experienced war, hunger, or maximum discomfort. In fact, simply considering the reality of such devastation for the United States is unthinkable—even against our "Christian" theology.

Yet God is on the throne, and his priority is *not* peace and prosperity at any cost. His goal today is the same as it has been since creation—to bring mankind to a saving knowledge of Himself. To that end, physical circumstances are simply spiritual tools.

The decade of the 90s turns completely on what happens within the Soviet Union. And the only answer is spiritual. Only massive spiritual repentance from among the Soviet people can develop a grass roots movement strong enough to effect change in the political direction of our world.

How can that happen in an atheistic nation oppressed for generations by spiritual and political forces? What could bring about such a radical change that events in the Soviet Union—and around the world—would be altered?

More important, is there a way for me, for my church, to be effective in changing the destiny of the world?

To answer these questions, you and I of the Church in America must be like the sons of Issachar, "who understood the times" and knew what they should do (1 Chronicles 12:32).

2

Communism: Time for a Change

Crop failures year after year.
Long waits in unending food lines. Empty grocer's shelves.
A thriving black market.
Devastating earthquakes. Bureaucratic red tape delays relief supplies.
Years on waiting lists for a small apartment. Husbands and wives forced to live apart.
Hundreds killed in uprisings among ethnic groups. Demands for more local control.
Discontent abounds.

Mikhail Gorbachev and the Soviet leadership of this decade face a domestic crisis of unparalleled proportions. Communist ideals, in place for decades, have experienced dismal failure in coping with today's political and economic environment.

In his best-selling book *Perestroika: New Thinking for Our Country and the World,* Mikhail Gorbachev reiterates that the Soviet Union finds itself in a struggle to survive as a serious nation. For this reason, he says, the country is too weak and vulnerable from massive internal problems to have foreign policy objectives.

Even Presidents Reagan and Bush agree with him.

New Policies

Now entrenched in a ten year policy of reform and "openness," Gorbachev has made commendable strides toward convincing the free world that the Soviet Union is non-aggressive and solely concerned with a desperate domestic problem of a failing economy.[1]

With his new policies of *glasnost* (openness) and *perestroika,* (restructuring) Gorbachev proposes fundamental changes in the ideology and practice of Soviet communism. The Russian people wait with careful anticipation, and the world looks on amazed at Gorbachev's unprecedented reform measures.

Is the age of the all-knowing, all-powerful Marxist-Leninist party over? Is the almost mythical image of the Communist Party—originated by Lenin, made rigid by Stalin, and held sacred by millions—rapidly disappearing?

An avowed atheist, Gorbachev's faithfulness to the ideology of Marxism seems inconsistent with hopes for peace and freedom. In the words of *Time Magazine* writer George J. Church, "He could be the most dangerous adversary the U.S. and its allies have faced in decades—or the most constructive."[2] In spite of his flexibility and experimentation, Gorbachev's anti-American attitude, temper, and pride are cause for concern among some U.S. officials.

Are Gorbachev's new promises of ideological openness and economic restructuring compatible with the history of oppressive communist constraints? Can the ideology of Marx and Lenin be integrated with Gorbachev's openness?

In order to fully grasp the radical nature of Gorbachev's glasnost policies and perestroika proposals, the fundamental nature of communism must be understood.

The Perfect Society

Karl Marx and Friedrich Engels, in their 1848 work titled *Manifesto of the Communist Party,* laid the foundation for the communist rule that would follow seven decades later.

In communism the social, political, and intellectual institutions are considered the inevitable, unchangeable results of a centralized and socialistic system of production. Other influences, such as religion, tradition, custom, and genetic inheritance, are considered secondary to economic determinism.

Marx and Engels labeled the family as "an institution of capitalism" and, therefore, inconsistent with socialist ends. The term for the family is "public prostitution."[3] Parental concern for the health, education, and spiritual well-being of their children is given no place in a Marxist society.

Marxists believed communism could design an environment that would develop perfect character in the people. This character would be immune to emotion, greed, and self, thus creating a perfect, universal man.

Not only skilled in every working trade, the universal man would be immune to crime, war, child abuse, drug addiction, racism, and all other vestiges of the prevailing economic system of capitalism. Marxists assumed that once capitalism had been destroyed, all anti-socialist attitudes and activities would disappear. A society of abundance, harmony, joyous creativity, and peace would emerge.

The Bolshevik Revolution

What prompted Marx and Engels to create such a man-centered, socialistic philosophy? A look back into Russian history gives us some clues.

Before World War I, the Russian people were subjected to a czarist system based on elitism. The common man shouldered the most difficult burdens and reaped few rewards. The intelligentsia of that time, however, produced noteworthy achievements in the arts, mathematics, and medicine. As the war continued and these intellectual advances became less common, the seeds of Marxist revolution ripened.

The Bolshevik Revolution initially began after military mutinies and political upheaval forced Czar Nicholas II to abdicate the throne in February 1917. A provisional government established in Petrograd proclaimed civil liberties and generous reforms while continuing its efforts in the world war.

Despite being emancipated, the serfs continued to live in medieval conditions. Any positive changes were slow and painful.

At this crucial time in history, Lenin gathered a unique group of individuals who possessed great intellect, ability, courage, dedication, and a clear vision of Marxist ideology. If Lenin had been a Christian, he would have been called a revivalist. He insisted on bringing revival to Russia through the premise that every member of the Communist Party must be a devoted, sacrificial worker. Even the name given to the communists (Bolsheviks) meant "majority," reflecting upon the massive involvement of all the communists.

Most of Lenin's band had forsaken a life of privilege and ease for the deprivation and danger of revolutionary activity. Dedicated to eliminating the vices caused by capitalism, these Marxists sought to create socialistic conditions that would ultimately result in the promised "new man."

Rather than reflect positive change, however, the revolution actually worsened the conditions of most ordinary Russians, at least from 1918 to the 1950s.[4] The murder and exile of the country's elite stifled its creative powers and destroyed the intelligentsia. During the decades that followed the revolution, the communists imprisoned, exiled, or murdered the successors to these Russian artists and scholars. This sterile and repressive new political system was worse than anything experienced under the czars.

The economic ignorance of Lenin and his comrades also crippled the domestic economy, which had been the most rapidly developing of the European nations before the war. The dismal results of the Leninist revolution were blamed instead on the remains of an ineffective capitalistic system that tainted the society. Communists believed the new man would arise from the new generation being born into the pure and self-perfecting socialist economic system. A community-oriented, unselfish, and productive worker would eventually result.

Stalin's Reign of Terror

Lenin, who was encrypted inside the Kremlin after his death in 1924, is still revered as the heart of Soviet communism. Lenin and Joseph Stalin, his successor, had a combined rule lasting thirty-six years.

Stalin, also a Marxist, believed that the economic system generated genuine character and ideas. Stalin refused to allow this economic determinism to take its natural course, however, opting instead to embark on a reign of terror unprecedented in the history of the modern world.

The most detailed account of Stalin's victims was recently reported in the Soviet press. The weekly tabloid, *Arguments and Facts*, said 15 million people died under Stalin's regime. Mass graveyards filled with human skulls and bones have been discovered at different sites throughout Russia.

Dissident Soviet historian Roy Medvedev records that more than 40 million people were arrested, killed, or otherwise repressed in the bloody political terror of Joseph Stalin. These figures, released for the first time to the Soviet public in February 1989, came as no surprise. Almost every Soviet living today had relatives who suffered under Stalin.[5]

No official figures have ever been given for the number of people imprisoned in gulag camps or killed during this tyrant's rule. Western sources, however, have estimated that an average of seven to eight million people were being held in the gulags in any given year between 1937 and Stalin's death in 1953.[6]

A prominent Soviet economist has stated that 17 million people passed through Stalin's labor camps during his reign.[7] With the population estimated between 158 and 166 million people, over ten percent of all Soviets, including millions of Lenin's colleagues, found themselves in labor camps.[8] Stalin's forced labor camps, however, were a deviation from established Marxist principles.

In addition, an astounding twenty million Soviet citizens died during World War II as compared with three million in Germany and two million in Japan.[9] The U.S. lost 405,399. Many view the relatively large number of Russian deaths as an indirect result of Stalin's methods.[10]

Collectivization Fails

Collectivization began in 1929 when Stalin reversed Lenin's New Economic Policy (NEP). The NEP had permitted the private sale of grain and the operation of small businesses for a profit. Such limited private enterprise diverged from Marxist thinking and had the potential to create capitalists and invite impurity into the system. Lenin believed, however, that those infected could be physically controlled by the police as long as the communists retained dictatorial power over all instruments of the state.

The "profit incentive" actually worked quite well from 1924 to 1929. Food production was stepped up, and the Russian standard of living increased. In reversing Lenin's NEP, Stalin eradicated the farmers and small businessmen who had profited from those policies. An estimated five million families were deported during Stalin's collectivization of agriculture.[11] He classified all who had farmed profitably as "Kulaks" and ordered "the liquidation of the Kulaks as a class."[12]

History records the failure of collectivization. Extremely poor harvests caused grain production to drop by 40 percent.[13] And although Stalin purchased the necessary machinery and equipment to produce one-third of the world exports in 1931 and almost half in 1932, Russia could not even produce a sufficient volume of agricultural goods for her own people. This combination of factors caused wide-scale hunger and famine in the Soviet Union. Untold millions died of famine-related deaths.[14]

Despite Stalin's rhetoric encompassing Marxist economic views, he pursued a cult of personality that was denounced three years after his death.[15] Although adhering to a "basic economic law of socialism," the reality of history indicated Stalin simply pursued the prediction that under socialism, conditions will, and in fact must, improve.[16]

The Spread of Communism

Why didn't the people revolt and demand Stalin's overthrow? Strong police oppression and the reign of terror had rendered most citizens politically paralyzed and unable to rise up in rebellion.

What about the rest of the world? How did other countries view Stalin's diabolical dictatorship? Amazingly, Stalin's policies gained worldwide acceptance and support, allowing him to proceed virtually unchallenged in the communist world. The United States, in particular, voiced little if any protest to Stalin's reign of terror. Victory in World War II brought great prestige and respect to Stalin and the Soviet Union.

By mid-century, communism, despite its obvious failures, had reached a pinnacle in world acceptance. Communism had become an all-encompassing world view, offering ideological answers to the world's problems. Socialists possessed a rather optimistic outlook; with history on their side, the triumph of communism was inevitable.

Within only a few years, Marxist inroads would be made into:

1. The western hemisphere—through Cuba
2. The continent of Africa—through Angola and Mozambique
3. Southeast Asia—through North Korean expansionism and Vietnamese insurgency against the French.

Rather impressive for a small revolutionary movement less than forty years old.

Khrushchev's Secret Speech

The period that followed Stalin has been described as a time of "revolutionary" reform, not unlike, some say, the current Soviet policies and direction.[17]

In the power struggle following Stalin's death, Nikita Khrushchev faced opposition from those who controlled the Soviet police state. Khrushchev neutralized his opponents through the execution of the chief of the Soviet Security Police (KGB). Although a politically guarded secret, the execution forced Soviet leaders to acknowledge the extent of influence and power that Stalin had given the KGB to control the government and the populace.

Khrushchev's regime revealed Stalin's massive crimes, and millions of prisoners were released. When Khrushchev eased restrictions on society, many believed that communist systems could be changed for the better.

Khrushchev's now famous "secret" speech on the subject of Stalin to the twentieth Soviet Party Congress in 1956 is noteworthy. Khrushchev described Stalin as "capricious and despotic of character," whose "persecution mania reached unbelievable dimensions." He also attributed to Stalin "brutal violence . . . barbaric tortures" and the "moral and physical annihilation" of those who opposed him. Stalin's crimes were so gigantic, Khrushchev said, they included the "mass deportations from their native places of whole nations."[18]

With such unexpected response to Stalinist repression, personal freedoms increased and evangelical religion flourished under Krushchev. Despite the rhetoric of the cold war theme so prevalent in the West, life was surprisingly better for most Soviets.

This theoretical change in Soviet ideology distinguished Khrushchev from his predecessor. The result, however, was an ideological struggle between the Soviet Union and China, led by Mao Tse-tung, who was an avowed Stalinist.

In the 1960s, the bitter disputes, threats of war, and ideological accusations fragmented the leftist forces all over the world and diminished their unity. After Mao's death in 1976, the cruelty and oppression of China's Cultural Revolution was exposed and discredited.

A more pragmatic approach to socialist productivity brought further confusion within international movements that had relied on Maoism as the only solution. The U.S., basking in the glow of Marxist confusion, nevertheless had its hands full with Cuba, Khrushchev-phobia in Europe, and the imminent conflict of Vietnam.

In the 1970s, the Soviet Union experienced the uninteresting stability of Leonid Brezhnev. During this time, doctrinal diversification and exploration were unstoppable. The previous certainty that the world would be changed for the better through Marxism now yielded to another frightening alternative: the extermination of humanity through nuclear arsenals.

Communism Today

Seventy years after the Bolshevik Revolution, the world's communist and Marxist forces are more diverse and open-minded and less certain of their beliefs than at any time since

the 1920s. The watchword of the Marxist-Leninist movement, "workers of the world unite," today has a shallow
ring.

The Third World, once the most promising arena for rapid
socialist expansion under Lenin's theory of imperialism, has
showed an amazing lack of interest. Nationalism and strong
religious beliefs (Hinduism, Islam, Buddhism, etc.) often take
precedence, making socialist ideologies ineffective in many
of the poorer nations of the world.[19]

The Stalinist model of a central economic plan—one central source directly allocating producer goods, setting prices
and wages, and deciding the mix of goods and services best
for society—may have worked well in theory at one time.
Today, however, such rigidity in economic principle is hopeless and impractical.

Although history verifies its failure as a world political
and economic system, Marxist-Leninist ideology has been
around for more than 140 years. Communism is probably
here to stay—in spite of the fact that it is clearly antithetical to systems of democracy and free enterprise.

Consider the mandate in the following statement made
by Lenin:

> As long as capitalism and socialism exist, we can-
> not live in peace; in the end, one or the other will
> triumph—a funeral dirge will be sung over the
> Soviet republic or over world capitalism . . . As
> soon as we are strong enough to defeat capital-
> ism as a whole, we shall take it by the scruff of
> the neck.[20]

Is this mandate to exterminate capitalism at whatever cost
being served today? We only have to look at the regimes in
Angola, Afghanistan, the Third World, and Central America
for the answer. Does the vision of advancing the supreme
socialistic society justify men fighting and dying in hot spots

all over the world? Sometimes the answer is no, as in Afghanistan.

The Soviet troop pull-out in Afghanistan, however, doesn't mean that the communists are giving up. Their puppet government has been left intact with full Kremlin support. Pulling out only saves face for the military hierarchy and buys more time for Gorbachev.

World history proves that communism does *not* equal peace. World wars do *not* become obsolete after the triumph of communism.

The blood of the martyrs bitterly confirms that where communists have consolidated control, no country has ever subsequently become noncommunist—even if it takes Soviet tanks (as in Hungary and Czechoslovakia) or Chinese troops (as in Korea) to reassert control.

Will Lenin's mandate one day bring communist insurgents to the shores of *our* country? Or will they be satisfied to tenaciously hold on to previously obtained prizes of nations and peoples?

America Beware

Is Mikhail Gorbachev any different from his predecessors? Perhaps the most important sentence in his speech to the General Assembly of the United Nations on December 7, 1988, provides the answer: "We are not abandoning our convictions, our philosophy or traditions."

Most Americans, however, seem unconcerned, believing there exists little risk of military threat from abroad.[21] Many feel that what is happening in the Soviet Union has little or no social consequence either for the United States or the world.

Yet a cursory reading of today's newspaper reveals that Gorbachev faces many problems: the nuclear issue, environmental concerns, a struggling economy, the shrinking industrial working class, natural disasters, and the overall discontent of the people with communism. Have these created the need for a new kind of response, even perhaps a new Soviet party? Will all these issues leave the Marxist-Leninist with more questions than answers?

Every American must take note of what is going on in the Soviet Union and why. The larger significance of these issues, however, may only raise another concern—the very survival of man himself.

3
Gorbachev: Here Today Gone Tomorrow

Mikhail Sergeyevich Gorbachev was born on March 2, 1931, in the small farming village of Privolnoye near Stavropol in the southern part of the Russian republic. Each year Gorbachev returns to this village to visit his widowed mother in her original one-story brick cottage.[1]

As a young boy, he witnessed the struggle of local peasants during Stalin's collectivization of privately owned farms. Mikhail also knew firsthand the horrors of armed conflict, having lived through the Great Patriotic War. Exposed to extreme famine, death, and destruction, Mikhail became determined at an early age to work for political and social change.[2]

After receiving the Order of the Red Banner of Labor as an eighteen-year-old agricultural worker, Gorbachev entered Moscow State University in 1950 to pursue the study of law. There he became known as an ideological loyalist—one to watch out for should any deviation occur from the Stalinist line that was in vogue at that time. A Komsomol (Communist Youth League) member since age fourteen, he became a Komsomol organizer at the University with the highest recommendation of Stavropol communist officials. At age twenty-one he was made a full party member.

During his university days, Gorbachev became enamored with Lenin. Although recognizing the failures of the socialist system to meet the needs of the Soviet people, Gorbachev nevertheless was attracted to Lenin's ability to adjust his methods while pursuing goals.

Gorbachev's philosophy of Marxism-Leninism is expressed by him in his book, *Perestroika*:

> Many decades of being mesmerized by dogma, by a rule-book approach, have had their effect. Today we want to introduce a genuinely creative spirit into our theoretical work.[3]

Politics, not the practice of law, dominated Gorbachev's interest while working at the university. With responsibilities as a propaganda activist, Gorbachev undoubtedly found it advisable to take a positive public position regarding Stalin's vicious anti-Semitic policies. This last of Stalin's Jewish purges was launched prior to the dictator's death in early 1953.[4]

During law school Gorbachev met and courted Raisa Maximovna Titorenko, a philosophy student one year younger than Mikhail. Married in 1954, the couple lived apart for several months until married student housing became available.

Prepared and Promoted

After graduation from law school in 1955, and unable to get a job in Moscow through local party structures, Gorbachev was forced to return to his hometown region of Stavropol. In less than a year he rose from his first job within the local Stavropol comsomol to its first secretary. Then by 1962, at the age of thirty-one, Gorbachev himself was selecting party members for promotion throughout the entire Stavropol region, an area similar in size to South Carolina with approximately 2.4 million people.

Taking additional courses in agriculture, he became First Secretary of the region at age thirty-nine. During this period Gorbachev expressed interest in the press and developed his communication skills. Locally, his concern for the people and his reputation for incorruptibility and hard work made him a popular party official.

As late as 1978, few people outside of Stavropol had ever heard of Mikhail Gorbachev. But that was soon to change. Because of his position as area First Secretary, Gorbachev was the host official for two local, well-known mineral spas. There he met Mikhail Suslov, then chief ideologist for Leonid Brezhnev and KGB chief Yuri Andropov. Both Suslov and Andropov were discretely disgusted with the corruption and inefficiency of the Brezhnev regime.

When the Communist Party Central Committee Secretary in charge of agriculture died in 1978, Gorbachev was appointed, probably with the approval of Suslov and Andropov. At age forty-seven, Gorbachev became number twenty among all Soviet leaders.

As overseer of agriculture for the entire nation, Gorbachev faced his first economic crisis when the grain harvest fell from a record 230 million tons in 1978 to only 155 million tons in 1981. Despite these severe agricultural problems, Gorbachev was made a candidate member of the Politburo and a full member one year later. At age forty-nine, Gorbachev was twenty-one years younger than the average age of his Politburo colleagues.

It was at this time that Gorbachev began to prepare himself for national leadership through meetings with academic experts in various areas of expertise. He was especially interested in seeking solutions for the ailing Soviet economy. By 1984 Gorbachev was already under consideration to succeed the ailing Andropov as General Secretary.

Gorbachev's appointment as General Secretary and as Politburo member was made in 1985 by a majority of the 307 member committee.

Struggling for Party Leadership

Since coming to power, Gorbachev has taken on the Communist Party in direct confrontation. He has denounced the cruelty of the Stalin era, rebuked the corruption of the Brezhnev era, and swept away one of his outspoken top lieutenants to relative obscurity. Yet Gorbachev still faces serious opposition. In fact, several Central Committee members have hinted privately that the Kremlin leader may face an ouster attempt at any moment.[5]

Although the leaders of such opposition are not publicly known, the anti-Gorbachev forces supposedly enjoy wide grass-roots support among Communist Party and KGB functionaries. Those in opposition not only see their power and positions threatened but are convinced that Gorbachev's reforms threaten the very foundation of the socialist system.

The Central Committee is composed of the country's top officials and has the power at any time to change members of the Politburo (which has day to day operational control over the government), the Secretariat (executive members of Politburo), and the government. While the Central Committee can initiate any economic or governmental reform, it cannot add new members. This must be done only at party congresses usually held every five years.

In June 1988, Gorbachev convened the nineteenth All-Union Conference of the Communist Party in Moscow.[6] The five thousand delegates were assembled to solidify his position of leadership within the party and to neutralize opposition still remaining on the 307 member Central Committee.[7]

In an effort to protect his position, Gorbachev had replaced 40 percent of the current membership at the party congress in 1986.[8] In addition, some fifty-one voting members of the Central Committee have retired, died, or were demoted to jobs that normally would not warrant committee membership.

Since additional lame ducks would develop, Gorbachev risked the Conference. He wanted to work through the local party leadership from each Soviet district as a way of getting his loyalists to Moscow as appointed conference delegates. Yet practically no local leadership changes were forthcoming, leaving many Brezhnev appointees in attendance. In some cases Gorbachev supporters were the ones who drew fire. "Gorbachev proposed the idea of a conference to get rid of the conservatives. Now they are trying to get rid of him," one analyst said.[9]

Sweeping Political Reforms

Under the pressure of initiating political reform first, Gorbachev went all out at the June 1988 All-Party Conference. Proposing some thirty pages of theses, Gorbachev called for sweeping political reforms that would establish a stronger legislature, institute the office of president, and limit elected party officials to ten years in office.

The conference was unprecedented in Soviet and worldwide media coverage. Delegates and party officials engaged in open debate and confrontation. "For the first time since before the First World War, and the early 1920s, some of these things are being debated openly," one veteran Western Kremlin observer stated. "That's really very extraordinary."[10]

Having considered proposals for four days, six resolutions of the conference were submitted to the Politburo and then to the Central Committee for "practical work to implement the decisions of the . . . conference."[11]

The documents, released by the official news agency Tass, called for "reforms of the political system, the democratization of party, state and social life."[12] Proposed political changes included multi-candidate (not multi-party) elections to a new 2,250 member Congress of People's Deputies, which would evidently choose a strong president and full-time parliament of 400 members. This election, held in March 1989, was preceded by a December 1988 review of the 20 million members of the Communist Party, which Gorbachev wants reduced "significantly."[13]

Gorbachev reiterated the purpose of his movement is to remove the party from day-to-day administration of the economy and government. By reducing the party bureaucracy, he hopes to transform the Soviet Union to prevent the repression of the Joseph Stalin years and the corruption and stagnation of the Brezhnev administration.

In trying to evaluate the extraordinary happenings of the conference, former U.S. Secretary of State Henry Kissinger expressed the uncertainty of most observers:

> I ask myself, in part, are we witnessing here an exercise in democracy or are we witnessing a purge of the opponents of Gorbachev, this time by a method that is different from the one they've used before, and I think it's a combination of both.[14]

Arkady Shevchenko, the highest level Soviet defector, is utterly convinced that the process of change in the Soviet Union is irreversible:

> Globally Gorbachev is the first Soviet leader to realize seriously that the base itself is weak. There is an enormous struggle going on against the change, but the serious disagreement is about how fast, how far? No one who replaces him can ever erase the process of glasnost—the trend is going in his direction.[15]

The reforms, despite the difficulties and the resistance they have spawned, are proceeding according to schedule.

Gorbachev's KGB Connection

In addition to his political foes, Gorbachev faces other formidable challenges: a passive public, Brezhnev party "apparatchiks," managers upset by all the reforms introduced, and military commanders who face cut backs in spending and changes in leadership.

In such a situation, the role of the KGB has become crucial. No anti-Gorbachev plotting would be possible without at least tacit support from the vast security police apparatus.

Besides gathering intelligence abroad and guarding the Soviet Union's 37,000 mile border, the KGB's 700,000 employees protect state security internally.[16] Such a pretense enables the KGB to control all aspects of Soviet life while enforcing the Communist Party's political and ideological monopoly.

The KGB's array of political organs not only includes an army of plainclothes police and countless paid informants, but also offices that the agency maintains in every government ministry, major industrial enterprise, newspaper, and cultural and scientific body.

No one is surprised that the KGB is the only state body to have escaped Mr. Gorbachev's criticism and significant reform since he launched his campaign to restructure the Soviet Union in April 1985. Some, saying Mr. Gorbachev owes a debt to the KGB, refer to his tutelage under former KGB head Yuri Andropov. Experts also verify the widespread rumors that Chairman Viktor Chebrikov, the KGB boss at the time of Gorbachev's appointment to General Secretary, clinched Mr. Gorbachev's selection as party leader by threatening to unveil secret, compromising dossiers on the two other Politburo members contending for the job.

Ironically, loosening the controls to achieve a more productive society and economy isn't possible without the full cooperation of the police machine that has effected these controls over many decades. Yet it's obvious that Gorbachev would be asking the KGB to implement a self-destructive reform.

Perhaps this is why KGB Chairman Chebrikov in October 1987 publicly accused obvious beneficiaries of glasnost—cultural figures and journalists—of having come under "the secret services of imperialism trying to discover new loopholes to penetrate our society."[17]

Two weeks later the party's number two man at the time, Yegor Ligachev, Mr. Gorbachev's arch rival, at a meeting of editors, bitterly condemned the two official publications, *Moscow News* and *Ogonyok* for "excessive liberality."[18]

Such a scenario provided the backdrop for Mr. Gorbachev's September 1988 televised visit to the Siberian city of Krasnoyarsk. A day that changed the course of history.

Gorbachev's Power Play

As the Soviet Union and the world watched, the people of Krasnoyarsk openly expressed their anger and displeasure over their govenment's mismanagement of economic affairs.

Armed with the complaints of the people, Gorbachev wasted no time. Moving with the quick precision of a surgeon, the Soviet leader set out to undercut his adversaries.

On Monday, September 26, in the absence of Yegor Ligachev and several others thought to be in conflict with his policies, Gorbachev convened a special Central Committee meeting for Friday, September 30.

To underscore its urgency, Gorbachev called back trusted colleague Foreign Minister Eduard Shevardnadze from a United Nations visit in Washington. In addition, Defense Minister Dimitri Yazov was summoned from India, and Marshall Sergei Akhromeyev, the armed forces chief of staff, flew in from Stockholm.[19]

Gorbachev convened an unusual meeting of the 1500 member Supreme Soviet for Saturday, October 1. Normally giving perfunctory approval to Central Committee decisions, this parliamentary arm of Soviet government meets only twice a year, with the next regular session scheduled for October 27.[20]

Apparently Gorbachev couldn't wait a minute longer. Obviously referring to his recent Siberian trip, Gorbachev lashed out at the Supreme Soviet, stating:

> We need practical movement ahead, a genuine improvement of the situation in all directions of our work, and especially where people's living standards are concerned. People see and understand our problems and difficulties, but they demand more decisive and energetic steps.[21]

In bold moves, Gorbachev reshaped the party hierarchy by terminating four Leonid Brezhnev holdovers from the Politburo, including Soviet President Andrei Gromyko, a veteran of Soviet foreign policy since the days of Joseph Stalin.[22]

Gorbachev reduced the central party bureaucracy by nearly one-half. Yegor Ligachev, reportedly more critical of Gorbachev in recent weeks, was transferred from his job as the party's chief ideologist and the head of the Central Committee's Secretariat to an agricultural post.[23]

Even more significantly, Gorbachev became President as well as General Secretary, replacing Gromyko. A somber Gorbachev made the following statement to the parliament:

> The soviets [government councils] must become the highest authority on their territory and eliminate the shortcomings of stagnation. The party will facilitate the enhancement of the role of the soviets. The soviets will take on their shoulders the major burden of state work. As the situation changes, we must change accordingly.[24]

The next to go was KGB chief Viktor Chebrikov, who was reassigned to a position as party secretary. His new job is to head a new commission (one of six created as a result of the June party conference) on legal affairs reporting to the Central Committee.[25]

Vladimir Kryuchkov, a sixty-three-year-old career KGB officer, became Chebrikov's successor. While having no apparent rank in the senior Kremlin leadership, Kryuchkov has headed the KGB's foreign espionage and overseas operations for the past ten years.[26]

With the western world aghast at such rapid consolidation of power, there remains little doubt who the immediate winner is in this round of Kremlin musical chairs.

A Western diplomat made this observation of the recent Soviet shake-up:

> [Gorbachev] may look like a different breed of Soviet leader, but he certainly demonstrated that he knows how to play the Kremlin power game. He has shown us a side that we always suspected was there, and it is a lesson not to be taken lightly.[27]

"Gorbachev has strengthened his own power over state security," said Robert Legvold, head of the Harriman Institute for Soviet studies in New York. "It's an important step in his consolidation of power."[28]

No Guarantees

What has really happened in the realm of Communist Party politics? Are Gorbachev's measures purely defensive to pre-empt any kind of coup attempt lurking in the background, as the one that toppled Nikita Khrushchev?

Is it a typical muscular ploy of aggressive Soviet politics centralizing power and security for a few regardless of the rhetoric of "democratization" and "openness"? Or is it the expected progression of normal events in dealing with political inefficiency and economic crisis?

Regardless, the results are clear: Gorbachev is in control.

Ligachev and Chebrikov, despite maintaining places of responsibility within the structure, must get with the program of reform or find themselves suffering the brunt of even greater retribution—possibly even banishment—as an example for all local politicians who would stand in the way of Mikhail Gorbachev.

Soviet officials are advising the people on the streets not to doubt the sincerity of the political structure, to be there when they are needed, and to support "glasnost" in its entirety. To all who will listen, Gorbachev is saying the changes are real and they will last.[29]

Despite his overseas popularity, Gorbachev's reforms have brought only slow and insignificant changes to the Soviet people. As a result, the past loyalties of local party officials to the Brezhnev structure of graft, corruption, and party favorites present formidable opposition.

Although such widespread reform opposition within the Soviet Union may be difficult to fathom by Americans familiar with Mikhail's and Raisa's charm and personality, it does suggest that the Soviet propaganda machine has been far more effective outside the country than within.

Reform is critical to Gorbachev's game plan. Without reform, no vehicle exists to effect change or replacement of local party leadership through popular voice. Perhaps Soviet human rights champion and physicist Andrei Sakharov answered for the Soviet people when he stated:

> Today it will be Gorbachev, tomorrow it may be somebody else, and there are no guarantees—everything boils down to one person. It's extremely dangerous for 'perestroika' as a whole and for Gorbachev personally.[30]

Why would Gorbachev take such risks? What has forced this powerful leader to take such drastic and decisive measures? To discover the answer we must go to the source of the Soviet dilemma: the failure of communism.

4

The New Age Messiah?

The week prior to the December 1987 Washington summit with President Reagan, Mikhail Gorbachev used an American television program to gain the favor of the nation. Completely dominating NBC's Tom Brokaw, Gorbachev pushed his own agenda. Issues such as Afghanistan, Soviet Jewry, the Berlin Wall, and human rights became diverted as unnewsworthy to propagate Mr. Gorbachev's message of INF, peace, and cooperation.

That interview changed America's attitude toward Gorbachev and the Soviet Union—a change that will last for years, perhaps for a generation. The very next day an ABC News poll put Gorbachev's popularity at a 59 percent favorable rating, just four percentage points behind the most popular U.S. President ever.[1]

"No Soviet leader has ever enjoyed the level of popularity in this country that Gorbachev has achieved," stated one U.S. survey subsequent to the December 1987, Washington summit.[2] "The guy is a PR genius," remarked one spectator watching Gorbachev work a Washington street crowd.[3] "He out-Reaganed Reagan," said the President's former press spokesman, Larry Speakes.[4]

In one poll, those with post-graduate educations considered Gorbachev better informed than Reagan by a significant margin: 48-23 percent. "No doubt this man *is* different from any previous Soviet leader," Americans generalized.[5]

Good First Impressions

Our nation's leaders responded with an overwhelmingly favorable impression of Mr. Gorbachev. Jim Wright, Speaker of the House of Representatives, spoke with Gorbachev personally in the Kremlin. Upon Wright's suggestion the U.S. use defense funds to feed the hungry rather than for nuclear warheads, Gorbachev was quoted by Wright as saying, "Thank God."[6]

When this story was related to Robert Schuller's Crystal Cathedral congregation in California, listeners inferred that Gorbachev is a spiritual man, a lover of peace for sure, perhaps just like most of us—even a closet Christian. Former President Jimmy Carter, in July 1987, called Gorbachev the "most humanitarian" of the world's leaders.[7]

Billy Graham, who participated in three meetings with Gorbachev in Washington, was greatly impressed with the Soviet leader. The *Dallas Times Herald* carried Graham's evaluation of the Soviet leader:

> There's a great warmth about him. I think he is the first real personality the Soviet Union has had since Lenin. He also understands the modern world better than any Soviet leader I've met.[8]

Tatyana Zaslavskaya, a leading sociologist describes a visit with Gorbachev:

> I sat next to him. It is incredible what power and drive emanate from him. One feels as if it were a strong field of energy. His vitality is extraordi-

nary, and yet, although you feel this tension, he is a good listener and waits for you to finish.[9]

Quite a contrast in personality from past Soviet leaders who have presented a stagnant image to the world.

In this age of baby boomers, however, Soviet ideologues were right on target with Mikhail and Raisa. Now the entire West is familiar with Mr. Gorbachev's carefully developed public image. His suits are pre-ordered from western tailors, and his attractive wife Raisa has a doctorate in Marxism-Leninism philosophy.

The Soviets have carefully portrayed Gorbachev as a national hero, an accepted world leader, and a reformer. Their well executed, worldwide program of information and disinformation has been a success. The resourceful Soviets have used diplomats, pastors, artists, athletes, businessmen, and performers to achieve their ends. Even Dr. Andrei Sakharov, a Nobel Peace Prize winner now living in Moscow after years of forced exile in Gorky, helped to propagate Gorbachev's image.

A Change in Policy

Years of training and preparation have now enabled Mr. Gorbachev to take on the very best head to head—and win.

Even President Reagan, standing within the walls of the Kremlin fortress with Mr. Gorbachev smiling at his side, recanted his previous condemnation of the Soviet Union's "evil empire." When questioned by reporters about his scathing remark made seven years earlier, Reagan stated, "You are talking about another time, another era."[10]

The change in policy statements and positions was a massive redirection from earlier presidential speeches. "What we have decided to do is talk to each other rather than about each other, and it's working just fine," the President remarked at the Moscow summit.[11] "We think of you as friends," Reagan said.[12]

This most anti-communist U.S. President in history actively went on to support Mikhail Gorbachev's battle to reform Soviet society. By personally approving the delay of the Moscow summit one week, Reagan hoped to help the Soviet leader. By scheduling the summit closer to the called emergency session of the June 28, 1988 Communist Party Conference, Gorbachev's chances of staying in office were greatly enhanced.

"I think the improvement in U.S.-Soviet relations and arms control will probably be remembered as Reagan's greatest achievement," said Senator Warren Rudman, (R-VT). For a conservative Republican president who as recently as 1983 described the Soviet Union as "the focus of evil in the modern world," Rudman observed, "that's ironic."[13]

Soviet strategists and planners point out that when President Reagan met with Mr. Gorbachev in Moscow in June 1988, it was the first time since World War II that a Soviet leader has been rated more favorably than a U.S. president in European public opinion polls.

A European Bestseller

Gorbachev's book, *Perestroika: New Thinking for Our Country and the World*, has made him the bestselling author in the Netherlands, selling more copies than anywhere else in Western Europe.

Exceeding five printings and 150,000 copies in Holland (population: five million), Gorbachev's book "breathes a kind of optimism," according to Marianne Fieleman of Spectrum Publishing Company, the publisher. "We're a reasonably sensitive people in terms of peace movements and so on," she said.[14]

This seems to be quite a contrast to the street riots and violence the Dutch used to welcome another peace proponent—Pope John Paul II—on his 1985 visit.

Polls indicate that Western Europeans find Gorbachev more trustworthy and credible than President Reagan on arms control. In addition, the West German news magazine *Der Spiegel* chose Gorbachev as its first Man of the Year for 1988 in recognition of his statesmanship.

Europeans, who are supportive of the expanded Soviet role in world affairs, now find fault with U.S. indecision in foreign policy. As they make efforts to reduce tensions with the Eastern Bloc, which most Europeans favor, our allies now wonder about America's diminishing role as a world power.

Christoph Bertran, the chief diplomatic correspondent of the West German newspaper *Die Zeit,* made this observation about the Soviet leader: "He [Gorbachev] is a charismatic leader, and the public likes someone who is a different Russian than we are used to. He also has to fight to get his way internally in the Soviet Union and this adds to the fascination with him."[15]

What has British Prime Minister Margaret Thatcher discovered about Gorbachev? "If he says he'll do anything, he'll honor it." He's "quite different from any other" Soviet leader she's known.[16]

Even the seven Western leaders at the Toronto, Canada, June 1988 Economic Summit broke precedence to say in a "political declaration" that they lauded Gorbachev for perestroika and for improving human rights. The message contained a promise to respond positively to such an "evolution."

With such endorsements one can actually walk the streets of continental Europe and find that international good will and favor is in the camp of the Soviets. Questions, apprehension, and doubt are associated with the U.S., its new president, and upcoming policies. It's a new ball game, and a new player is dominating the game.[17]

Peace Movements and the New Age

Europeans seem to have fallen under the Gorbachev spell, but what about Americans? While most people are content to wait and watch, certain groups are pushing the new Soviet agenda in the United States.

Popular support for Gorbachev in the U.S. comes from 27,000 peace organizations networking throughout the world with other groups to strengthen their base. One such group held a Soviet-American Citizens' Summit in Washington, D.C., February 1-5, 1988. They brought together 100 leading hand-picked Soviet citizens with 450 Americans from all walks of life. Their goal? To find innovative ways to create more favorable relations between governments.[18] Eighteen task forces set up at the conference continue the objectives.

Although most U.S. delegates were from the fields of religion, science, education, journalism, and the film industry, all the Soviet delegates were selected by the Soviet controlled Soviet Peace Committee headquartered in Moscow. The American principal organizational sponsor was the Center for Soviet-American Dialogue (CSAD) of Seattle, Washington, created by Rama Vernon, a New Age peace activist who has made twenty-four visits to the Soviet Union over the past four years.

The basis for bringing Soviet-American "citizen diplomats" together centers on searching for "commonalties," looking for common goals. Rama draws from her extensive background of yoga (meditation) and training in East-West psychology to provide unlimited contacts for the Soviets to work openly without fear of reprisal.

Barbara Marx Hubbard, Program Director of the Soviet-American Citizens' Summit (and a 1984 Democratic contender for the U.S. Vice-Presidency) described her ideas for a series of citizens' summits "to celebrate the whole world as a new world."[19] In 1986, Ms. Hubbard participated in the "World Healing Event." This Moscow affair was designed to usher in world peace and the New Christ, who failed to appear on New Year's Day 1987 despite the psychic energy created by millions meditating on peace worldwide.

With the total endorsement of Soviet authorities, Ms. Hubbard and the Center (CSAD) sponsored a second undertaking in 1987 in Moscow called "The World Instant of Cooperation." Designed to accumulate "psychic energy" through meditation, the New Age term is "social synergy." Barbara Marx Hubbard made the following statement about that event:

> Tears came to my eyes. Oh, yes . . . it's true. The attraction which Soviet and American people feel for each other is the pull of evolution, joining opposing elements together to create a new synthesis. When we learn to work together we will be partners to build new worlds on earth, new worlds in space, new worlds in the human mind.[20]

Following the theory of the German philosopher Hegel, which Karl Marx adopted as "synthesis," the conflict between capitalism (the way things are) and communism (a new idea) inevitably will produce a new synthesis (a new concept arising out of the death struggle between the thesis and antithesis). The synthesis or new concept will be "synergy" or new world enlightenment brought about by collective psychic energy accumulated through meditation by the masses.

The most logical forum for such pursuits? The established religious community. Twenty-four church leaders throughout the District of Columbia were among those who invited one hundred Soviets attending the Washington Soviet-American Citizens' Summit to fill pulpits. Most were non-believers.

Lulling the Capitalists to Sleep

Today everyone wants to get into the act of befriending the Soviets. A former women's editor of a leading newspaper was spurred on by three Soviet visits and the encouragement from a Soviet professor to promote relations between the superpowers. She gathered 2500 delegates from 241 countries in Dallas, Texas, in August 1988, at an estimated cost of $325,000, to confer on "Global peace—from vision to reality."[21]

Dr. Armand Hammer, whose Bolshevik ties began with the Revolution of 1917, has also been involved. In addition, other participants include hundreds of businessmen reputedly led by billionaire Sam Walton, actors, and media celebrities. Even Fred Rogers, of "Mr. Rogers' Neighborhood," has presented ideas on "puppet detente."

Many are concerned that such activities, well-intentioned as they may be, only undermine national sovereignty. These coalitions of specialists, in dealing directly with the Soviet government (through communist controlled agents and institutions), establish international agencies and make deals that blunt the nationalistic policies of the U.S. government.

The words of Soviet ideologist Dimitry Z. Manuilsky, who taught at the Lenin School of Political Warfare, are timely. Yet, he made the following statement in 1930.

> War to the hilt between communism and capitalism is inevitable. Today, of course, we are not strong enough to attack. Our time will come in twenty to thirty years. To win, we shall need the element of surprise. The bourgeoisie will have to be put to sleep.
>
> So we shall begin by launching the most spectacular peace movement on record. There will be electrifying overtures and unheard-of concessions. The capitalist countries, stupid and decadent, will rejoice to cooperate in their own destruction. They will leap at another chance to be friends. As soon as their guard is down, we shall smash them with our clenched fist.[22]

Perhaps former President Richard Nixon's unsolicited advice to President Bush will prove to be prophetic: Deal warily with Mikhail Gorbachev or risk "being taken to the cleaners."[23]

The New World Leader?

"The most spectacular peace movement on record" has already been launched. All they need now is a widespread "religious" revival in the Soviet Union to reawaken a sense of national autonomy and unity. Rejecting biblical Christianity, this religion will involve the new mind—"the ascendance of a startling world view that gathers into its framework breakthrough science and insights from earliest recorded thought."[24]

In effect, the Soviets need a new "openness" to one another that spans religion, politics, and even philosophy. The untapped powers of the mind must be stimulated and awakened. Religious beliefs are to be exchanged for the recognition that we are all "gods," interconnected with a unity of consciousness that centers on new world order, peace, and individual self-development.

Soviet General Chairman Mikhail Gorbachev makes his priority as a leader perfectly clear in his book, *Perestroika*. He states implicitly that his "new thinking" is not limited to his country but is for the world. Where does Gorbachev place his emphasis? His words may surprise you:

> Today our main job is to lift the individual spiritually, respecting his inner world and giving him moral strength.[25]

Strange words for a politician or an economist. Spirituality, "inner" world, and moral strength are terms of religion or spiritual interest—buzz words of a new kind of revolution quietly taking over the cosmos. Akin more to mysticism than violence—words rather than guns. Some call it a "consciousness revolution" out of which Scripture says will emerge a coming world ruler, the Antichrist.

Claimed as a savior of the Soviet Union by most intellectuals, a hero by Soviet Christians, and the New Age Messiah by many in the West, Gorbachev's popularity is not limited to uninformed third world populations.

Time magazine evaluated Gorbachev as a "symbol of hope for a new kind of Soviet Union; more open, more concerned with the welfare of its citizens and less with the spread of its ideology and system abroad."[26] Here is a man who, in one commentator's words, presented himself as the leader the world had been seeking in the peace movement for the past forty years—ever since Hiroshima.

Miracle Man

With his eye on the next century, Gorbachev has been described as "the most formidable political presence of our era"[27] and the most fascinating leader since Franklin Roosevelt or Winston Churchill. Unfortunately, that makes all Soviet hopes for reform dependent on Gorbachev personally—not on institutions or other leaders.

"We need this man, we depend on him absolutely," said Mikhail Ulyanov, a well-known figure in the theater and cultural politics. "We want limited terms of office, but not for Gorbachev. Not yet, I don't think we can afford that."[28]

Gorbachev has risen from provincial austerity to an undeniably competent world leader in less than four years. As the first Soviet head of state to address the United Nations General Assembly, his influence on a world desperate for leadership has spread rapidly.

Asked to explain such an amazing transition, U.S. Soviet expert George Kennan admitted there was no simple explanation. "You know, I really cannot explain it," Kennan recently said in a television interview. "There are only partial explanations.... I think he's rather a miracle."[29]

"The [U.S.-Soviet] relationship is only as strong as Gorbachev himself" said Christopher Coker, a specialist in East-West relations at the London School of Economics. "We are putting a lot of faith in him."[30]

Yet "faith" is a religious word. Is this man Gorbachev more than a politician, an economist—a well-intentioned reformer? Could he be the New Age Messiah to whom the world will turn to save it from destruction and bring world peace?

Jesus Christ, the confessed Messiah of the first century, said that His Kingdom was not of this world. For a New Age Messiah, however, kingdoms will have both boundaries and subjects. But before Gorbachev can take on the world, he must first bring peace and order within his own borders.

5
The Dilemma of Diversity

Recent newspaper headlines reflect the growing turmoil among ethnic groups in the Soviet Union.

NATIONALISTIC UPRISING IN BALTIC STATES

MASSIVE DEMONSTRATIONS IN SOVIET GEORGIA

ARMENIAN-AZERBAIJAN RIOTING CONTINUES

One-half of the Soviet's 600 popular disturbances since early 1987 have been attributed to ethnic issues. "Major nationalist demonstrations" took place in nine of the fifteen Soviet republics in 1988[1] and continue unimpeded in 1989.

Diverse people create diverse problems, and Gorbachev certainly has his hands full these days. The peculiar dilemma of the Soviet Union centers on its multi-ethnic composition.

Extending across eleven time zones, with fifteen Republics divided into 130 territories and regions, divided further into 2,970 districts—with thousands of towns and urban settlements—political structures alone make change impractical. When a population of 283 million people converses in over 120 main languages (75 percent speak Russian), with 65 languages being literary,[2] political persuasion, much less unity, becomes impossible. The result—political indifference, even apathy.

Such apathetic resistance to "perestroika" need not be open opposition to undermine Gorbachev's reform movement. The lack of change itself is harmful enough because it keeps traditional controls in place.

Yet, open criticism of Russian policies by non-Russians is often interpreted as "stabbing perestroika in the back," as Gorbachev accused the Armenians in February 1988.[3] When violent, public demonstrations are used to express a grievance, the authorities always take a pro-Russian stance.

Solving Ethnic Tensions

Although the nationality issue has been a problem for every Soviet leader since Lenin, it is a particularly stressful issue for Mr. Gorbachev. Millions of ethnic non-Russian citizens of the U.S.S.R. wait hopefully for some clarification of Soviet policies related to ethnic tensions, regional problems, and nationalistic movements.

Perhaps that position became more clarified by Gorbachev in his three and one-half hour speech to the five thousand delegates at the June 1988 nineteenth Soviet Communist Party conference held in Moscow. While advocating broader economic rights for ethnic minority governments, Gorbachev emphasized that party leadership will not tolerate efforts to redraw boundaries, an obvious reference to the Armenian-Azerbaijani conflict.

In effect, Gorbachev rebuked an ethnic minority group (the Armenians) for raising political solutions as a means of ending ethnic problems. Apparently, ethnic groups cannot expect government intervention to protect their minority interests.

The government's stance disappointed half of the Soviet population. Gorbachev's lack of response just confirms his track record. Past policies have seemingly allowed more public criticism of the Soviet bureaucracy, but no substantive policy changes have ever taken place.

Former National Security Advisor Zbigniew Brezezinski calls the Soviet nationalism issue "the Achilles' heel of the Soviet System." "Serious problems to deal with," said William Webster, the U.S. director of Central Intelligence Agency.

Why is the issue of diverse ethnic groups such a particular obstacle for Gorbachev? Because it exposes glasnost for what it is and is not.

Openness: How Far Will it Go?

Gorbachev's constant touting of "glasnost" (openness) as the basis for all good accomplishments within Soviet society presents special concerns relating to minority interests. Soviet citizens have been encouraged to bring alleged deficiencies and criticisms of governmental policies to the attention of authorities. Such openness, however, eventually confronts the controlling interests in each of the Soviet Republics.

The more people (including Gorbachev) speak of redress of grievances the more encouragement ethnic minority groups receive to speak out. That is *consistent* with "glasnost." Yet ethnic Russians have long dominated party apparatus and suppressed all other ethnic groups. Adverse criticism of the way the Russians do business simply invites a defensive posture of Russian nationalism/chauvinism to develop. That is *inconsistent* with "glasnost."

The question is simply: To what extent will the Russians share *political* reform with ethnic minorities? Mr. Gorbachev, speaking for the ethnic Russian controlling interest, evidently has said, "not very far."

Mr. Gorbachev is also having particular problems because of recent concessions to existing religious interests. Again, under "glasnost," Gorbachev has tolerated a return to religious ideology.

All the major ethnic minority groups have religious foundational principles that underlie the existence of each group.

1. The Baltic area, the Ukraine, and Armenia have strong Christian ties.
2. The six south central Asia republics are almost exclusively Muslim.
3. The Jewish Autonomous Region and 1.8 million scattered Jews still embrace their cultural and religious traditions.

Encouraging religious pursuits only foments nationalism. Most minority groups lead simple lives centered around a strong identification with local religious tradition and culture. To satisfy their personal and community needs, minority groups depend on their religious interests rather than looking to the state.

The Soviet Communist Party apparatus is legally agnostic/atheistic and practically Russian. Until that structure changes, or personnel entrenched from within the Brezhnev dynasty retire and are replaced by reform-minded followers of Gorbachev, glasnost will be empty words to ethnic minorities.

One wonders how the Leninist exhortation of "He who is no atheist and fails to fight against religion is no Marxist" fits into the perestroika/glasnost policies of Gorbachev.

The Baltic Battles

With no clear winners in sight, a policy of uneasy compromise seems to be in vogue in much of the Soviet Union. The result: a certain venting of nationalistic sentiment is allowed, then the Communist Party cracks down on anyone attempting to organize nationalistic movements.

Nowhere is such a policy more evident than in the Baltic republics of Estonia, Latvia, and Lithuania. Open demonstrations were held by hundreds of thousands of patriots in these countries on August 23, 1988, to mark the forty-ninth anniversary of the secret pact between Adolf Hitler and Joseph Stalin. That pact described the three Baltic states as a Soviet sphere of influence, later becoming Stalin's justification for sending in troops in 1940 to forcibly incorporate the states into the Soviet Union.

Local police arrested some one hundred people in a September 29, 1988, massive demonstration in Vilnius, Lithuania. Soviet reaction was consistent with previous smaller groups that routinely were dispersed, arrested, or beaten even in front of western television crews.

With all three Baltic states heavily anti-Soviet, Gorbachev has no short-term solution to restore Soviet confidences. Out of a population of 1.5 million, 900,000 native Estonians live in Estonia. Despite military inductions, imprisonments, and deportments, Baltic nationalism causes extreme problems for Moscow.

In a bold move on November 16, 1988, Estonia declared their economic independence from the Soviet Union. Only days later, however, a parliamentary committee found their bid for sovereignty at odds with the Soviet Constitution. Gorbachev said Estonians were acting too emotionally, and that the tense, formerly independent Baltic republics would eventually settle down.

Lithuania is seeking similar autonomy. "If there would be a referendum on independence, of course it would pass," said one woman who identified herself as a "Lithuanian patriot, Communist Party member, and staunch supporter of Mikhail Gorbachev." She thought it more realistic, however, to work toward "greater democracy and political rights" within the existing system, she said.[4]

Now both Estonia and Lithuania have established the local language as official and restored the flag of the state.

Moldavia, a republic of 4.2 million people bordering Romania, has made similar demands in demonstrations involving thousands of people in January 1989.

"This morning we know how serious this is," said Tonis Segerkrantz, a twenty-two-year-old Estonian student the day after the Estonian parliament declared its sovereignty from the Soviet Union. "We are waiting now. Just waiting."[5]

Much of the activity centers on Lithuania's Roman Catholic Church, Latvia's Baptist and Pentecostal believers, and Estonia's Lutheran Church.

The Ukrainians

The Ukraine, a hotbed of simmering nationalistic revolt, contains the largest evangelical Christian community within the country, the Uniate Catholics, along with traditional Ukrainian Orthodox believers.

Such an independent culture, expressed for centuries by outstanding writers, educators, artists, and scholars, has been decimated over the past forty years. During that time, an intense Russification program forced the exchange of Ukrainian language, culture, and history for Russian.

To what extent have the Ukrainians resisted Russification? Over one-half of the political prisoners in Soviet camps and prisons are Ukrainian—despite the fact Ukrainians account for only 20 percent of the Soviet population. Ukrainian writer Vladimir Drozd expressed his concerns:

> And I thought, "Why does it have to be me"? You can understand my alarm, and even my fear. Fear for myself, fear for my family. Fear for all of us who can feel their hot breaths on our necks, can see their narrowed wolf-eyes—the eyes of those who do not want the "perestroika" . . .
>
> They get together every evening, sit late into the nights, cursing everything new that has come to our lives. Our every mistake or miscalculation

gives them unbelievable pleasure—"See what your precious reform leads to."

They watch all of us who speak out today in favor of renewing our society, those of us whose souls still live and who feel pain. And they make lists of our names, for when their day comes round again.[6]

Soviet tactics remain the same; only the label given to support the present policy changes.

German Emigres

Of the 26,000 Soviets allowed to emigrate through October 1987, ethnic Germans made up the largest group with about 1500 per month seeking exit visas to West Germany. Ethnic Germans, located within the Soviet Union for two centuries, number two million. Some 75,000 have already left Russia for West Germany.[7]

Still called "fascist," "Fritz," and other uncomplimentary terms in the Soviet Union, they are mostly rural, farm oriented, and politically uninvolved people. Scattered for thousands of miles over the Soviet steppes, in Siberia, and on the plains of Central Asia, the mostly Mennonite, Baptist, Pentecostal, or Lutheran Germans still speak German or a dialect in their homes. Their sense of pride can be found in any local community.

"You could tell where the Germans lived in any village," an old German emigre remarked in West Germany. "The house was better, the fences were neater, there were more flowers, more geese, more hogs."[8]

These Germans represent a powerful minority because of the constant efforts of West German authorities to have them released to their "homeland." The Soviet Union, able to obtain western currency in exchange for the release of German emigres, has felt the political leverage of this ethnic minority.

The Armenian Conflict

Most of the emigres to the U.S., numbering about 1,000 per month, are Armenian. The large burst in Armenian emigration, which has increased from fewer than 247 in 1986 to more than 6,000 in 1987, depicts the unhappy state of affairs in this predominately Christian republic.

Armenia, the smallest of the fifteen Soviet republics, is located approximately one thousand miles south of Moscow and has 3.4 million inhabitants. It has long been a target of Gorbachev's reform movement against corruption.

In February 1988, full scale hostilities developed, causing the deaths of at least thirty-two and perhaps seventy-eight Armenians, with hundreds injured, depending on who you ask. The dispute arose over demands of the 162,000 inhabitants of the Nagorno-Karabakh region located in the Republic of Azerbaijan but on the border with Armenia. Approximately eighty percent of the people in the region are Armenian Christian, but they have been forced to reside in the Sunni Muslim republic since the 1920s when the region was deeded to Azerbaijan.[9]

The Christians demand cessation of discrimination and propaganda by the Muslim government, improvements in health care, more physical benefits, and an end to the lack of education, news, and television programming in the Armenian language. The Armenian demands have resulted in strikes and demonstrations involving hundreds of thousands of people.

The Communist Party newspaper *Pravda* (Truth) acknowledged that "atrocities" had been perpetrated against the Armenian population in Azerbaijan. The Soviet government, to justify their refusal to cede the region back to Armenia, recently asked, "What if other peoples demand satisfaction of their narrow nationalist interests at the expense of others? What would happen to our union of peoples? What would happen to the economy?"[10]

Prolonged strikes and demonstrations involving up to 400,000 people have been met with an unprecedented Soviet curfew backed by thousands of Soviet police, troops, and dogs. The non-violent, Armenian demonstrations in the Nagorno region were met with extreme violence by the Islamic Sunni Muslims. The result? Large numbers of dead and wounded Christians. The bloodshed is a major indication of the Muslims' deep-rooted hostility against any contrary expression of control by either Christians or communists.

Located across the border from Iran, this region is potentially subject to the control of the Ayatollah's radicals. Such a possibility must give nightmares to all reform minded Soviet bureaucrats.

The Muslim Dilemma

Of the 283 million Soviet citizens, some 50 million are Muslims with 75 percent living primarily in the central Asian republics adjoining Iran, Afghanistan, and China.[11] This situation presents the Soviet Union with its greatest dilemma.

With the Muslim birth rate far exceeding ethnic Russian figures, simple arithmetic places the Russians in the minority in less than twelve years. Figured another way, the compulsory Soviet draft, if continued within the armed forces, will place a majority of Muslims among the Soviet troops.

In some respects the six Islamic republics—Azerbaijan, Kazakhstan, Kirgizia, Tajikistan, Turkmenistan, and Uzbekistan—represent a lingering colonial empire. Having struggled for self-autonomy since the 1920s when Russian troops forcibly occupied their territory, they are no strangers to conflict.

Ethnically oriented and intolerant of any religion other than their own, the Islamic republics are known for their extreme prejudice toward all Europeans. Hardly any Christians are known among this Islamic stronghold as these figures show:

14.5 million Uzbeks—twenty known Christians;
7 million Kazakhs—eight known Christians;
3 million Tajiks—less than ten known Christians.
2 million Turkmen—not one single Christian is
known.[12]

A majority of the Moslem population is under twenty-five years of age and very impressionable and teachable. Approximately 90 percent, however, read and write only the local language—not Russian[13]—despite intense Russification programs requiring compulsory study of the Russian language, culture, and history.

The Russification indoctrination has long since yielded to the even more radical voices of Khomeini, Afghani rebels, and other Shiite Moslem extremists.

Afghanistan: The Big Mistake

Shiite Moslem doctrine recognizes no political or geographical boundaries, as the western world has learned from Lebanon, Libya, and Iran. The Soviets have been dealing with this problem since December 1979 when its troops, then mostly comprised of soldiers from the central Asian republics, invaded Afghanistan.

Ethnically and religiously related to their Afghani ''cousins,'' the Soviet Muslim soldiers found their loyalties not just divided but leaning toward their ''enemies.'' When Soviet leaders quickly replaced Muslims with European Russian troops, this only caused greater schism and distrust between the Russians and their communist Afghan comrades. Those in authority began to question the loyalty of the entire ethnic composition.

In addition, the people on the streets back home in Moscow questioned why they should surrender their sons to a war unrelated to a white Russian majority interest. During the nine-year campaign against the Afghan insurgents, 15,000 Soviet soldiers were killed.

In spite of the Soviet pull-out of troops from Afghanistan in February 1989, Soviet involvement continues. Afghan Ambassador Abdul Samad Azhar said he expects the Soviet Union to continue arming his government. He told a news conference,

> We will not only rely on their material support and food supplies in the future, but also on their military supplies and their moral support.[14]

This leaves Gorbachev committed financially and militarily to Afghanistan—a Muslim nation with a communist government. Such a combination in itself defies the ideological principles of both the Muslim religion and Marxist thinking.

The six Islamic Soviet republics are no longer convinced that Afghanistan was only an anomaly. The Soviet Union, having the sixth largest Muslim population in the world, can no longer affirm that ideological principles are meaningless in a Soviet socialistic society.

An Islamic resurgence within the Soviet Union, however, poses the greater threat. With almost 20 percent of the total Soviet population and the birth rate among Islamics booming, the threat of a domineering Islamic radicalism is now reality in the minds of all Soviet leaders.

The Soviet Union is suffering from an ideological crisis in which its own citizens lack confidence in its principles. Yet, without the fear element, no moral affirmation exists to hold the Soviet empire in willing union. As the strong religious uprisings in Afghanistan and Iran creep into the Soviet Central Asian republics, Gorbachev knows he must do something soon. Since only artificial political and geographical boundaries exist, the crisis will only get worse.

That may be why the Soviets responded so quickly to a January, 1989 personal message from the Ayatollah himself. Almost immediately, Foreign Minister Shevardnadze was dispatched to Iran for sensitive talks.

The Soviets now wait to see what direction Iran will go after Khomeini's death. They would like to know how the transition will affect the Sunni leaders across the border and the balance of reorganization in Afghanistan.

Should any aspect of the Middle Eastern Islamic revival centered out of Iran spread to the Soviet Union, serious internal and international tensions will develop. For the most part, Soviet policy in the past has been to placate the Muslims, back out, and leave them alone as much as possible.

Jewish Emigres

While the Muslim community grows in strength *within* the Soviet Union, the Jewish community yearns to find freedom *outside* the power of communist control. The media focuses on a few Jewish refuseniks who are attempting to find self-worth and dignity within the U.S.S.R., but they represent only a token of the small group of 1.5 to 2 million Soviet Jews. Most long to escape the extreme hostility and persecution of the Marxist government who dominates their lives.

Although intensive Jewish emigration began in 1971, less than one hundred thousand have been given exit permits.[15] Leonid Brezhnev, through Jimmy Carter's persuasion, allowed an amazing 51,320 to exit in 1979.[16] The number, however, has declined appreciably ever since. Today 400,000 Jewish people are waiting to leave the U.S.S.R.[17]

Under Gorbachev's administration, only 914 were allowed out in 1986,[18] and 8,155 in all of 1987,[19] far less than the promised figure of 12,000 given by Soviet Foreign Minister Edward Shevardnadze to U.S. Secretary of State George Schultz.[20] In 1988, however, 20,082 Jews were granted exit permits, which was the second highest figure since 1980.[21]

The Soviets released two prominent Jewish activists in 1987. Vladimir Slepak, the "father of the refuseniks," waited seventeen years for his visa,[22] and mathematician Iosif Begun waited sixteen years.[23] In fact, all twelve Jewish prisoners of conscience were released from Soviet camps and prisons in 1987. New Soviet immigration regulations, however, effective January 1, 1987, allow only those Soviet citizens who have parents or children overseas to leave the Soviet Union.[24]

Jewish young adults want to know their "roots," learn about Jewish life, history, liturgy, and achievements of Jews worldwide. But, most efforts take place in locked apartments or houses in utmost secrecy. The zeal to leave, to conquer, to appear indestructible in the face of Soviet oppression, anti-Semitism, and atheism only grows.

Soviet Jews comprise the largest group of Jews outside the U.S. and Israel. Since the inception of the Revolution, they have fought a lack of religious freedom, language training, educational pursuits, and career opportunities. Joseph Stalin was especially aggressive in plotting to exterminate all Jews at the period of the Feast of Purim. His death was an amazing miracle, not unlike the salvation of the Jewish race under Esther. (See Esther 9:20-32.)

A Soviet newspaper recently admitted that Soviet Jews have suffered discrimination for decades and that dictator Joseph Stalin destroyed Jewish culture in the country. This public admission came as Jewish leaders from around the world converged on Moscow in February 1989 to celebrate the opening of the first cultural center for Soviet Jews in more than fifty years.

Nobel laureate Elie Wiesel, who attended the opening, said it's too soon to declare an end to the problems of Jews in the Soviet Union. "Glasnost has taken hold here," said Rabbi Marvin Hier from Los Angeles. "The question will be, can it continue."[25]

The Crimean Tatars

Another national group that has continuously been in the limelight of Soviet oppression are the Crimean Tatars— descendants of the Mongol Tatars, a Muslim Turkic-based race.

In 1944 Stalin ordered the entire Tatar community deported for "treason" and "collaboration" with the German forces while they occupied the Crimean peninsula. The existing autonomous republic was disbanded. Subject to extreme decimation of its ranks, 46 percent died within eighteen months of deportation from the Crimea.[26]

Without a homeland, Crimean Tatars were forced to begin clandestine political action groups that have continued to defy Soviet laws and authorities. In an effort to reclaim their homeland, they hold public demonstrations, meetings, and public campaigns. Although officially "rehabilitated" in 1967, administrative reaction failed to change.

When they were finally given an audience with the Gorbachev administration, the structure refused to allow the Tatars to return to the Crimea. The mandate was clear: no autonomous republic will be allowed to be re-established by the Tatars.

Without a homeland, a language, or a culture, the scattered Tatars still hope one day for their proud and great heritage to be re-established. The words of activist Mustafa Dzhemilev, who himself has been constantly in and out of Soviet camps and prisons since 1970, expresses the strength of the Tatar commitment:

> The authorities, of course, would like it if I finally bowed before their strength and power, reconciled myself to it and limited my requests to saving my own skin. But that will not be . . . No one would ever, under any circumstances, force me to renounce the fulfillment of my duty and obligations, imposed by honor, conscience and national dignity."[27]

In many ways this is the legacy that binds all ethnic minorities—Christian, Muslim, or Jewish; white skinned or brown; Oriental or European; Slavic or non-Slavic—against the Russian bear.

6

The Suffering Soviet Church

Gorbachev's glasnost policy has certainly caught the attention of the world. But is the Soviet leopard really changing its spots? One way to tell is to look at the Soviet Church. The state of Soviet religious freedom provides an accurate picture of what has actually happened since Gorbachev's policy of openness began.

The Russian Orthodox Church recently celebrated one thousand years of Christianity with full Communist Party approval. Quite a switch for a Marxist government that has tried to suppress religion in any republic trying to hold on to its centuries-old practices.

In spite of the oppressive, seventy-year control of the Communist Party over the religious life of the Soviet people, two powerful factors have co-existed:

> 1. The government has exercised unrelenting control and raised obstacles to worshiping freely.
> 2. Religious beliefs and practices have experienced far-reaching revival.[1]

These two principles go hand in hand and know no denominational or traditional boundaries in spite of the religious diversity in the Soviet Union. From Pentecostal to Russian Orthodox, when God is worshiped, suffering is inevitable and revival follows close behind.

The Russian Orthodox Church

The Russian Orthodox Church is said to have suffered more in this century than any other church in religious history.

From 1917 to 1953, an estimated 60 million Soviet citizens were killed directly or indirectly as a result of the Bolshevik revolution. Forty percent were executed by communist officials. Another 66 million were incarcerated in prisons or labor camps.[2] At least half of these two totals were Christian believers, most of these Orthodox, imprisoned for alleged political offenses.

Those who managed to survive their imprisonments were not released until 1953 to 1956. As late as 1976, ten million prisoners remained in Soviet prisons and camps, with 10,000 being political prisoners and 1,000 religious.[3]

Barrett's *World Christian Encyclopedia* describes the persecution suffered by Russian Christians. By 1913, the Russian Orthodox Church alone reached a count of some 87 million members totaling over 80,000 churches and more than 50,000 priests. Immediately after the Revolution, 10,000 priests, monks, and nuns were arrested and executed in 1922. By 1939 only about 1,000 churches remained open throughout the Soviet Union, mostly in the Ukraine, which had only four active bishops and a few hundred priests.

As a result of Stalin's overtures of unity to the church during the war years, the state permitted some 16,000 churches to re-open. The number of churches peaked in 1957 at 20,000, which included about half that were legally registered.

Under Nikita Khrushchev from 1959 to 1963, however, a massive state-orchestrated program of closures was carried out, leaving only 10,000 open churches in 1964. Despite a reduction in extreme harassment, church closings continued, reaching a 1975 low under Leonid Brezhnev of approximately 5,000.

The Russian Orthodox Church, now numbering approximately 7,500 open churches, has strongly been accused of servility to the Kremlin. Accusations of the church being permeated with graft and corruption have shaken its credibility. Today, the church faces internal challenges to remain pure and external challenges to unite the Soviet people as it has in the past.

Overseen and Underground

When Marxism came to power, Orthodox believers were persecuted more severely because of their association with the Tsar. On the other hand, the state extended degrees of religious tolerance—even openness—to the Soviet evangelicals.

Soviet history confirms that with each brief flirtation with freedom, the membership in evangelical fellowships increased proportionally. Since 1944 with the opening put forth through Stalin, an All-Union Council of Evangelical Christians-Baptists (AUCECB) was allowed to form.

This council was designed to drive all Protestant streams into one single river for purposes of control. Later over half of the congregations, comprised primarily of Baptists but also containing Pentecostal and Mennonite, were closed in the Khrushchev purges of 1959 to 1963 to a low of 2,000 churches by 1965.[4]

The AUCECB has seen their church congregations increase by over 300 since 1977, now totaling over 5,500 churches.[5] This is an increase nine times more than the Russian Orthodox Church has been allowed, yet far short in membership numbering approximately 550,000. Despite the generosity of Soviet authorities, most large cities, including Moscow, claim only one official Baptist church.

In order to keep evangelical fellowships open, compromises were made and great dissatisfaction developed within the AUCECB or registered Baptists. In 1961, the Council of Churches of Evangelical Christians-Baptists (CCECB), also known as Reform Baptists, "Initsiativniki" (Action Group), or unregistered Baptists, was formed. This new group protested the Registered Baptist accommodations to state restrictions and opposed the association of Pentecostals in AUCECB ranks.

The CCECB leader, Gennady Khruchkov, is still a wanted man, having lived "on the run" for over twenty-four years. Although small in membership, estimated to be 50,000 in 1,000 congregations, it could easily be triple in size, totally unregistered, and completely "underground." Its leadership, numbering approximately 200, has over the years suffered boldly for their faith, creating strong biblical examples for their membership of mostly young people.[6]

Pentecostals, Mennonites, and other evangelicals, if not content to fit in with Baptist structure and controls, have been forced to form independent groups. They meet outside the control of the AUCECB but with permission of local authorities (autonomous), or they become "underground" groups totally without the sanction of authorities.

No Altar Calls

Lenin's original constitution of July 1918 permitted the dissemination of religious propaganda, but constitutional changes enacted under Stalin on May 18, 1929, squelched such possibilities. These changes were finalized in a decree of April 8, 1929, which required all churches including the Orthodox Church to obligatory registration.[7]

Under this new decree, civil authorities had the right to refuse registration without reason; clergy were required to register and be approved prior to exercise of office; and a number of prohibitions limiting the life of the church were placed in effect. Separation of church and state was provided for, as well as separation of church and school. All religious education was prohibited for children under eighteen years of age.

In 1936, Article 124 of the Constitution was amended to allow Soviet citizens "the freedom to hold religious services and the freedom to engage in anti-religious propaganda."[8] Subsequent interpretations of this provision allowed only the meeting of acknowledged Christians to worship, subject to the registration authority of the state. The Soviet government totally forbids Christians to proselytize or share their faith—even inside the walls of a church. Pastors who make altar calls violate state regulations.

Because the government sanctions only atheistic propaganda, Christian literature, radio, or public expression of any type was prohibited. Even the identification of church buildings, written or verbal notice of public worship service, or communication with non-believers remained unlawful.

Atheism—The Godless Religion

During the early years of communist rule, while the church struggled to survive, militant atheism flourished. The League of Militant Godless numbered three million by 1930. By the end of World War II, organized groups of Godless Youth and the All-Union Society for the Dissemination of Scientific and Political Knowledge numbered tens of thousands.

The state formed anti-religious publications, created departments and specialized schools of atheism, and built Museums of Atheism. Today, the government continues to sponsor millions of atheistic lectures each year. Exhibitions, films, shows, and thousands of book titles published in millions of copies are carried out under the Soviet freedom to "engage in anti-religious propaganda."[9]

In 1965, in Byelorussia alone (a republic in the European part of the Soviet Union that contains large numbers of Christians), 5,500 atheist lecturers and political instructors worked to erode Christian influence. In addition, 1,400 propagandists and 23,000 workers called "agitators" conducted individual work with believers.[10]

Under Khrushchev in the late 1950s and early 1960s, the state made extreme efforts under a five year plan to eradicate every vestige of religion. Penal code modifications resulted in increased penalties for infractions of laws relating to religious activities. New laws enabled the government to legally deprive Christian parents of the custody of their children, a practice that was already in effect in some regions.

In 1966, the Council of Ministers of the U.S.S.R. created the Council for Religious Affairs to combine both Orthodox and non-Orthodox cults and religious activities. Its powers seem to be absolute, yet written and published authorization is virtually non-existent.

In 1976, a Soviet publication surfaced in the West dated 1971, which gave some insights into the Council's basis for persecution of religious acts. While the Soviet church remains in the dark about official restrictions, practice has proven that under state registration, the church:

1. Has no legal standing
2. Can own no property
3. Cannot manage its income
4. Cannot engage in charitable activities
5. Must subject its programs to local scrutiny and approval (including sermon content)
6. Is prohibited from baptizing those under eighteen year of age
7. Cannot involve children in its activities (under eighteen years of age)
8. Cannot conduct activities outside the church building
9. Must subject church leadership to state approval.[11]

Since 80 percent of all Soviet decrees are never disseminated publicly, including those of a religious nature, churches find it increasingly difficult—if not impossible—to comply with unknown requirements.

Persecuted Pentecostals

Compared to other denominations and religious groups, the Pentecostals endure the greatest persecution. They are mostly unregistered (Crypto-Christians) and doctrinally prohibited from military service because of the oath of allegiance required of all inductees. This makes the Pentecostals prime targets for Soviet anti-religious efforts.

Historian William Fletcher, in his book *Soviet Charismatics,* suggests that the Pentecostals will be *the* evangelical group that will dominate Soviet evangelical growth and expansion over the next few years. Suited particularly well to urbanization and the Soviet mind-set, Pentecostals have become increasingly more attractive to the young, educated, city professionals as well as to the rural, less educated agrarian.

The rise is partly due to the faithfulness and courage exhibited by believers such as Vasily Barats, a forty-two-year-old engineer from Moscow, and his wife Galina. Long a leader in unregistered, unofficial Pentecostal circles in Moscow, where no registered Pentecostal services are allowed, Vasily was first arrested and incarcerated in a psychiatric hospital in 1980. He was later given five years of hard labor, and his wife, Galina, was sentenced to six years hard labor plus three years of exile. Understandably, both suffer from heart failure and poor health.

Released back to Moscow on November 11, 1987, both Barats petitioned for 2,800 Pentecostals to be allowed to emigrate from the Soviet Union. In May, 1988, Vasily was forcibly removed from Moscow and transported to the Western Ukraine. In spite of government attempts to block his return to Moscow, Vasily rejoined his wife in September. The visa office has refused their application to emigrate because they lack a residence permit, which has been consistently denied them in Moscow and the Ukraine. Today, they live under constant surveillance and harassment from the authorities.[12]

The Barats are not alone in their suffering and desire to leave their homeland. Some estimate as many as 30,000 to 50,000 Pentecostals are awaiting similar action on their exit visas, many from far eastern regions of the Soviet Union.

The Way of the Cross

The largest banned religious group in the Soviet Union today is the Ukrainian Greek Catholic Church, which dates from 1596. Today called the Ukrainian Catholic Church, Eastern-rite Catholics, or Uniates, they have consistently held allegiance to the Papal See in Rome and have been severely repressed since the 1930s under Stalin.

After mass revivals in the war years, the Uniate church was forcibly annexed to the Russian Orthodox Church in 1946. Without church buildings, seminaries, or authority to ordain priests or hold services, the four million adherents are served by three illegal Catholic bishops and some 330 priests with many younger men assisting.[13] It is called the Catacomb Church.

In July 1988 some 6,000 worshipers gathered in a field in rural western Ukraine to celebrate the first public mass since 1946. When police arrived and commanded them to disperse, they refused.

The continued rise in such activities is due partly to the legacy left by men such as Joseph Cardinal Slipyj who refused a top Russian Orthodox church position in 1945 in order to preserve the Catholic body. Sentenced ultimately to seventeen years incarceration through three terms, he still refused positions of Orthodox leadership.

In 1963, one year after his release from prison, the Soviet government permitted Slipyj to emigrate to Rome. Prior to his death in 1984, the church elevated him to the office of cardinal. Limping on frostbitten feet, the cardinal said he endured the arctic temperatures of Siberia, the rags, and the maltreatment because he "had to suffer . . . moral and physical maltreatment and humiliation, torture, and enforced starvation . . . As a prisoner for the sake of Christ, I found strength through my own Way of the Cross . . . I was not alone."[14]

From within a Soviet prison, another Ukrainian Catholic Church leader wrote his wife that the day will come when "our children will be free of Communist prejudice and hate toward Christ. Bars are not a prison. A person can still be free in spirit. They have lost!"[15] Half a lifetime—over twenty-three years in Soviet prisons and camps—could not dissuade Josyp Terelya from giving himself to his church.

These heroes of the faith should include Latvian Baptist Janis Rozkalns who throughout four years of recent imprisonment, shared at great risk a secret Bible with fellow inmates in his Soviet labor camp. Teaching, converting, even baptizing camp colleagues despite incredible hardships—including outdoor isolation cell interment in 40 degrees below zero temperatures without adequate clothing—symbolizes today's search for faith and hope from a country void of meaning in life.

Silencing the Church?

While objective evidence of the persecution of the church is not published officially in the Soviet Union, *the fact* of the persecution of believers, however, is not denied but officially confirmed. Yet those who have tried to set the record straight with accurate figures as to the severity of the oppression have been cruelly persecuted themselves.

Deacon Vladimir Rusak, in one sermon that began a pilgrimage of suffering and imprisonment, said:

> During the period from the revolution to the war, that is roughly twenty years, about 300 ark-

hierei [members of the Church's upper ranks] were annihilated: metropolitans, arch-bishops, bishops. Almost 200 of them disappeared without a trace. Before the war, there were only four bishops in office in all of Russia. . . .

Our church has been adorned and fortified by tens of thousands of martyrs. There are no monuments to them where we might offer flowers. . . and our sympathy. Many of them do not even have a grave: they are at the bottom of the river, they are in pits, they are burnt.[16]

Oppression and hostility, however, has not silenced the church. Nyole Sadunaite, affectionately called "Joan of Arc," stands out as a common example. Arrested in 1974 for her uncompromising witness, this beautiful Lithuanian Catholic nun has become a symbol of resistance and victory for the Christians in the Baltic republics. After three years in prison, then three more in exile in Siberia, she is back on the streets sharing her faith and her work with the church.

Then as recently as March 1988, Sister Sadunaite was assaulted by two men as she was on her way to a memorial service for a fellow religious activist. Punching her in the stomach, she was warned to cease her religious work and to "take the smile off her face." The reason for her spiritual strength has been expressed in her autobiography, published in the West entitled, *A Radiance in the Gulag:*

To attain his ends, God often chooses the most unlikely people, and that's what I am. "What appears to the world to be weak, God has chosen in order to confound those who are strong."[17]

Has Glasnost Made a Difference?

Recent Soviet emigre psychiatrist Dr. Anatoli Koryagin made the following statement from Switzerland:

Amid a false sense of euphoria in the West about the extent of *glasnost,* there is a greater need than ever to stress that persecution of believers in the Soviet Union still goes on . . . The Leninist dictum "that the eradication of religion is our State duty" is still in force.

Many hundreds of people are still in the camps and psychiatric prisons of the Gulag for no other reason than their belief in God, their desire to profess their faith and live out their lives in accordance with its teachings.[18]

Vladimir Titov, a Moscow Baptist and human rights activist, was released on October 9, 1987, from the psychiatric hospital where he had been held since his arrest in November 1982. Titov, a former KGB officer converted in prison while serving time for his political activities, estimates that 90 percent of all inmates in special psychiatric hospitals in the Soviet Union are not mentally ill, but are being "treated" for their religious or political beliefs.[19]

Despite some 156 known religious prisoners in prisons, camps, and gulags, Soviet officials admit to less than a dozen individuals presently serving time for "violating the law of religious legislation."[20]

Fedor Burlotsky is the chairman of the recently formed Soviet Commission on Humanitarian Problems and Human Rights and an expert advisor to Mikhail Gorbachev. When Congressmen Frank Wolf (R-VA) and Chris Smith (R-NJ) recently presented him a list of religious prisoners at an international consultation in Holland, Burlotsky said, "Many prisoners on your list are criminals who are also religious people trying to find a defense on religious grounds."[21]

The list was officially accepted by Yuri Smirnov, a member of the Council of Religious Affairs and the U.S.S.R. Council of Ministers. Obviously the Soviets' view on the religious prisoner issue is different from the West's.

Gorbachev himself in a February 1986 interview with a French journalist stated that "in our country . . . persecution of citizens for their beliefs does not exist."[22]

"There are no prisoners of conscience" in the Soviet Union and "so-called religious prisoners were in fact criminals arrested for committing crimes," echoed Konstantin Kharchev, director of the Soviet Council of Religious Affairs in Chautauqua, New York, in August of 1987.[23]

One week later, however, in a private conference with Senator Richard Lugar (R-IN), Kharchev admitted to "very many mistakes" being made in the past, "which were connected with such rude matters as administrative struggles with religious organizations."[24] Unexpectedly, Kharchev then promised all "prisoners of faith" would be released by November 1987.[25] They weren't; although by the end of 1988, approximately two-thirds of the known religious prisoners had been prematurely released.

Andrei Sakharov, himself a former prisoner in exile, believes two thousand religious adherents presently remain in Soviet prisons and labor camps. Because the Soviet law regards all religious conscientious objectors to forced Soviet military induction to be criminals, the number could be much higher.

A Grass Roots Change

While Christians are led to believe that the state is preparing a new law regarding religion, nothing concrete has emerged. Archbishop Makari, of the Russian Orthodox Church, said at a conference held January 17-20, 1988, on the Church, State, and Society in Contemporary Russia, "Unfortunately, I am afraid that the new legislation is not going to be ready this year." Expressing hope for future progress, Makari acknowledged that some state officials are "not ready for this and would like to take more time to study and perhaps convince others that it is a necessity for the present life."

We are "working very hard to bring the Gospel to the people," Archbishop Makari continued. "We are emphasizing the preaching of the holy Gospel in our churches" and attendance at services has increased "more than ever before"—we are experiencing a "renaissance," he said.[26]

Alexander Ogorodnikov, a Russian Orthodox Christian who has served more than eight years in Soviet camps and prisons, expressed his doubts about fundamental changes.

> Is there any change in the attitude of the state toward religion and religious believers? The Soviet regime has always seen religion as one of the main obstacles to communist ideology and has therefore sought to destroy the Church.[27]

Changes in religious life are "coming not from the top, but from the grass roots," Ogorodnikov said in direct reference to the Orthodox leadership.

> The Church hierarchy, which has passed through the hard school of compromise, seems to be content with the status quo and does not strive toward greater freedom for religion; for freedom would oblige the hierarchy to engage in the true service of the Church, to speak the word of truth to the people—something for which the hierarchy is unprepared, and which it fears.[28]

Many think that the government will give a greater moral role to the Church only if it is sure that the Church has become a secure part of the Soviet establishment. If true believers have their way, that will never happen.

Hearts Ready to Receive

To millions of Russians, Orthodox Christianity is not just a patriotic and nationalistic spirit reborn in the people. Their faith is more than merely an attitude of the past reflected by cupola adorned churches as national monuments. It is faith in Jesus Christ born out of hearts seeking to know and love God. Their hearts, broken by the oppression they see around them, are ready to receive anything God has for them.

In the words of Father Gleb Yakunin, an Orthodox priest restored to the priesthood after a term of imprisonment, "a person cannot be renewed in his personal life unless he repents. This is true of the Church, too."[29]

While suffering has purified portions of the church, persecution has made compromisers of others. Suffering does not make one a Christian—in the Soviet Union or anywhere else. Personal repentance, an individual acceptance of Jesus Christ as Savior, and obedience to God's Word remain the true marks of discipleship.

Our prayer in the West should be that God would take this suffering remnant, equip it as an effective spiritual army, instill it with godly leadership, and give it vision to engulf the Soviet Union in the knowledge and love of the Lord Jesus Christ. Throughout the Soviet Union today, many hearts are being prepared to receive Him. May they not be disappointed.

7

Russia's Search for God

At the Moscow International Book Fair in 1987, a U.S. Christian publication display gave away three hundred Christian books and Bibles from September 8-14. People lined up for hours just to gain entrance to the booth.

"I can't imagine there are this many Christian books," one woman whispered when she saw the few titles displayed on the table. "But that's only a tiny sampling of what's available," John Van Diest, publisher of Multnomah Press, explained. "There are thousands of other titles published each year in America alone." The woman walked away shaking her head.

"I met you here two years ago and asked for a Bible," one Russian said to Van Diest. "Can I have one now?" he asked. Disheartened by a negative response, the man asked sadly, "Do I have to wait another two years?"

People cry, beg, and literally steal to get books worth almost a month's salary. John Van Diest emphatically stated, "I believe thousands, maybe millions, would accept Christ in Soviet Russia if the message were made clear and available."[1]

Why this hunger for God in a nation controlled by an atheistic government? Is the thinking of modern Soviets moving away from Marxism?

Today's Soviet citizens look elsewhere for hope and spiritual satisfaction. The idealism of the 1917 revolution stands three generations behind them, and the unifying purpose of World War II lies two generations in the past. One thing is sure—they know what *doesn't* work.

Recent Romanian emigre Josef Tson, in a November 1987 issue of *Eternity* magazine, called socialism "mutually shared poverty . . . there is no communist country of economic success; there is no communist country where the people cherish to live."

With 80 percent of the world's refugees coming today from communist countries, almost every dissident states that nobody in his homeland believes in Marxism as an ideology. A new spiritual hunger thrives in communist countries.

Igor M. Ilinsky, a researcher for the Young Communist League, concluded that a religious revival has evolved to fill the ideological void. One recent poll of young people defined a "growing fascination" with religious literature and services, especially among the well-educated.

Approximately 34.5 percent of the Soviet population are practicing Christians and nearly 20 percent are Islamic. After adding 2 million Jews and other religionists to those figures, the bastion of atheism admits to an obvious ideological failure.

Soviet authorities themselves, in recently released statistics, acknowledge 10 to 20 percent of their people are religious believers. Konstantin Kharchev, the director of the Soviet Council for Religious Affairs, made the following observation:

> We are not seeing a mass departure from religion
> such as happened in the first years of Soviet power.
> In some regions, there is even a rise in the number of believers.[2]

The Soviet Church: Alive and Growing

The World Christian Encyclopedia reveals some amazing statistics on the state of religion in the Soviet Union. Despite wars, revolutions, and state persecution of all religion, the Soviet Union has 40 to 50 million Russian Orthodox believers, many of whom are young men and women. These are joined by Armenian Apostolic church members and Eastern-rite Catholics (Uniates).

In addition, evangelical Christians include Baptists, Lutherans, Mennonites, Pentecostals, and Crypto-Christians (underground churches of varying denominations), and total at least 64 million *practicing* Christians, a term defined as those adults practicing once a year or more.

These figures do not include children, since they are prohibited by law from participation until age eighteen. Nor do the statistics include some 20 million isolated radio church believers scattered across the Soviet Union. These Christians are generally prohibited by geographical remoteness from attending religious worship services.

Mid-1980s estimates now number:

> 152 Christian denominations
> 87,900 congregations
> 64,662,100 members

Total affiliation is numbered at 96,726,500 (members plus children, non-member attenders, isolated radio church members, and certain Crypto-Christians).

Lenin apparently selected the wrong group of people to change idealistically. With deep emotion, sincere concern for spiritual issues, and expressed passion for God, Russians have not adjusted well to a dispassionate, scientific solution to finding their place in the universe.

One Soviet radio listener expressed his feelings in a letter to a Western Christian radio broadcaster:

> I'm not a believer. I've never been baptized, but your programs interest me . . . When one compares the Church and the Communist Party, he can only conclude that the Church is the best moral educator of society. If one takes a long, hard look at our Soviet society, which is supposedly heading forward to a bright future of communism, it becomes apparent that this includes corruption, money-grabbing, treachery, robbery, pilfering, alcoholism, and drug abuse. I'm not saying that these things totally pervade our society here, but they do occur all too frequently . . .
>
> The average Soviet has heard since kindergarten that God doesn't exist. But later, when he grows up, he comes to the understanding that believing in communism is simply ridiculous. Even the leaders of communism don't believe in it, but they have to somehow deceive the people.[3]

Despite seventy years of cultural devastation and religious repression, the church is alive in atheistic Russia. Open churches stand out against drab surroundings, and the excitement inside is obviously contagious.

Official Soviet writings themselves admit to a concern for religious uprisings. The central newspaper of the Soviet Communist Party Central Committee acknowledged in October 1984 that large numbers of young people were drifting toward religion. To counteract the trend, the paper called on schools and youth organizations to intensify atheistic propaganda efforts.

A similar article in the Soviet armed forces magazine focused concern on increased signs of religiosity with recruits. "Step up atheistic work" the article urged instructors, recognizing "time and again one sees the glint of a copper cross on the chest of a recruit."[4]

Pravda, in an editorial dated September 28, 1986, admitted that the church is not only surviving, but "has also been trying to attract new members, particularly youth."[5]

In October 1986, Radio Free Europe Research reported,

> A process of religious reawakening has been gathering momentum in most East European countries over the past two years. Interest in religious ideas and participation in religious observances has been growing among the public, and more and more citizens are committed to sustaining religious values in the face of the state's ideological efforts against religion.[6]

A *Moscow News* article of August 16, 1987, described how the one Orthodox church allowed in the city of Kirov (population 400,000) "is so crowded on Sundays and feast days that worshipers cannot raise their hands to cross themselves."[7] Worshipers have been trying officially for twenty-five years to receive permission for another church.

The publication *Ogonyok,* in its March 1987 issue, published a letter from three hundred believers in a small town in the Caucasus region of the Soviet Union. After having received official permission to renovate a dilapidated wooden hut into a church edifice, the authorities confiscated the result—a beautiful church building complete with crosses and cupolas. Authorities converted the structure into a kindergarten "in case it attracted young people to religion."[8]

Changing Soviet Attitudes

Rampant alcoholism, drug addiction, social alienation, teen-age suicide, and increased crime point to the failure of communism to create the perfect society. In addition, the need for legitimate charitable functions to help victims of Chernobyl and the Armenian earthquake have forced the communist state to look at the church in a new perspective.

Some communist officials have even begun to express appreciation for the qualities of Christians. Yuri Aslanov, an inspector for the state Council for Religious Affairs, which controls the church's activities, was recently quoted as saying:

> My generation was brought up to believe that religion was backward, and that attitude persists through inertia . . . But now, the state is beginning to appreciate that believers are good patriots and, in their morals, often better than atheists.[9]

A Soviet historian, allowed access to the weekly publication *Ogonyok,* surmised that "in the 20th century, the exploration of space and study of the atom turned up various nuclear phenomenon, making it possible for the scientist to be a believer," he said.[10]

"Christianity is not ideology, either bourgeois or socialist," the historian Dmitri Kikhachev continued. "It is a world view plus ethical norms for behavior in everyday life. Christianity is a universal religion applying equally to black people and Chinese. As Christianity is international, so it is a great religion."[11]

Both eastern and western commentators, however, believe it's premature and naive to assume the Soviet state now promotes religious growth. There is not a nationwide movement orchestrated from a central source.

Instead, each local success for religious effort seems to be spontaneous, outside of any large campaign effort. Nor is there any indication that church leadership of any denominational persuasion is taking the lead in such matters. This strongly indicates that the balance of power within the Soviet Union between church and state is still overwhelmingly on the side of the state.

Many Soviet Christian activists believe that today's work in the Church is more important than ever before. Real change, they say, will only come about through pressure applied at every local level of government.

Release of Christian prisoners and relaxation of some controls, they believe, are due solely to campaigns in the West on behalf of Christians. Soviets also believe economic pressures have forced Gorbachev to seek improved relations with the West.

Confronted with overwhelming economic and political problems, the survival of Marxism nevertheless seems keyed to its ability to quickly and satisfactorily meet social and moral needs. We're "a military giant, but a moral midget," one Soviet emigre was quoted as saying.[12]

Gorbachev, Glasnost, and the Church

Reams are being written and spoken about the depravity of the Soviet system that brought Mikhail Gorbachev to power. Not the first reformer in Soviet history, Gorbachev succeeds Nikita Khrushchev, who himself pushed through a number of internal changes in the early 1960s. Yet Gorbachev can distinguish himself from Khrushchev in *one* important way: by allowing religious reform.

While Khrushchev did liberalize some individual rights, he viciously purged the Orthodox Church and evangelicals in a determined effort to stamp out all religion within the Soviet Union. Perhaps this despicable inconsistency limited Khrushchev's successes and ultimately undermined his political base, resulting in his ouster.

Does the Soviet Union acknowledge that religious freedom is a fundamental human right? Their oppressive practices seem to indicate just the opposite of signed declarations. The Soviets have inked the following human rights agreements that include religious freedom:

1. United Nations Charter
2. Universal Declaration of Human Rights
3. International Covenant on Civil and Political Rights

4. International Covenant on Social, Economic, and Cultural Rights
5. Convention Against Discrimination in Education
6. Helsinki Final Act
7. United Nations Declaration Against All Forms of Religious Intolerance

Now is the time for the Soviets to comply with the conditions of the legal relationships it has made with the rest of the world.

Today Gorbachev is forced to look carefully at religion's role in the ongoing changes of glasnost. Why is he feeling pressured? Because world opinion favors expansion of Soviet religious liberties. The unexpected outcry of many religious adherents and leaders is also putting pressure on Gorbachev. The continued focus on religious rights issues by Carter and Reagan administration negotiating teams has weighed especially heavy on the Soviet Union.

After a 1987 visit with Soviet believers, James Stark, an Orthodox Christian of Russian descent, observed:

> Everyone is positive about Gorbachev's leadership and policy direction, but there is an edge of realism to their new found joy. They attribute the release of some prisoners of conscience, the opening of a few churches, and some positive articles in the newspaper to pressure upon the Soviet government.[13]

Glasnost can no longer exclude the church and Russia's rich religious heritage. To what extent will Gorbachev respond? Who will raise the issues?

A Communist and An Atheist

Through the Russian Orthodox Church's millennium (one thousand year) celebrations in June 1988, Gorbachev made generous offers to rewrite Soviet laws guaranteeing freedom of conscience. Such anti-atheistic overtures impressed much of the world, including President Reagan. In private, the former president has said these are signs of "spiritual regeneration," leading to questions of just how "religious" Mr. Gorbachev really is.

Every question asked, every comment publicly made by Soviet officials does make us wonder—what is the nature of the Soviet religious policy?

All foundations of policy emanate out of the precepts of Lenin. In an unprecedented meeting with Russian Orthodox Church officials on April 29, 1988, Gorbachev emphasized that Lenin's decrees always enabled the church to carry on its activities without any outside interference.

Yet both Marx and Lenin took strong positions against religious belief. Marx wrote in a personal poem, "I wish to avenge myself against the One who rules alone."[14] Lenin stated that "Religious ideas, every idea of God, even flirting with the idea of God, is unutterable vileness."[15]

The Museum of the History of Religion and Atheism in Leningrad prominently displayed a 1918 poster that expressed the sentiment of the Communist Party:

> The sooner workers and peasants are freed from
> the influence of religion and the church, the
> sooner they will be able to reconstruct the world.[16]

Gorbachev has acknowledged that Christians suffered and mistakes were made in the 1930s. That, he says, was the result of Stalin's "cult of personality." According to Gorbachev, it is Lenin's precept of avoiding "offending religious freedoms" that will be the policy of his government. Yet this is inconsistent with another statement of Lenin: "the eradication of religion is our governmental task."[17]

Gorbachev himself, in 1986, called for "a firm and uncompromising struggle against religious phenomena."[18] Now, however, he exclaims that believers will "have the full right to express their conviction with dignity," and he pledged the state would not interfere.[19]

While such inconsistencies are not uncommon for public officials, it would appear that for the time being at least, the inconsistencies favor the church.

How hopeful these new developments are for Soviet Christians is too early to predict, says Dr. Mark Elliot, director of the Institute for the Study of Christianity and Marxism, Wheaton College. In fact, should Gorbachev and his reforms survive, Elliot says, Christians may be no better off. The *Evangelical Missions Quarterly* carried the following remarks by Elliot:

> With all of the items on his agenda, there is no particular reason he should invest his energy or stake his political future on making life easier for Christians. Gorbachev is, after all, a communist and an atheist.[20]

Bibles Bound for Russia

In spite of Gorbachev's ideology, glasnost *is* bringing changes for the better, especially in the attitude of the public and the government toward the Bible.

The official Soviet youth newspaper, *Komsomoskaya Pravda,* in a 1986 article by Russian author Yevgeny Yevtushenko, gave three reasons why Bible reading should be allowed: the place of the church in Russian history; the necessity for neutrality of the State regarding formation of individual beliefs; and the failure of atheism itself as a positive source of morals. Yevtushenko undoubtedly influenced millions of young Soviets with this article.

Soviet television followed such an article with a series entitled "Religion and Politics" in early 1987 with participants openly discussing their desire for Bibles and Christian literature. The presentation ended with the moderator stating, "If the public wants Bibles, they will have to be published."[21] Most Soviets know that is easier said than done.

Out of the 85,000 book titles and 13,000 periodicals printed in 1987, with a combined total of over one billion copies of literature, the Soviet government produced almost no religious literature.[22] The only exceptions were several government publications printed for denominational use.

Before 1988 the state had permitted only six official shipments of Scripture into the Soviet Union. The largest influx of religious materials occurred in 1979 when 25,000 Russian Bibles and 5,000 concordances were imported. Prior totals for Soviet evangelicals amounted to less than 100,000 copies.[23]

During the first nine months of 1988, however, more Bibles and other Christian literature were officially imported into the Soviet Union than in all the years between 1920 and 1987 combined. Requests for literature are initiated by registered or autonomous Soviet church groups. After approval by Soviet governmental agencies (Ministry of Religion and Cults), the requests are referred abroad to Bible societies and mission agencies.

The United Bible Society announced some astonishing figures in the *National and International Religion Report* of October 1988:

—The Russian Orthodox Church received 100,000 Bibles. In addition 100,000 New Testaments with Psalms were slated to be sent later.

—The Baptist Union (AUCECB—Registered Baptists) received:

103,000 Russian Bibles
68,000 Ukrainian Bibles
10,000 German Bibles
2,500 each Latvian and Estonian Bibles
2,000 Georgian New Testaments

—The Lutherans received 8,000 Bibles.
—The Pentecostals were sent 2,200 New Testaments.

In addition, the unregistered Christian groups are finding themselves on the receiving end for the first time. For years, these underground churches had supplied the registered congregations with Scripture that had been printed on illegal presses or imported covertly at great risk to their people. Now Bibles and hymnals from the West are finally reaching these brave believers.

Miscellaneous titles in Christian literature exceeding 160,000 pieces have also been unofficially transported through the mail and by personal travel, accounting for tens of thousands more. In addition, one million New Testaments with Psalms were authorized as millennial gifts for the Russian Orthodox Church in 1988.[24]

Who Benefits?

These shipments of Scripture made available to official church structures have caused considerable controversy both inside and outside the country. Church leaders have complained that some groups have been totally ignored while others, like the Pentecostals, have received small quantities pre-determined by an unfair quota system.

Furthermore, each copy was sold for a price of 30 to 35 rubles, approximately one week's salary, making the purchase of literature impossible for many Christians. This is discouraging to Western sources who intended the Bibles and hymnals as gifts.

Even with such help, barely 15 percent of Bibles and 6 percent of New Testaments currently within the country have been imported officially. Despite recent shipments, estimates indicate less than 1 percent of the Soviet population has a personal copy of the Scriptures. At best there's only *one copy of the Bible for every 133 Soviet citizens.*[25]

Bibles and some Christian literature are now available to selected libraries and educational institutions for public access, but these will have a positive effect on only a limited number of Soviet citizens. The accessibility to university libraries by most believers is impractical and will provide very limited access to the church as a whole.

Recent revisions in Soviet customs regulations now permit Soviet citizens (and presumably foreigners) to bring formerly prohibited objects (including religious literature) into the country. But the quantities are not expected to make an appreciable difference. Besides, these benefits are limited primarily to citizens traveling abroad. Few believers fall into that category, except those in high church positions.

But other significant changes have been made. A long article in the March 25, 1988 edition of the Soviet newspaper *Izvestiya* stated:

> It will be possible for almost anything to be sent by post, hardly any restrictions will remain, except on computers, video equipment of all types and food products. The sending of religious objects, also copies of the Bible, the Koran, etc., is allowed.[26]

The new policy, however, is of limited use to Soviets who have no accessibility or contact with the West. Unless such efforts are initiated outside the country, the church as a whole within the Soviet Union will not benefit.

The Dividing Line

Many believe the real test of the state's position on religious issues centers on the banning of 1929 legislation prohibiting, among other activities, the teaching of religion outside the immediate family.

One Russian Orthodox group presented an appeal both to Mr. Gorbachev and U.S. Senator John Heinz on his May

1987 Moscow visit. They complained of being prohibited from any "expression of social activity." Help us "change from being second-class citizens to full members of our native land," the petition pleaded.[27]

Not unlike other public expressions of dismay, one group of thirty-two Soviet Christians from many denominations called a public press conference in Moscow on September 11, 1987. They formally read and later presented to Soviet authorities a series of suggestions and changes they feel are necessary for Soviet religious freedom to exist.

Despite the overtures, however, no fundamental change has appeared in official religious thinking. Under Gorbachev, in 1986, the Communist Party rules retained the provision that Party members must actively struggle against "religious prejudices."[28] Atheism is still a prerequisite of the ruling ideology. In his first speech to party officials on religion in twenty-two months in office, Gorbachev stated:

> We must be strict above all with Communists and senior officials, particularly those who say they defend our morality and ideals, but in fact help promote backward views and themselves take part in religious ceremonies.[29]

Western visitations, hopeful Soviet promises, isolated cases of individual church successes, controlled Scripture importation, or expanded immigration policies will not accurately gauge Soviet reform. How will the West know that the Soviets are becoming responsible participants in the world community? When certain fundamental changes take place. Only then will glasnost be more of a hope than a delusion.

First the church must be granted full legal status, allowing:

1. Ownership of church property
2. Religious propaganda
3. Charitable work
4. Full freedom for church off premises

5. Religious education, particularly with children
6. Public interaction of church members in local society
7. Independence from state regulation
8. Unlimited international contacts
9. Conscientious objector status
10. Unlimited literature production

In a document entitled "Appeal for Religious Freedom in the Soviet Union," a project of the James Madison Foundation, these points were made available to Mr. Gorbachev. He knows what the churches want. The issue is not a case of being uninformed, but lacking desire.

Actually, the issue doesn't seem to be politics or economics. The "perfect man" the Marxists have been trying to develop over seventy years is admittedly more reflective of a Christian than the current Marxist product. Perhaps another wall divides people more significantly than barbed wire, an Iron Curtain, or cultural abysses. Perhaps social, economic, and moral deficiencies of civilization are only symbolic of the existence of this other wall from which no human is immune.

This wall divides man from God and ultimately divides one man from another. Perhaps Mr. Gorbachev is most interested in keeping this wall intact, despite the prior rhetoric and the suave gestures of human sensitivity.

As Alexander Solzhenitsyn has observed, "the dividing line between good and evil is not set by boundaries between countries, but is found in every human heart."[30] Perhaps the dissolution of the "evil empire" Mr. Reagan spoke of will not be evidenced as much by military concessions as religious reform. Mr. Gorbachev now has that opportunity.

Waiting for Change

If changes in religious liberty don't come from Gorbachev, it is unlikely they will come at all.

Soviet poet Irina Ratushinskaya explains why. A veteran of four years in Soviet labor camps, this thirty-three year old woman had been prohibited from writing poetry in the cold, damp isolation of her cell. Nevertheless she continued to write using small matchsticks on soap, memorizing the verses, then washing away the writing. In all, she memorized some three hundred poems.

Two days prior to the Reagan-Gorbachev summit of October 1987 in Reykjavik, Iceland, this brave poet was released. *Christianity Today* quoted her as saying:

> Most of our people don't have communist ideas. We are tired of such life, tired of promises. We see we are not free. It is hard for Westerners to understand a society where people, from childhood to old years, are forced to lie, are afraid to speak freely, are afraid to trust even their relatives. People know if they protest someone's sentence to a labor camp, they will be sent to labor camps themselves. Changes will occur only when the people find within themselves the strength not to be afraid and not to obey orders blindly.[31]

Citizens in the West, particularly well-intentioned Christians who think they can passively await change from within the Soviet Union at the hands of the people, may find their inactivity will only bring damage. "There is no grass roots in the Soviet Union that has the opportunity to impact directly on Soviet policy," stated Zbigniew Brzezinski in a 1986 radio interview.[32]

Soviet citizens experience extreme futility at their inability to change the system. *Christianity Today* carried the following comments by an Estonian believer:

> The Americans told us how important it is for Christians to work for peace and disarmament. Of

course, I want peace. But don't Americans understand that in Russia it's not the citizens who make such decisions? A government-assigned Intourist guide accompanied the Americans, so I couldn't speak openly to them. They didn't even seem to understand that we can't talk freely in such circumstances. I wanted to tell the Americans that if they truly wanted to help, they could bring Bibles to us.[33]

From a populace perspective, the Russian church is unable to change Soviet legislation. And for self-serving reasons, the church denominational hierarchy is unwilling to pursue change.

Incapable of determining its own future, the church hopes this time that external circumstances of time and failure will force changes from Soviet officials. But the crumbs of "democratization" sporadically strewed under Gorbachev's table to a spiritually starving people are not enough. Gorbachev makes no secret of his aim—to make the system more efficient, not to change it.

So the Soviet church finds itself looking to the West. This is a significant time for all believers around the world. The Church must respond to this time of unprecedented openness and freedom while the door remains open.

Part Two

Gateway to Reform

8

Glasnost: Hope or Delusion?

An older woman asked her son to explain glasnost to her. The young man asked, "Mother, do you see these two buckets?"

"Yes," his mother replied. "One is empty, and one is filled with stones."

"Watch very carefully," the son said. He picked up the bucket filled with stones and poured it into the empty bucket. Then he asked, "Mother, *now* do you understand glasnost?"

The mother shook her head and replied, "But son, nothing has changed. One bucket is still empty, and one bucket is filled with stones."

The son said, "That's right. But when I poured the full bucket into the empty bucket, didn't you hear all the noise? *That,* Mother, is glasnost."

Is this Russian joke an accurate portrayal of life under glasnost? Is Gorbachev's new policy of openness a cause for hope or only a deceptive smoke screen? What significant changes, if any, has Gorbachev made under glasnost?

Confrontation in Krasnoyarsk

Surrounded by the drabness of mass housing blocks and the polluted air of the large industrial center, Gorbachev hit the streets in September 1988 with TV cameras rolling. His goal? To record good reports from the pleased residents of the Siberian city of Krasnoyarsk.

Instead, what the party leader heard was mass grumbling with open statements that all perestroika had brought them was longer lines and higher prices.

"Go into our stores, Mikhail Sergeyevich. You'll see there's nothing in them," shouted a man.

"The housing situation is terrible," one woman added, urging others to "go on, tell him what it's like."[1]

Confronted with reality, Gorbachev returned to Moscow and featured the video tapes from Krasnoyarsk over national television for three days, obviously with a much larger purpose in mind. While Gorbachev hoped the situation would put pressure on his comrades in the communist hierarchy, the event sent a clearer message to the Soviet public. "It's okay to say what we think. He will listen to us. Glasnost is here!"

Although perestroika (restructuring) is the process for change, glasnost (openness) is the key to the reform. This new openness is the main agent that Soviet leader Mikhail Gorbachev hopes will expose the resistance, mismanagement, and corruption of mid-level bureaucrats reluctant to part with the privileges of power.

Many differ in their interpretation of openness. "The fact that we were allowed to come," Robert Bernstein said of the group of human-rights monitors from thirteen countries, "is a good indication that things have changed for the better."[2]

Others have described the changes more as a "remarkable increase in sophistication and shrewdness." Nevertheless, Russians are invigorated and hopeful.

New Freedoms of Speech

Soviets are enjoying new writing opportunities through newspapers, magazines, film, and theatre revisions. Intellectuals from varied backgrounds compared the previous limited reforms of Nikita Khrushchev in the 1960s to today's possibilities as "that being a trickle, this is a flood."[3]

"This is the closest I've ever felt to freedom of speech," admitted a Soviet woman writer in her sixties.[4]

Some call it a war of ideas in Moscow. Current issues that would have been considered improper for public print only a year ago are now the subjects of public debate in open forums: the wounded psyches of soldiers returning from Afghanistan, religious persecution, censorship, homosexuality. Even the works of Aleksandr I. Solzhenitsyn are being read, and the deeds of dishonored former leaders are being exposed. The revival of talk and expression, after decades of intellectual oppression, has exploded in the press and over the airwaves.

Glasnost has also resulted in greater candor among those reporting domestic affairs in official government publications. Many publications feel free to debate government action, criticize officials, stir up controversy, and publish readers' opinionated letters about the bureaucracy—without consulting the censors of Glavit, the organization that protects state and military secrets.

Articles on crime, prostitution, corruption, and AIDS are interspersed with news of disasters such as airplane crashes, accidents, and related subjects formerly unheard of in a Soviet publication. All publications report massive increases in circulation figures with the official government newspaper *Izvestiya* selling 8 million copies a day, up from 6.7 million two years ago.[5]

Glasnost, a fifty-five page unauthorized commentary whose editor had served nine years in prison for his dissident views, was allowed to circulate freely. Two weeks later a second edition of the magazine, now up to 184 pages, was distributed. Did this dissident fear censorship or reprisal from the Soviet government? Sergei Grigoiyants, the forty-five-year-old editor, boldly responded:

> If they tried to close me down, every American television network would bring their cameras. It would be an international scandal.[6]

The creation of a new independent magazine on religious questions, called *Vybor* or *Choice,* was also announced, as were regional ethnic publications from the Ukraine, the Baltic area, and elsewhere within the fifteen Soviet republics. The lack of codified law on publishing, coupled with Gorbachev's more liberal policies on private and cooperative enterprise, created a growing interest in private journalism and publishing.

Across the country many ambitious Soviets have applied to local officials to open cooperative book publishing enterprises. The government newspaper *Izvestiya* in September 1987 attacked the phenomenon in an article labeling it a "primitive" activity, no longer necessary because the Communist Party, which in practice controls all publishing, has proven its superior wisdom in all intellectual matters.[7]

As a result, the Council of Ministers in October 1987 ordered a halt to the creation of independent publishing and printing cooperatives. Authors of fiction, however, will be permitted to publish their works through the state publishing houses at the author's expense.

All Talk and No Change

Such an intellectual hunger brought on Directive Number 315 of the Ministry of Communications, limiting 1989 subscriptions to 1988 levels. Citing the boom in subscriptions and alleging a tight paper supply, forty publications have been affected by the squeeze.[8]

The general consensus of many readers and editors is that the paper shortage is only a subterfuge to stifle progressive, popular publications. Communist Party newspapers and magazines, however, may print as many copies as they want.

Affecting book publications as well, one editorial writer compared the publishing situation with the scene in state-controlled grocery stores where there is "no decent sausage or fresh chicken but only awful looking cans and fish heads."[9]

"If it cannot be liquidated, it can at least be limited," said *Literary Russia* editor Georgi Dolgov, speaking of anti-reform bureaucrats against "glasnost."[10] Yet as many Soviet citizens complain, the new frankness, criticism, and demands put on officials have produced few results.

One Soviet, who wrote a letter to the *Magnitogorsk Worker,* gave his appraisal of what had really changed under glasnost:

> It seems to me, in the struggle to rectify short-comings, we are talking more than we are doing. The newspaper is writing "hot" material. And yet, so far, changes are few.[11]

Outspoken articles, now accepted in Moscow publications available to western access, are routinely reaching into the heartland of the Soviet Union as well, a sign that the official policy of openness has made some impact outside Moscow.

The loosening controls over the press are reaching the provinces, yet the new openness cannot be confused with independence. Soviet newspapers are official organs, with each publication tied to an official organization. On the local level, the main newspapers are the mouthpieces of the local Communist Party. Editors devote their front pages to the same expression of announcement and speeches as the Moscow-based national party newspaper, *Pravda*.

Information remains tightly controlled. With few exceptions, certain areas of government, defense, foreign affairs, and the KGB are out of bounds for journalistic criticism. Major stories such as the Chernobyl nuclear accident or the Matthias Rust plane landing on Red Square remain back page items in Soviet newspapers.

Small groups of people control the role of the press, the issue of public opinion, and certainly the changes in party leadership at all levels of government. Some act in opposition to Gorbachev's reform policies; others act in compliance with orders from above.

Soviet political clubs, film producers, travelers, social initiative clubs (that lobby for political and economic reform), musical expression groups, rock bands, theatre, environmental, and cultural groups (such as Epicenter a coalition of fourteen such groups) find new possibilities of public meeting and expression through authorized "social organizations."

Even nonparty members may be nominated and elected to local and national legislative bodies—if cleared by a party screening committee. The government often provides meeting places for these groups. The ground rules party officials imposed, however—including registration by name and no foreign reporters—are found by most participants to be objectionable.

The murky waters of glasnost vacillate between what is approved and what is not yet clearly defined. No one is entirely sure how far to go in trusting an official embrace. As a result, fear of government reprisal still keeps many, including Christians, from proceeding too quickly.

Human Rights: Progress or Camouflage?

Has glasnost made a difference for the ordinary Soviet citizen? Looking back to glasnost's inception, no clear picture for the future of communism emerges from the rhetoric of Mikhail Gorbachev. Western human rights advocates, who have denounced repressive and restrictive Soviet practices, are not convinced of lasting change. Why are they dubious despite glasnost? Gorbachev's amendment of oppressive laws and structures lacks consistency and clarity.

Gorbachev, calling for greater "democratization" of society, has to date only *discussed* abolishing laws that concern political (religious) offenders, ending the abuse of psychiatry, and permitting more independence of trade unions.

A suggestion was made to a high Soviet official that granting immediate emigration permits to the 15,000 to 20,000 Jewish refuseniks would make Mr. Gorbachev the most popular man in the West. "But he already is," was the smiling reply.[12]

While asserting in its 1,358 page study of human rights around the world that Soviet changes were "more than cosmetic and less than fundamental," the State Department still voiced reasons for optimism.

Since February 1987, 314 "prisoners of conscience" have been released. Amnesty International estimated in October 1988, that about 150 people were still being held in Soviet prisons, labor camps, and psychiatric hospitals for "the nonviolent exercise of their fundamental human rights."[13] Approximately 200 religious prisoners have been released within the past two and one-half years, and the Soviets claim to have freed 67 of the political prisoners by the end of 1988.[14]

Does this mean religious persecution has ended and that the communist government now views Christianity differently? Janis Rozkalns, a Baptist pastor, was given this message by the authorities on his premature release from a Soviet labor camp in late 1987:

> You have not been amnestied; you have not been pardoned. You were released on instructions from the top. When instructions come to imprison you again, we shall do so.[15]

"It is still a one-party dictatorship," U.S. Assistant Secretary of State Richard Schifter said. "The KGB is still an all powerful organ of repression."[16]

Glasnost: The Flying Crocodile

In an effort to evaluate glasnost, we must eventually resort to the opinions of those who once lived within the socialist system and are now free to express their opinion.

"An economically flourishing and democratic communist society is as possible as a flying crocodile" said Alexander Zinoviev, an exiled Soviet writer living in Munich, West Germany.[17]

"Glasnost is not a new policy" said Ivan Svitak, a Czech exile. "It is an improved lie, a new temporary facade. Glasnost is an ideology of reforms without actual reforms."[18]

Russians often use the slang expression *pokazuka,* which means "for show." Any traveler to the Soviet Union has experienced countless empty gestures perpetrated by Soviet officials to deceive foreigners looking for reform. Perhaps that term is applicable here.

Some say that communist systems cannot change, no matter what. Others believe as long as the Soviet Union is a police state and the communist ideology is its major export, the West should support policies that promise to destabilize the communist rule in Russia. Still others hope the Russians are, quite simply, coming to maturity as a nation.

How should the West respond to Gorbachev's overtures of change? We must ask pertinent questions and press for relevant actions until we find out whether glasnost is the harbinger of a new era or only a cruel ruse.

9

Perestroika: Too Little Too Late

Time Magazine, in naming Gorbachev its 1987 Man of the Year, described him as one who became a "symbol of hope for a new kind of Soviet Union: more open, more concerned with the welfare of its citizens, and less with the spread of its ideology and system abroad."[1]

Two years earlier, in March 1985, Mikhail Gorbachev became the General Secretary of the Communist Party of the U.S.S.R. What motivated such a decision? The Central Committee, driven by a sense of impending crisis at home and abroad, hoped to narrow the base of world power with the Gorbachev appointment.

How bad had things become? With Soviet Marxism unattractive to the world ideologically, inept militarily, and with unabated economic and social problems at home, the Soviet Union of March 1985 distressingly resembled the Russia of 1916-1917.

What better time to employ risky new measures, "a new word," a "new relationship" in the same spirit as propounded by Karl Marx at the turn of the century?

Those new measures have come to be known by the Russian word *perestroika* or restructuring. Described by some as an "upheaval" or "from the ground up," perestroika has become the slogan of the Gorbachev era. Since mid 1985, Soviet citizens and the entire world have been listening to Gorbachev's call for restructuring.

On the Verge of Crisis

What does perestroika actually mean? The definition of perestroika has evolved as Mr. Gorbachev unfolds his program of social and economic change. At first reorganization was not even mentioned. Now the term not only encompasses drastic structural changes but a whole range of social and economic revisions, calling for greater "democratization" and "openness."

Mikhail Gorbachev, in his best-selling book *Perestroika,* made the following two statements:

> The Communist Party made a critical analysis of the situation that had developed by the mid-1980s and formulated this policy of perestroika or restructuring, a policy of accelerating the country's social and economic progress and renewing all spheres of life.[2]

> Any delay in beginning perestroika could have led to an exacerbated internal situation in the near future which, to put it bluntly, would have been fraught with serious social, economic and political crises.[3]

In Gorbachev's own words, "stagnation" became a common choice in describing the Soviet economy. National income growth rates had declined by more than half over the past fifteen years. In world advancement, the Soviets found themselves losing one position after another. The gap in the efficiency of production, quality of products, scientific and technological development, the production of advanced technology, and the use of advanced techniques began to widen to the disadvantage of the Soviets.

Prior to Gorbachev's public statements, the government published few statistics on living conditions. Comparisons with other countries based on figures for Gross National Product (GNP) became meaningless. Nevertheless, certain conclusions concerning the dilemma facing Gorbachev are apparent. The Soviet standard of living is falling further and further behind most industrial European countries.

The Soviets are plagued by considerable concealed unemployment, inflation, poor and inadequate housing, inadequate food and medical care. Forty percent of all blue collar workers are physical laborers; the hardest physical jobs are often done by the women.

Informed sources estimate that the 1976 per capita consumption in the Soviet Union was 20 to 30 percent of that in the United States. An unemployed American lives much better than the average Soviet citizen. In fact, the average per capita income in the Soviet Union is lower than the official poverty level in the United States.

With the present growth rate of production of goods and services within the Soviet Union, the per capita consumption of Soviet citizens is estimated to reach the 1976 United States level as follows:

> Meat—74 years
> Fruit—62 years
> Cars—176 years
> Housing—142 years
> Telephones—188 years
> Roads—298 years[4]

At the Plenary Meeting of the Central Committee in April 1985, Mikhail Gorbachev admitted, "the country was verging on crisis."[5]

Life Under Perestroika

For many, if not for most Soviets, life still has not improved much—especially in actual conditions. Most ordinary people simply don't understand what restructuring means for them—what is expected of them or what to expect in return.

The *International Herald Tribune* printed some revealing information on the state of the Soviet economy. Vasili Ryndin, a Stavropol collective farm manager, made this assessment of the situation under perestroika in that article:

> You have to imagine the mistakes, the stagnation that we had. It was so over-planned that local leaders could not act or think for themselves. Now, day and night, I think about how to earn more money, because now the government has made me responsible.[6]

Looking back at the collectivization policies of Stalin in the 1930s, the Soviet system did not permit private enterprise except on a very limited scale. In the past Soviet workers have been content to wait for their orders to be negotiated between ministries in Moscow, perhaps five thousand miles away.

Many people still find it uncomfortable to take the initiative. Press reports from the Ukraine indicated 1987 spring crops failed to get planted as farmers awaited orders from above.

Basic shortages still exist. The government strictly rations meat and butter in many areas—each person receives only 2.2 pounds of meat and 14 ounces of butter per month. Even such necessities as soap and toilet paper are often not available in the stores.

Because of the poor quality of goods and services, plants have initiated higher standards. Employers are pushing for greater discipline and a crackdown on drinking. A new national commission that implements stricter quality controls has the power to reject products that fail to meet state standards.

Reform—A Long Way Off

Another revolutionary concept developed as part of perestroika is "self-financing." Local enterprises must now meet costs and pay their own way with a minimum of help or interference from above.

The profit incentive, coupled with self-financing, is a phenomenon in socialist economics. Profits mean jobs for managers, higher wages for employees, and fulfillment of consumer demand quotas initiated by the state.

"Cooperative" is also a new word in the socialist economic dictionary. So far, private profit efforts have been implemented only in a limited way through cafes, services, taxi drivers, etc. Much of the Soviet effort in cooperatives has been a public relations gimmick pushed through massive advertising campaigns in the U.S. and elsewhere.

But such common capitalistic principles, for years antithetical to socialism, also mean big potential problems in the short run:

—About three thousand bureaucrats were put out of work in a restructuring of agricultural agencies in one area.

—Fourteen percent of Soviet farms operate at a loss, and potential foreclosures seem inevitable.

—Wages have been held up at factories where products have been rejected by quality control boards.

—In Moscow, economists talk about sixteen million workers being dislocated over the next fifteen years as industry and agriculture trim back their work forces.

—Basic food prices, heavily subsidized by the government, will most likely go up as they have in other socialist states recently, some as much as 46 percent.[7]

In addition, the few durable goods that are available are so heavily taxed that the average consumer cannot come close to affording them. For example, the largest Soviet passenger car, a Volga, retails at $25,600. Most of the increase above the wholesale price of $5,460 consists of taxes.[8]

Publicly, most workers seem to support restructuring, but people wonder when—or if—this latest in a long history of Soviet reform will bear fruit.

Disillusioned Youth

Economic reforms, however successful, address only part of the grievances, particularly for the young people. The millions of post-war born citizens of the Soviet Union and Soviet bloc countries possess a different mind-set from their parents.

These young adults are more familiar with the Soviet invasion of Budapest in 1956, the construction of the Berlin Wall in 1961, the takeover of Prague in 1968, and the present Soviet occupation of Afghanistan rather than the heroic accomplishments of the Soviet motherhood in World War II.

The *Dallas Times Herald* recently published a revealing story about disillusioned Soviet youth. Membership in communist party and youth organizations is falling. As economic prospects diminish, the frustrations of life in a closed society have brought about unprecedented alienation at levels unpublicized in the West.

Teen-age drug addiction, alcoholism, and crime have soared in the past decade. The director of a communist youth union made the following evaluation of the youth climate:

> Young people are cynical. They see little hope for a future. Living standards are going down and unemployment is going up. We are all in the same boat. And the boat is sinking. Somehow, we have to regain the youth's confidence without changing the system.[9]

Pent-up frustration has thrust the young people of the socialist countries into varying phases of reform movements rather than nationalistic flag-waving. Young people complain about studying computers on blackboards and being educated in areas where jobs don't exist. Other common complaints include:

1. Travel restrictions
2. Alternative media, music, and literature restrictions
3. Obligatory military service
4. Implied allegiance to the Soviet Union (in Eastern bloc countries)
5. Government indifference to the East bloc ecological crisis
6. Educational backwardness throughout the bloc[10]

Yugoslavia has 850,000 unemployed youth. Czechoslovakia has a serious drug problem—young addicts have increased twenty-fold in twelve years. Hungary has the world's highest rate of teen-age suicide.

Pressed to explain the high rate of crime and the drug and alcohol abuse among youth, Soviet sociologists invariably blame parents for setting a bad example. Rarely do they mention the ills of a communist society, such as the oppressive boredom or the inability to travel freely. Never would they recognize spiritual and moral needs.

Why does the communist system have few prescriptions for youth crime? According to Marxist ideology, no motive for crime exists under communism. "Young people grow up saying the party is not for them," one party leader lamented.

Membership in communist youth organizations keeps dropping all over Eastern Europe, despite the fact that joining is considered indispensable to a career. There is no other way to get into college. High school students in the party might number close to 100 percent one party official said, but once they get into college, it drops to 10 percent.

"Marxism is in a state of regression among young people," another communist leader said. "The question is: When will it stop?"[11]

The Thriving Black Market

Housing remains scarce in every socialist country. Thirteen million Soviet citizens live in communal apartments where two or more couples share the same bathroom and kitchen.

In addition, public health services are inadequate, pollution is the worst in Europe, and even the public water supply in many areas (including Prague) is considered unhealthy. In fact, thirty million Soviets do not have pure drinking water.[12] As a result, the influence of Marxism is so weak that citizens have taken matters into their own hands in nearly every sphere of life.

Nowhere is this more evident than in the second economic system of the Soviet Union and its socialist allies. The "black market" or shadow society is tolerated by communist authorities because the Marxist economic system has neither the means nor the purpose to build a better life for its working people.

Communist authorities have been forced not only to patronize the second economy, but authorize it as well, using it to achieve the slow moving successes of the restructuring process. Official corruption, lies, graft, and greed have destroyed four to seven decades of what little social value remains in socialism.

Hedrick Smith explains in his excellent book *The Russians:*

> Practically any material or service can be arranged [under the table] from renting a holiday cottage in the country, buying a raincoat or a pair of good shoes in a state store, getting a smart dress made

by a good seamstress, transporting a sofa across town, having the plumbing fixed or soundproofing installed on your apartment door, being treated by a good dentist, sending your children to a private playschool, arranging home consultation with a top-flight surgeon, to erecting buildings and laying pipe in a collective farm. This counter-economy has become an integral part of the Soviet system, a built-in, permanent feature of Soviet society.[13]

Pulling strings, or *blat* as the Russians call it, is an essential lubricant of life.

Forty percent of Czechs and Slovaks are engaged in the second economy, which provides everything from farm goods to automobile repairs. In Hungary, government officials say 70 percent of their employed people work in the second economy; Bulgarian officials estimate that 50 percent of their country's workers take part.

A Romanian commercial transporter, in a personal interview, estimated that sixty-five percent of all goods imported into Romania are illegal contraband. How do the good get in? Through border check points using sophisticated systems of payola.

The Soviet Union spends $22 to $26 billion a year on privately provided services, which has created thousands of Soviet millionaires over the years. This compares with $72 billion a year for services through the official economy.

One Russian chemist, who distilled vodka at his institute, owned a small car for five years and never once took it to a gas station. The gasoline always came to him regularly on Friday afternoon—supplied by the drivers of cars for state enterprises and government motor pools. These drivers would come to areas where private car owners park their cars. Then gas was siphoned from the state drivers' tanks—gas bought by their agencies with subsidized government coupons—into the private cars.

Hedrick Smith explains this procedure:

> Everyone is so used to the operation that when
> the drivers come by, you just hold up two, three,
> or four fingers for twenty, thirty, or forty liters.
> The gas doesn't cost the driver a kopek so he
> makes a ruble profit, and it costs me only about
> one-third of the regular price.[14]

Black market activity is motivated by both economic
incentive and a desire for greater personal freedom. Many
young people and neighborhood groups have organized
entertainment and other social activities outside the framework of the Communist Party or municipal government
authority to help meet these needs.

Have Things Changed?

Some suggest that the spread of social and economic
activities outside the government's reach threatens the very
foundations of the communist system. The *Houston Chronicle* carried this assessment by one Czech sociologist:

> Our analysis of the social structure and way of life
> for the last fifteen years shows a certain depletion.
> We have many empirical research proofs showing
> a total breaking up of social development.[15]

Difficulty in supplying medical care, housing, and social
services present an aura of hopelessness that is dominant
and irreversible. Many people work two jobs in an effort
to deal with the high costs of consumer goods. What's causing the price increase? Government reductions in the subsidization of food, health services, education, public
transportation, and housing.

The long hours that people must work and the constant
stress associated with keeping food on the table has con-

tributed to the drop in life expectancy in most of the socialist countries. While many promises have been made and new policies worked out on paper, have things really changed in the Soviet Union?

Most of the key Soviet officials who brought on *the need* for such changes are still in place under Gorbachev. "With people like that still around," Robert Bernstein, chairman of the U.S. Helsinki Watch Committee said in Moscow, "it doesn't exactly inspire public confidence in the leadership's commitment to change."[16]

Against this background, how does one view Gorbachev's call for "restructuring"? Are these unprecedented changes a critically needed response to rescue the system from itself? Or can we expect Gorbachev to reassert the supremacy of the ruling parties in areas where control is slipping away? Only time will tell, and in the meantime, the Soviet people are the ones who suffer.

10

Problems in Paradise

Once a Frenchman, an Englishman, and a Russian were discussing the nationality of Adam and Eve. The Frenchman said, "Adam and Eve must have been French. Who but the French would think of something so romantic as a man and a woman sharing an apple in a beautiful garden?"

The Englishman said, "No, Adam and Eve must have been English. Wasn't it so proper for the man to let the woman have the first bite of the apple?"

Finally, the Russian shook his head and said, "No, comrades. Adam and Eve were definitely Russians. Who else would have only one apple to eat between two people, not even have enough clothes to wear, and still have the audacity to call it paradise!"

A former communist party member, in referring to his Marxist ideology, sarcastically said, "Isn't it a beautiful idea to build paradise on earth? Communism is the only ideology that promises that."[1]

Unfortunately, the Soviet dream has fallen woefully short of its ideals. How much time Mr. Gorbachev has to resolve these problems in paradise may well determine his very existence.

Gorbachev's dilemma faces him at every turn. On the one hand, the downtrodden working women demand more pay and privilege. On the other, the emerging middle class of professionals expect more and more from glasnost and perestroika.

Second Class Citizens

When Tom Brokaw of NBC news interviewed Mikhail Gorbachev on December 7, 1987, the Secretary General disclosed his personal practice of routinely consulting his wife and confidante Raisa Gorbachev in most matters of state policy. While not causing unusual response in the West, the remarks were deleted by Soviet censors when broadcast over Soviet television.

Despite discussion of the Berlin Wall, Afghanistan, and other politically controversial subjects, the issue of Gorbachev's consulting his wife was the only topic deleted, even censored. Although Gorbachev's relationship with his wife might be exceptional, Soviet advisors undoubtedly believed such an image before a country of 150 million men would be devastating at a time when Gorbachev needs tremendous domestic popular support.

At the same time, he cannot afford to alienate the female population either. Especially when women comprise:

75 percent of Soviet doctors
Over 70 percent of Soviet teachers
Over 60 percent of all Soviets with a college education.[2]

Despite educational and legislative equality, the majority of Soviet women are underpaid and overworked. They commonly fulfill most of the manual labor jobs in construction, road maintenance, and agriculture. Women are paid depressingly low salaries commensurate with their practical (if not legal) status as second-class citizens.

The Moscow weekly *Navaya Vremya* (New Times) recently wrote:

> If all types of work are arranged in pyramid form of the qualifications necessary and the status attached (which means wages or salaries), we find the following picture: Each of the layers is more densely populated by women than the one above it. The same applies more starkly to the pyramid of administrative or educational posts.[3]

In June 1987, while at a women's congress, Mr. Gorbachev alluded to inconsistencies between practice and form when he asked: "Can we draw the conclusion that everything is in good order? Frankly, no."[4]

No greater exploitation of female labor in an industrialized country exists than in the Soviet Union. Women are at the mercy of the state when it comes to where they will live, what kind of job they will have, and even if they will marry and have an apartment.

In areas where Soviet population trends are dominated by females, and the labor force still is recovering from a devastating world war, the females of the Soviet Union will do anything to get the prospect of a husband, an apartment—and a residence permit in Moscow.

The "propiska" or residence permit, which is usually issued at the place of one's birth, locks Soviets into involuntary commitment for life. Having one's residence permit changed to another city is only remotely possible. Relocating to another city without a job in that city is against Soviet law. One is not entitled to employment without first presenting a valid residence permit for that city.

Housing, if available (a rarity), is not permissible without a valid residence permit. Therefore a single female born in a small Ukrainian village is normally doomed to a lifetime of servitude within that environment unless she takes advantage of a work opportunity to another remote area desperately in need of habitation (Siberian projects for example).

Living on the Edge

A program, mainly for single females, called "limitchiki" (literally "those living on the edge"), provides work in industrialized cities (mostly Moscow).[5]

As a result of the poor planning of the socialist economic system, the industrial enterprises of large cities are always in dire need of workers. Some plants in Moscow employ 90 percent of their workers "limitchiki."

Most of this work consists of hard physical labor in factories that are not air-conditioned, using antiquated equipment and necessitating little sophisticated training or skill. Local citizens have no desire to work under such conditions for minimum wages. Because they already have residence permits authorizing them to live in the city, they can simply look for other employment.

Lacking adequate employees, employers resort to work pools outside urban areas. There they can find women working in collective farms or rural villages who long to experience culture, social activity, and economic advancement. The majority simply want a good salary, an apartment in Moscow, and a marriage with a Muscovite that will give them the coveted residence permit to remain permanently in Moscow.

With no apartments available, the single women are often housed in hostels, two to four per room, with nothing to do after their hard physical labor but to pursue their own devices toward sanity and self-respect. Single adults, mostly women, comprise about 8 percent of Moscow's population.

Should a "limitchiki" survive the rigor of daily doldrums and exploitation, she has no hope of obtaining a permanent residence permit for at least five to six years. To be eligible for an apartment, one must wait until she has been in

Moscow at least ten years. That means a twenty-year-old "limitchiki" must expect to wait until she is forty years old before she can hope to obtain her own separate apartment. Until then she must struggle through life at the hostel. Listen to the plight of Nina Vasilyevna, a Moscow limitchiki:

> I am 37 years old and manager of the hostel, but I am also a "limitchiki" and have no rights. I am still a "girl" like everyone else. Everyone can see who visits me. Thank God, the city security guard at least lets through my guests. This is a big city, but no one cares about me. Other girls manage to marry, some move, I have nowhere to go. I have decided to bear a child without a husband as it is my last chance.[6]

Even those single females fortunate enough to find a husband and obtain the cherished resident permit must live apart from their spouses for years without hope of their own apartment. No end to the frustration is in sight.

Over the past fifteen years more than 700,000 workers have relocated from the provinces to the capital. Now the rate seems to be 300,000 to 400,000 people every five years, primarily because of decrease in machine-tool replacement and renovation, slow down of automation, poorer labor discipline, and more public disorder.[7]

Without "limitchiki," Moscow plants would have long since closed for lack of a work force. Bringing in new workers is far easier for the Soviets than updating the technology or improving the conditions of those already here.

Gorbachev's dilemma is that he needs the working class on his side. He knows that the immediate social and economic problems must be met before he can count on the backing of the proletariat. To do this, the Soviet leader must rapidly transfer personnel resources in the form of scientists, technicians, and educators away from military goals to meet the needs of the people today.

The Emerging Middle Class

In spite of the huge blue-collar class structure, a new group of people is appearing among the work force.

The economic changes brought about by perestroika have resulted in an unusual phenomenon: the sudden appearance of a middle class in Soviet society. The emergence of this new, powerful class—comprised of economists, scientists, technicians, doctors, lawyers, educators, and other professionals—is suddenly the force to be reckoned with by the Soviet party structure.

In the past, the Communist Party knew how to deal with the Soviet people. During the 1950s, Stalin's style of industrial development was centered on discipline, slave labor, and quantity rather than quality. The techniques were simple, and workers were easy to control. While Stalin's ideology purported to espouse the value of the working class, it only succeeded in enslaving the people.

Czechoslovakia in 1968 and Hungary in 1956 attempted to chart a new course, but Soviet tanks ended most hopes for substantial change. In the past ten years, Poland, however, has been more successful. In fact, all change—even a Solidarity union—emanated from worker's demands.

At the same time that Solidarity was gaining in power, Eastern European nations and the Soviet Union were also producing their own new class structure. As a result, Gorbachev's bureaucracy seems to derive its legitimacy not from the proletariat (working people) but from a reform-minded middle class of professionals and technicians.

In our highly technological age, middle class professionals are the key to accumulating and transmitting necessary statistical data and information technology. They are also absolutely essential to production.

Gorbachev now realizes that for the Soviet Union to deliver in the area of its greatest weakness—information technology—he must satisfy this ever increasing class of professionals. Then he can induce them to work more efficiently to achieve his goals. But to accommodate middle-class demands, Gorbachev may have to yield authority and make necessary concessions in order to refuel his reformist programs.

What do members of the middle class expect? Their more sophisticated consumption needs are reflected in quality of life, information, goods, and travel. Middle class workers want more selection and greater supplies of food products. They want improved health care, uncensored news reports, access to overseas products, and freedom to travel within the Soviet Union and around the world.

To keep the growing middle class happy, Gorbachev will have to resolve crucial issues that affect the daily lives of Soviet citizens. Without an improved quality of life, specifically the redress of obvious social and material needs of the people, the rise of the middle-class may be short-lived.

Gorbachev's Dilemma

Marx said the dominating social class always represents the dominant means of production. Without a doubt the reform measures of Mikhail Gorbachev will only be as effective as his response to accommodate the demands of this new middle class of technocrats.

Gorbachev knows that middle-class professionals are more difficult to control than blue-collar workers. They are more open to new ideas and less intimidated by police threats. In addition, they are more difficult to coerce, responding more readily to incentives and opportunities.

For the Soviet Union to reach its twenty-first century goals, Gorbachev must quickly mobilize his army of middle-class revolutionaries and intelligentsia. If he cannot, his reform goals will be in shambles. And if he cannot initiate his reform policies, his support might never extend beyond the intellectual and middle class bureaucracy he has now enamored to the working class he also desperately needs.

The national free health system, old-age pensions, child care, and a host of related social service needs are at a critical crossroads. The people expect reform, but overhauling the Soviet's social welfare system is like sandblasting a charred, old castle with a toothbrush.

Sub-Standard Health Care

Medical care standards within the Soviet Union have fallen to a disastrous level. While life expectancy levels continue to increase in the United States and most of Europe, Soviet citizens have not yet caught up. Let's examine the discrepancy in life expectancy estimates:

Soviet men: 66 years   Soviet women: 73.9 years
U.S. men: 71 years   U.S. women: 78.7 years

Since 1976, deaths from heart disease have simultaneously risen 50 percent in the Soviet Union and declined 25 percent in the United States. Mortality rates in the Soviet Union related to cerebral arterial disease (strokes associated with high blood pressure) doubled within the past twenty years while they have declined 50 percent in the U.S.[8]

In addition, the Soviet medical system is antiquated and unprofessional. Svyatoslav Fyodorov, a respected eye surgeon, admitted that "we are trusting our patients' lives to absolutely unreliable technology."[9] Forty percent of new medical graduates cannot read X-rays or cardiograms.

Soviet doctors have not made any major advances in surgical techniques in the past thirty years. During that same time, not one important drug has been developed. The average Moscow drugstore sells only ten of the most standard thirty-nine drugs commonly available in the West. None of these are manufactured within the Soviet Union.[10]

Devastating Statistics

Although the Soviet birth rate is on the increase, the lack

of good medical care has resulted in a higher infant mortality rate. According to 1986 figures, 25.4 Soviet infants die for every 1,000 live births, compared with 10.4 in the U.S.

Despite the Soviet national average of 1.94 births per couple, such figures still fall short of 2.5 births per family, which Soviet demographers have determined to be the "replacement rate" need to assure a stable population.[11] The birth rates in the non-Russian republics, primarily the Asiatics in Soviet Central Asia, are far outstripping the Russians. At the current rate, by the year 2000, the Russian population will, for the first time in Soviet history, be a minority ethnic population group of 49 percent. Such statistics put fear in the hearts of Soviet leaders.

At the same time, an even more serious phenomenon affects the birth rate of Soviet citizens. Alexandra Biryukova, a high-ranking female official in the Kremlin, recently decried the chronic shortage of contraceptives in the Soviet Union, saying it contributes to an estimated 6.5 million abortions a year (compared to 1.5 million in the U.S.). She told a news conference: "It is not normal when the number of abortions is about equal to the number of births."[12]

A recent article in the *Moscow News* contained the account of a Russian woman's abortion experience. Yekaterina Nikolayeva reveals the effects of socialized medicine at its worst and portrays the emotional trauma faced by almost every woman in Soviet society.

> As I stood in line at the door of a hospital operating room waiting for my abortion, the doctor said, "What are you waiting for? Come on, don't stare." As I entered the room, he removed a pair of blood-stained rubber gloves.
>
> My hands started to shake. I felt scared, hurt, and on the verge of tears. But the doctor only shouted, "Hurry up, you! I'm sick and tired of your stupidity!"

> After the abortion, the doctors left for the day
> without checking on me, and I finally got up and
> went home on my own in a nightgown and robe.[14]

In spite of Soviet efforts to stem the high abortion rate among women, abortion remains the most common form of birth control, with ten abortions not uncommon for a Soviet woman.[13]

Bring Your Own Bedpan

As in any welfare state, hospital services relate directly to the quality of treatment vs. money available. Bribes and corruption abound. Patients constantly "tip" attendants, surgeons, and physicians to provide the most common of care needs such as bedpans, towels, sheets, and even the availability of the surgeons themselves.

Many patients are forced to bring their own surgical equipment or to secure medicines on the black market. Western coffee, cigarettes, or other products have always been the effective mode of payment for any adequate medical treatment.

Little food exists for inpatient care, and Soviet health care authorities have refused to raise the daily food allowance for patients. Only recently have kiosks been permitted on premises for patients to buy snacks. A statement recently published posthumously by one critic stated:

> I drove up to the hospital and . . . visitors with
> bags and bundles were stretching from the gates
> to the numerous buildings. They were carrying not
> presents and flowers to the patients, but food.[15]

At the 71st anniversary of the "Great October Socialist Revolution," one of the Communist Party slogans was: "Working people in health care! Raise the quality of medical assistance, display more attention and charity toward people!" Hopefully, this slogan will become more than a faded poster hanging in the drab, grey halls of Russian hospitals.

This devastating health care crisis caused by tremendous financial and sociological strains has resulted in some soul-searching in this social paradise. New approaches are being considered, including private health care, steady dismantling of state subsidies, acceptance of individual charity, and the exploration of a national insurance program.

State commitments have been made to increase the national health budget (from 4.0 percent today) to 8 percent of national income by 2000.[16] An effort is also under-way to decentralize the health system, giving regional authorities budgetary controls based on local determination of needs. The Soviets are exploring Western approaches to welfare systems, including private assumption of realistic patient costs. The first fee-charging hospital opened in 1988 with anticipated annual profits of 15 percent.[17]

Despite these reforms, bringing medical doctors' pay up to the level of a skilled worker will take years. The salaries of most medical doctors, both male and female, has been severely depressed the past twenty years. Now, under Gorbachev a phased pay increase has been put into effect. (Gorbachev has a twenty-eight-year-old daughter Irina who is a physician herself and married to a physician).

Where Will the Money Come From?

Money must fuel these reforms. Where will it come from? Most likely from shutting down the enormous food and housing subsidy programs now in existence. This will bring intense psychological change as well as physical hardship to many.

For generations now, degrees of socialist successes have been measured in price *cuts.* Now to explain communist advances in terms of *increased* costs of living might bring on even worse rioting than in 1962. At that time Khrushchev's price increases led to seventy deaths. In Poland four such situations resulted in massive political uprisings.

With Gorbachev having announced officially the potential loss of 16 million jobs over the next twelve years, unemployment is also a social issue for the first time confronting authorities.

In all welfare states, many people subsidize the needs of the few. This means that demographics play a major role in balancing income with expenditures. With Soviet pensioners now numbering 60 million (over 20 percent of the Soviet population) and projections estimating 70 million in ten years, all costs of benefits are born by the state.[18] Monthly pensions of 36 rubles ($49.30) have been increased by Gorbachev slightly, adding to the strain.[19]

Leonid Brezhnev must share part of the financial blame for the ailing Soviet economy. With increasing numbers of old-age pensioners to support and increased dependence on food consumption, Brezhnev chose to heavily subsidize the cost of food. As Soviets have moved from a traditional diet of bread and potatoes to one including meat, eggs, and butter, government funding has increased. Today the food subsidy program represents one-fifth of the national budget.

Balancing the Budget with Vodka

Brezhnev chose to balance the budget through the sale of alcoholic beverages. When Brezhnev died, alcoholic sales were four time higher than the last year of Nikita Khrushchev's administration. The result? An epidemic of alcoholism.

Having declared alcoholism to be domestic enemy number one, Gorbachev in May 1985 raised the price of a bottle of vodka to the equivalent of two day's wages for an average worker, cut production of vodka in half, raised the legal drinking age to twenty-one, sharply curtailed sale hours, and introduced higher penalties for public drunkenness.[20]

According to official figures, liquor sales were reduced to half. Health-wise that was good news; economically, however, such figures were devastating. Why? Because the national budget was strongly dependent on alcohol sales, and balancing the budget in 1988 was nearly impossible.

Gorbachev's war on alcoholism did have some short-term benefits: life expectancy tables experienced an upswing, after many years of decline; alcohol related deaths decreased 32 percent; and crime came down.[21]

In the end, however, Gorbachev realized it was a losing battle. Sugar almost disappeared from store shelves to account for some two billion bottles of moonshine. Drunkenness increased, and nothing annoyed the working class like Gorbachev's anti-alcohol campaign. In response to such gripes, the government now permits two hundred additional shops in Moscow to sell vodka, and many more opened for wine and beer. Officials have also restored longer sale hours. Unfortunately, crime rose 4 percent in 1988.[22]

With some 15 to 20 million alcoholics/problem drinkers (official acknowledgement 5 million) in the Soviet Union, there are efforts to obtain pledges of sobriety from all trade-union members (99 percent of the adult population). In addition, alcohol education is compulsory in the schools.

The Armenian Earthquake and Chernobyl

The unexpected chaos of the Armenian earthquake of December 1988 has further complicated any structured plans for national reform. According to the U.S. Agency for International Development's official figures, 23,312 people were confirmed dead. There are 130,000 injured with 107,437 evacuated as of December 1988.

The earthquake completely leveled 58 villages and a town with a population of 50,000. One hundred villages were damaged. Imagine replacing over 21,000 residences, 83 schools, 88 kindergartens, 84 hospitals, and hundreds of stores and public buildings immediately. Food losses include 24,000 head of cattle, 45,000 sheep, and 8,000 pigs. Damage to agriculture alone is estimated at $3.1 billion while physical damage is expected to total more than $13.3 billion.[23]

In addition, the clean-up expenses at the Chernobyl nuclear accident and the hundreds of people left physically disabled and dependent on government medical care are costing millions of dollars. And that may be only the beginning. Three years after the incident cancer rates have doubled among regional residents; half the children in one locale have thyroid gland illnesses; and livestock are being born without heads and limbs.[24]

The Chernobyl nuclear plant accident has also put the Soviet government on edge in regard to nuclear energy. Gorbachev, facing tremendous public outcries from anti-nuclear power opponents, cancelled construction of a Black Sea nuclear site. Subsequent anti-nuclear demonstrations have surfaced—from the Far East to the Barents Sea—protesting the docking of Soviet nuclear powered vessels.

The added strain on the economy, brought on by the Armenian earthquake and Chernobyl, forces Gorbachev to look for new ways to bolster the system since the old ways obviously haven't worked.

A Different Story

The recent natural and nuclear disasters in the Soviet Union have opened a plethora of possibilities for social activism and responsibility. For the first time since communism came to power, new ideas and approaches to age-old problems are being considered.

New programs are proposed for the mentally ill—the first fundamental revision of the Mental Health Code in twenty-seven years. Over seven million physically disabled citizens and 300,000 orphans reside in state-run nurseries, schools, and vocational schools, most of which have severely restricted accessibility to help.

In Soviet society, the words "charity" and "needy" once depicted something improper, disgraceful, or unproductive. That's why the Soviet Union finds itself five decades behind in expressing any desire to help others.[25] Now, however, one sees officially organized, sanctioned youth groups aiding the elderly and disabled, providing relief services and even vehicles to Soviet orphanages around the country. The children's fund, authorized for Aleksandr A. Laveykin by the Communist Party Central Committee, now measures its assets over $200 million at the official exchange rate.[26]

"Intervening to help the fate of others is one of the oldest Russian—and human—virtues," Mr. Laveykin said. "Tolstoy and Dostoyevsky always helped the needy. This feeling has always been there in our people."[27]

Soviet TV exposure has brought on other volunteer efforts involving people from all walks of life. In Moscow alone, over a six month period, twelve community groups formed with causes as broad as cultural interests, children's needs, or artistic endeavors.

In addition, government efforts to provide individual financing of private homes to eradicate the housing shortage by the year 2000 are being made. Meetings are also set to reform the country's vast public-education system by the 300 member Communist Party Central Committee, affecting 40 million students and 3 million teachers.[28]

Facing the problems in this communist "paradise" is one thing. Finding lasting solutions is quite a different story. A story in which the final chapter may be written before the main character gets his act together.

11

No Money—No Reform

A Russian motorist pulled up in front of an Intourist Hotel near Red Square in Moscow and double parked, blocking the entrance. Despite angry threats from a Soviet policeman that the car would be towed, the driver shrugged nonchalantly and walked off.

A bystander explained the man's actions, suggesting that such a threat has no credibility. "That cop couldn't get a tow truck here in a week." [1]

The Soviet Union is a land where shoddy craftsmanship and grudging service are the norm. Machines don't run, and attempts to repair them are greeted with shrugs. Human resources are squandered on make-work jobs that turn productivity statistics into a cruel joke. People have money but nothing to buy with it.

A western journalist working near Moscow had a grueling experience with a rented Zhiguli, an elderly Fiat built under license in the Soviet Union. A short trip resulted in two flat tires, a broken jack, a search for a mechanic, an official declaration by the police as to the delay, and a broken gas cap while filling the tank with gas. While the inconvenience overwhelmed the journalist, the local people calmly accepted the fact that one usually needs *two days* to fix a flat in Russia.

"Hey kids, do you think Gorbachev will be able to make it?" the journalist asked several young teenagers at the Soviet service station. "No, his ideas won't work," they answered. "How can you change all this?" the person asked, gesturing all around.[2]

Gorbachev is facing a formidable task. Not only must he modernize a stagnant communist system, but he must overcome a long history of failure in which every effort at reform has become mired in defeat. Over the years, the Soviets have encountered economic setbacks with civil wars, world wars, and Stalin's terror. Despite a brief respite under Khrushchev in the mid-1960s, the Soviet Union continued to degenerate further during the Brezhnev years. Only recently has Gorbachev roused the sleeping bear from its slumber.

Glasnost and perestroika are asking the Soviet workers to roll up their sleeves and get to work. Yet Gorbachev himself admits that his message, which is balancing "on the narrow margin between the possible and the impossible" is meeting with reluctance, skepticism, and even resistance.[3]

The economic promises held out to those willing to work harder and demand better results are threefold:

1. More and better housing, where chronic shortages exist.
2. More consumer goods to buy, where empty shelves or long lines frustrate shoppers.
3. Better services and modern conveniences for the nation's long deprived consumers.

According to Soviet economists, however, none of the plans proposed will materialize in less than five to ten years. Nevertheless, the hope of change is certainly in the hearts of the Soviet people.

For Better or Worse?

Immediate change for the better remains an illusion. Actually, restructuring has brought on more social problems than it has corrected: unemployment; increased cost of living for the masses; substantial price increases for basic commodities; and diminished privileges of the ruling elite.

Such reforms run up against party officials, economic bureaucrats, and planners who see any change as upsetting their comfortable lives. Even ordinary workers feel endangered when they are faced with the demands for higher quality and greater productivity.

The state of the Soviet economy satisfies no one. In fact, the Soviet economy is in desperate need of help. Nikolay Shmelyov, a Soviet author whose work appeared in the June 1987 issue of *Novy Mir,* made this observation:

> We now have an economy which is out of whack and plagued with shortages, an economy which rejects scientific and technical progress and is unplanned and—if we want to be totally honest—unplannable.[4]

Gorbachev himself, in a recent speech to editors of leading newspapers and journalists, admitted, "We have revealed a real turmoil in the minds of many people—workers, intelligentsia and leading cadres, not only below, but at the top."[5]

Party functionaries face losing jobs and power. Some in military high command see the untouchable status of the armed forces threatened. Those facing the greatest unemployment risk are the party's ideological, educational, and propaganda arms of the government. These people represent a powerful minority of writers, journalists, academicians, "semi-intelligentsia," and thousands of teachers of Marxism-Leninism in universities and high schools.

As the people desire new freedoms of expression, a distrust for intellectuals, culture, and the media has arisen. This attitude generates extreme prejudice toward the younger generation and suspicion surrounding the instant affluence of entrepreneurs in the cooperative enterprises. Added to all this is an ever increasing western influence.

Yet the greatest hazard to reform comes from the stubborn minds and entrenched practices of the bureaucrats. That is why Gorbachev is in a hurry.

From Peasants to Profits

The current Soviet population is approaching 290 million people with a per capita income of only about $6,000. Part of the reason for the low income level results from the Soviets' agrarian mentality.

Despite the fact that the peasants were freed from serfdom in Russia in 1861, 80 percent continued to work as part of village collectives. Later, after the revolution, state farm systems engulfed the populace. This government control resulted in four substantial restrictions:

1. Individual initiative was squelched.
2. Farming privately owned small plots was prohibited.
3. Crafts and other similar products of home industry were likewise stifled.
4. The entire Soviet agricultural output was controlled.

Although the Soviets industrialized rapidly after the revolutionary process, inefficiency and confusion led to economic disaster. As a result the current reform plans were initiated. After years of government supervision, however, there are no trained technicians or managers eager to assume responsibility. No one is prepared to step from a controlled to a competitive economy, or to let the market determine prices.

Although Gorbachev's first five-year plan held out the prospect of a quick return, only 1986 and 1987 came close in projected economic growth (3.3 percent compared to 4 percent). Previously, 1985 growth measured less than 1 percent. But western experts consider the accomplishments to be an aberration.

Statisticians predict the initial stimulus of the reform movement plus a better than expected agricultural harvest cannot sustain long-term growth. Agricultural growth rates have consistently been less than 1 percent per year, despite mind-boggling investments in this area. In 1987, agricultural production rose by 1.8 percent to a value of $766 billion,[6] despite the need to import an additional 700,000 metric tons of soybean products above the existing contract with the United States.[7]

Although the Soviet Union produces "six times as many tractors as the U.S., we buy your wheat. You don't buy any of ours," stated Nikolay Shmelev of Moscow's Institute of U.S. and Canada Studies.[8]

Through 1991, the end of Gorbachev's initial five-year plan, growth is expected to average no better than 1 to 2 percent a year. Mark Kramer of Harvard's Russian Research Center says, "I wouldn't be surprised if it dropped below that."[9] Such figures are consistent with the prior twelve years when growth slumped to an average of 2 percent per year.

A Bankrupt Economy?

Obviously Gorbachev must move quickly. He can't hesitate much longer. January 1, 1988, was a turning point. On that date, 60 percent of the Soviet economy began operating in reform conditions, i.e. "profit incentives," "self-financing," and "cooperatives."

This means that a majority of the Soviet economy becomes subject to bankruptcy if a profit cannot be made. By October 1, 1988, fifty factories had been declared bankrupt. The government itself announced a 15 percent budget deficit, which forced the Politburo to consider cutting the budget and making the *ruble* a convertible currency.

Such drastic economic measures would cause runaway inflation because of the ruble's anticipated drop in value. This would result in soaring consumer price increases for already scarce food and personal products.

In addition to food scarcities, unemployment has become a crippling problem. Azerbaijan has 250,000 young men out of work; even more are unemployed in Kazakhstan. All over the Soviet Union workers fear increased layoffs and job loss due to a stagnant Soviet economy. The government predicts an estimated 16 million jobs will be lost during the reform movement prior to the year 2000.

Most Soviet citizens don't think in terms of business incentives but only whether or not they will be able to maintain a reasonable standard of living. In fact, the average worker often wonders if he will even be able to feed his family.

At any given daytime moment, half of Moscow can be found waiting in line. The typical Soviet woman may stand in line at a cheese shop for forty-five minutes. First, she may wait fifteen minutes in one line to make her selection. Usually white and yellow cheese are her only options. Then, after waiting fifteen minutes in another line to pay, she returns to the first line and endures another fifteen minute wait before picking up her purchase. At the next shop she must go through the same process for eggs.

Shortages of food are most acute outside the city. Each day one million people journey to Moscow with cash in hand, hoping to buy anything worth taking home. Every year a half-million tons of meat and meat products alone are carried off by residents to remote Soviet cities who stream into Moscow.

A joke goes: What is long, green, and smells like sausage? Answer: The Moscow to Tula train.

With sugar unavailable, potatoes in short supply, and coffee beans selling at seventeen dollars a pound, the average Soviet has no hope for tomorrow and little expectation for today. Few women, who constantly must shop for whatever is available, venture outside their homes or offices without the expandable string bags known as *avoski,* or "maybe" bags, on the chance they will encounter something worth buying.

"It's not correct to say that there is a shortage of meat now. There is a virtual absence of meat," complained Vera Kudryavtseva, a forty-two-year-old wife and mother living in Moscow. "Sometimes you get lucky and run into a line for meat on your way home from work. But if you go out looking for it, you can't find it anywhere."[10]

Every consumer fears the inevitable—price increases. The heavily subsidized food has largely disappeared from state stores in many towns. Private farmers' markets and new cooperative stores have plenty of food but at prices beyond the reach of ordinary citizens.

Although the price increases will not go into effect until 1989 at the earliest, a public passivity—if not hostility—toward the reform movement has developed on an individual basis. No one gets excited about the reality of food costs doubling.

Raising Money for Reform

Where then will the cornucopia of benefits and quality goods promised by Mr. Gorbachev come from? Foreign money from exported goods is out of the question since only 7 to 8 percent of Soviet products meet world standards. The remainder languishes in warehouses worthless for international sale.

Petroleum exports account for half of the Soviet Union's hard currency earnings, but these have to be set in dollars to conform to international business practice. The weakness in petroleum prices has resulted in fewer dollars for the

Soviets and much less in terms of other major currencies, such as the Japanese *yen* and the West German *mark*. This is important to the Soviets because most of their import obligations, with the exception of grain which largely comes from the U.S., are paid in European or Japanese currencies.

After oil earnings began declining in 1985, the Soviet Union compensated by increasing its sales of gold for hard currency. Once again, motivated by its desperate need for cash, the Soviets also increased their sales of platinum 26 percent in 1986.[11] The Soviets are second to South Africa in the world's production of platinum—the metal used primarily in the auto industries and by jewelers.

With few ways to generate income, who is keeping the Soviets afloat?

Western banks, despite the worst Soviet economic slump since the 1920s, are advancing the Soviets $700 million a month.[12] But Gorbachev wants even more. Moscow has borrowed $6 billion from Western banks in the past two years to cover shortfalls in hard currency caused by a weak dollar and declining world oil prices, according to Central Intelligence Agency (CIA) studies and other sources.

But where is the money going? The answer is obvious when we look at Soviet expenditures. Weapons procurement absorbs 35 percent of the Soviet gross national product (GNP), many times the U.S. rate of 6 percent.[13] In Europe, the Soviets have built up alarming advantages in their conventional forces over two decades, necessitating U.S. weapons to be more flexible and resistant to aggressive action.

Superpower treaties reducing medium and short-range missiles and ultimately long-range missiles are, in part, a means to an end for the Soviets. The end involves East-West trade and loan credits for Moscow and its East European allies.

Gorbachev needs a weapons downturn to permit extensive agricultural irrigation and energy development—

especially after Chernobyl and the earthquake in Armenia. Machinery, factory retooling, consumer goods, housing, and more competitive exports are essential to growth. He needs to modernize his conventional military forces, to provide oil drilling and pumping technology, to acquire advanced robotics and computer technology for factory automation.

Most of all, Gorbachev needs time. The urgency of implementing these objectives insists that loan guarantees be issued in order that such transitions begin immediately.

Waging the Economic War

Gorbachev must raise cash by borrowing more from the West or by exporting more to it. Such an economic interdependence is new. No longer is the West subject only to a large scale frontal military attack by the Russians. The second war is economic, and its goal is to secure Western capital and technology for the Soviet Union.

Ironically, however, to fight the economic war, Gorbachev must *reduce* military spending and borrow more from Western sources. Such reduced military spending will no doubt relieve international tensions, further accelerating the availability of Western capital. Freeing resources from defense and applying them to tools of productivity and increased living standards will provide the Soviets a credit worthy reputation.

Such easy availability of resources, often without obligation or conditions as to how the money may be used, has caused Senator Bill Bradley (D-NJ) to reflect:

> The West, while not overstating its importance, should treat its capital as a strategic asset and develop a plan for its flow eastward.[14]

In the absence of Western capital and technology, the Soviets can increase domestic investment only by decreasing military spending. Yet to date, they have not been forced

to make the choice, despite the fact that Western financial
institutions routinely force harsher decisions on struggling
third world democracies where people are starving.

The huge foreign borrowing by Moscow over the past two
years—a total of $15.5 billion altogether from government
and private creditors—raised the gross debt of the Soviet
Union to $38.2 billion at the end of 1986.[15] But where is
the money going? Almost half that amount went to Marxist
allies such as Cuba, Vietnam, and Nicaragua.[16]

Japanese and European banks provide the bulk of these
new private loans at very reasonable rates. Eighty percent
of Western loans or credits are free to be spent by the Soviets
as they please. In 1985, a group of Western banks advanced
$500 million to East Germany. Within days, a check for $20
million was reportedly deposited in a Nicaraguan account
in Panama.[17]

Senator Bradley affirmed his position:

> The flow of capital should be limited and propor-
> tionate to the degree of systemic reform. I ques-
> tion the wisdom of helping the Soviets avoid the
> choice between civilian investment and military
> build-ups.[18]

Yet, the Soviets continue to get more. In January 1988,
it was announced that a $77.8 million Swiss issue in obli-
gations due from the Soviet Bank for Foreign Economic
Affairs, in the form of public Eurobonds, would be offered
for the first time since 1917.[19] Then, the Soviets seized the
crown jewel of Western credit procurement on May 10, 1988,
when a group of West German banks granted them a $2.1
billion line of credit, the largest Western financial package
for Moscow over the past seven years.[20]

European bankers expected 1988 to be the beginning of
a major borrowing binge by the Soviets facilitated through
Secretary Gorbachev's public relations blitz, beginning in

Washington with the signing of the INF Treaty. History has confirmed the bankers' highest hopes.

By the end of 1988, U.S. allies, including Japan, had granted or were considering credits to the Soviet Union totaling $12 billion. Some are arguing for more liberal limits on the sales of high technology as well.[21]

Jockeying for Trade Position

When Mr. Gorbachev came to Washington in December 1987, one of his major goals was to lobby for Soviet membership in the World Bank, the International Monetary Fund, and the General Agreement on Tariffs and Trade (GATT). The IMF and the World Bank normally make loans to poorer countries while GATT organizes the world trading system.

Among the *communist* members of the World Bank, the monetary fund, and GATT are Poland, Hungary, Romania, and Yugoslavia. China, a member of the World Bank and IMF, has observer status in GATT. Membership in the 95 nation GATT would help the Soviet Union improve its trading position in Western markets where the execution of trade agreements are normal ways to do business.

Why are the Soviets suddenly jockeying for trade position? According to Tass, the Soviet volume of foreign trade dropped 4.6 percent in 1987.[22] Moscow is vigorously seeking foreign trade agreements with Western businesses to boost its failing economy. In fact, nearly thirty joint ventures have been announced and at least sixty are pending. Membership in the World Bank and the IMF, each having 151 members, would help Moscow tap private credit markets.

The Reagan administration, in a January 20, 1988 statement, reiterated that the President's policy opposing Soviet membership in the major economic organizations "remains unchanged." The document said the U.S. could consider endorsing Soviet participation in the organizations only if

Moscow's talk of economic reforms was "translated into positive action."[23] President Bush is not expected to differ in this assessment, at least not immediately.

Moscow has long been seeking an end to the high tariffs that the U.S. applies to imports from the Soviet Union. Such tariffs are mandated by 1974 legislation barring most-favored-nation (MFN) treatment, which carries low duties, to countries that do not permit free emigration.

Only Hungary and Yugoslavia maintain MFN status within the East bloc nations; Romania voluntarily renounced such privilege in anticipation of its termination by Congress.

To improve their world image, the Soviet Union allowed 20,082 Jews to emigrate in 1988, the highest number since 1980 when 21,470 were permitted to move abroad (up from only 914 in all of 1986). The number of emigres is still too small to warrant any major policy reversal, but that could change at any time.

Gorbachev is a shrewd wheeler-dealer, and Western financial institutions seem more than eager to help him out. The easy availability of hard currency has allowed completion of reform promises and goals all of which, whether economically, militarily, or socially oriented, serve only one function—to enhance the Communist Party and the one in authority, Mikhail Gorbachev.

How the U.S. and the West respond to Gorbachev's economic overtures could determine the future of the Soviet Union and the world.

12

East Meets West

Imagine Moscow with a Pizza Hut adjacent to Lenin's Tomb or a McDonald's one block from the Kremlin. Unthinkable only a few months ago, such a vision is now reality under the perestroika policies of Mikhail Gorbachev.

Desperate for Western expertise, the Soviet government took a major step in opening its economy by permitting joint ventures with Western businesses in 1987. Since then, American, European, and Japanese companies have flocked to do business within the Soviet Union.

The Soviets' desire to trade with the West is nothing new. With its non-convertible ruble, it desperately needs to earn foreign currency for two important reasons:

1. To buy those products its ailing economy cannot manufacture
2. To replenish its sagging hard currency reserves

Any activity by the Soviets outside the borders of its bloc nations has to be financed with Western convertible currency. Every diplomatic expense, travel of sports and artistic personalities, any business venture, espionage activity or financial grant has to come out of hard currency accounts.

Where does this money normally originate? Either from the West directly (borrowing, grants, etc.), or from the sale of Soviet assets in foreign trade payable in a Western currency.

Seventy percent of all Soviet exports are made up of oil and gas products, with oil accounting for one-half the Soviet Union's hard currency earnings. The drop in the oil prices, the devaluation of the dollar, and an over supply of oil in recent years has resulted in a 2.2 percent drop in foreign trade in 1987 for the Soviets—a significant loss of hard currency reserves.[1]

Because the Soviet Union lacks most-favored-nation status, the tariff on U.S. imported goods from the Soviet Union is 38 percent, compared with an average of 2.8 percent levied on U.S. imports in general. That, coupled with the Soviet reputation for products of poor quality, finds them running a merchandise trade deficit with the U.S. totaling $650 million in 1986.[2]

Trade statistics in 1985, for example, showed the Soviet Union imported about $2.6 billion worth of U.S. goods (68 percent corn, soybeans, and fertilizers). On the other hand, Americans bought only $600 million in Russian products (mostly gold, fuel oil, and mineral products).[3]

The Best of Both Worlds

Thrust by necessity into a competitive world economic market, from which they have voluntarily isolated themselves over the years, the Soviets must now change their approach.

For the first time in the history of a Soviet trade show held in New York City on December 8, 1988, the purpose was not politics but *profits*. In fact, in an effort to sell their wares, the Soviet participants themselves (cooperatives, foreign trade organizations, and enterprises) not the Soviet government, footed the bill, to the tune of $2 million.[4]

In the past, Soviet enterprises were not allowed to deal directly with their Western counterparts but had to pass through Foreign Trade Organizations (FTOs) under the jurisdiction of the Ministry of Foreign Trade. Since January 1988, however, new legislation authorized twenty-one other ministries and seventy-two state enterprises to arrange their own business affairs with the non-communist world.

Such legislation, called the "Law of the State Enterprise," allows the enterprises to maintain their own foreign currency reserves. In addition, this new change in policy has enticed hundreds of foreign companies with high hopes of cracking a market of 280 million potential customers.

The Soviet dream of the "best of both worlds"—hard currency benefits and access to Western technology—centers around the new socialist phenomenon of joint ventures. In a joint venture, Western businesses will be allowed an ownership of 49 percent in a Soviet situated joint stock company. The Western participant's venture will be tax-free for the first two years and, thereafter, will be taxed at the rate of 30 percent after deductions.[5]

Of course, the Soviets want the Western technology and expertise while at the same time *earning* rather than expending hard currency. Potential benefits for the Western entrepreneur are cheaper production costs and ready access to an enormously untapped market. For example, the Soviets' and East European allies' volume of business with Europe and Japan is only 1 percent of their total economic output; with the U.S., a minuscule 0.1 percent.[6]

Legislative resolve and vision from the top, however, are not guarantees of success. "Many [Russian officials] don't know what's going on, and hardly anyone dares to make a decision," complained Herbert C. Lewinsky, the president of an Austrian industrial conglomerate, one-third of whose exports go to communist bloc countries. "It's incredible what's happening in the Soviet Union today, but the problems are enormous."

Although the Soviet Union is the world's biggest untapped market, Western partners can repatriate profits only if the venture earns hard currency. For example, one United States partner in a joint U.S.-Soviet industrial venture negotiated to receive a cut of the improved yield from the Soviet oil refining and petrochemical industry. How will the U.S. Company take payment? Mostly in gasoline and diesel fuel.

Gold in Glasnost

One innovative U.S. concern, Roma Food of Piscataway, New Jersey, plans to launch as many as twenty-five pizzerias with a Soviet partner. Profits, however, will not be in cash but come from peddling Soviet mushrooms, champagne, and cut glass in Europe.

For most of the 450 U.S. businessmen jetting to Moscow for trade meetings in response to extensive Soviet advertising, their efforts will most likely be measured in increments of problems, patience, and disbelief rather than profits.

Mr. Lewinsky recalls that during a 1987 conversation in Moscow concerning joint ventures, senior Soviet officials suddenly looked disturbed. "They had started talking leasing with us, but they didn't know what it was," he recalled. The next day, Lewinsky sat down with a group of about ninety Soviet bureaucrats to explain the concept.[8]

Despite the Soviet optimism, only twenty-nine joint venture agreements have been inked. What discouraged the potential Western partners?

1. Restrictions on taking home profits in Western currencies
2. Steep taxes
3. Majority Soviet ownership
4. Burdensome visa requirements
5. Poor transportation networks
6. Questionable supplies of material

7. Competitive bureaucracy structure
8. Uninformed and unskilled work force
9. High cost of Soviet hotel accommodations
10. Doubt about how the joint venture law will operate[9]

Moreover, any industrial venture involving transfer of "dual use" technology, i.e. technology useful in industry and the military, will not be allowed by the U.S. government.

Pepsico (owners of Pizza Hut), Occidental Petroleum, Monsanto, McDonalds, Honeywell, Dresser Industries, and Cummins Engine are some of the larger U.S. firms discussing joint venture with the Soviets. Dozens of agreements with Italian, Japanese, German, Austrian, and other companies are also under consideration.

The largest U.S.-Soviet joint venture announced to date involves Armand Hammer's Occidental Petroleum Corporation and Combustion Engineering, two U.S. firms signing separate agreements to build massive Soviet industrial plants totaling more than $25 billion. U.S. firms are already engaging in typically capitalistic competition. Amid accusations of corruption and bribery, Coca-Cola signed a six-year contract with the Soviets, breaking a twelve-year monopoly in the country by Pepsi Cola.

Capitalist greed compels Americans to do business with the Soviets, no matter how difficult the circumstances, how onerous the obligations, or how detrimental the end results. As one U.S. businessman stated, "In the bottom of our hearts, we don't trust the Russians."[10] Yet, for some businessmen, the "gold in glasnost" overrules all other considerations.

Playing Catch Up

The Soviets have acted very shrewdly in trying to step up their domestic economy with the help of Western joint ventures. They have jockeyed for position in the world trade market and have borrowed millions of dollars from Western financial institutions.

Money alone, however, won't sustain the Soviet reform movement. Gorbachev realizes that the Kremlin leaders will never be willing to preside over the Soviet Union's decline into a third-class power. To prevent such occurrence, nothing must hinder the desired onrush of computerization and other forms of high-tech modernization needed to achieve super-power greatness, both militarily and economically.

In a *Chicago Tribune* article dated September 18, 1986, Soviet officials admitted to a five-year lag behind Western technology. Western experts say it is more like ten years, and likely to grow as the pace of Western innovation speeds up.

How far behind are the Soviets? America's electronic marvels will make roughly 50 billion more computer calculations per day than Soviet machines in 1990, a technological gap that is expected to widen dramatically by the turn of the century. No wonder the Soviet Union is often described as a Third World country with rockets.

"The problem with the Soviet economy is technological backwardness," Duke University Professor Jerry F. Hough has written. "The Soviet model was good for heavy industry and growth in the smokestack period of industrialization, but is terrible for heavy industry in the current electronics-computer phase."

The Soviets may produce more steel and machine tools than the U.S., Harvard economist Marshall Goldman says, but in this day and age, "it is not so much a question of more, but rather of better." In that same article Goldman also made the following observation:

> The Soviet Union must . . . find some way to foster innovation and master the production of the new high technologies, including information technologies—computers, computer-aided design and manufacturing (CAD-CAM), microprocessors,

fiber optics, ceramics, electronics, copying machines, robots, lasers, optics, and bio and medical technology.[11]

The brilliant skills of a few Soviet technicians, however, remain locked in research institutes primarily related to space and military development.

Where Are the Computers?

One can travel in the Soviet business community among planners, economists, and managers—persons who are surrounded by figures and statistics—and never see a single computer or printer. The few businesses that do have computers use them for bookkeeping not for inventory, design, or manufacturing. Moscow's 917 high schools recently had a total of fifteen computers on hand. Most students have no idea what a computer is.[12]

The Soviet Union has an estimated 100,000 mainframes and minicomputers, compared to about 1.3 million in the U.S.[13] Most have limited accessibility in scientific institutes where rumors abound that they are used mostly for plotting horoscopes, playing chess, and printing underground literature. Many simply sit idle.

As for microcomputers or personal computers, the Soviets have only 100,000 in the entire country, compared with over 13 million in the United States.[14] *Pravda,* the Communist Party newspaper, recently said the Soviet Union needs 28 million microcomputers to catch up with the West.

Yet to use a computer, a Soviet citizen must find one to buy. One computer theoretically on sale to the public, the BK-0010, lacks both storage and printing capabilities. Described as being a vintage Commodore 64, with virtually no available software and no compatibility with Western computers, it is available only to a tiny minority. Two thousand supposedly went on sale in 1986, yet diplomats report them unavailable at Moscow's only electronics store.

Besides the BK-0010, the Soviets also produce a machine called the Agat, closely based on the Apple II and used in schools. A range of larger computers based on small to medium-sized IBM mainframes of the mid to late 1970s are also available. Yet personal computers for the home, even if available, remain a far-off dream.

The Agat, the copy of the Apple II, costs about $3,600, or three times what one costs in the U.S. This is the equivalent of eighteen month's salary for an average worker. Even pocket calculators, at 50 to 70 rubles ($75-$105), cost a week's salary, one reason why the ancient abacus remains the most common calculator for many Soviets.

Gorbachev's reform policies remain optimistic. In March 1985, the Communist Party leadership ordered a crash computer literacy program for the nation's secondary schools. One newspaper called the program, "like learning to ride a bicycle without a bicycle."

By 1990, when the current five-year plan ends, the Soviet Union is scheduled to produce a total of 1.1 million personal computers. The U.S. produced 5.5 million in 1985 alone. Of this 1.1 million, 400,000 will go into schools. The hope is to have personal computers in one-third of the nation's 60,000 secondary schools "by the early 1990s."[15]

Even a personal computer magazine is in the offing for Soviet consumers. *PC World U.S.S.R.* will be paid for by Western advertisers buying advertising space with Western currency. What kinds of Western products will be available to Soviet consumers and how will they be purchased? No one is quite sure since complex Soviet foreign investment laws and U.S. technology transfer regulations (applying to export of high-tech equipment) are applicable.

Out of Step with the Times

The political fears of an information explosion have been partially responsible for the Soviets' late computer age entry.

Production, quality control, central planning that discourages innovation, and an out-of-step leadership that realized too late the importance of computers also played important parts.

For all the rhetoric about democratization, the Soviet Union remains a closed society in which a Western-style revolution in information technology seems far fetched. The Marxist-Leninist system is based on the tight and centralized control of all sources of information.

The unregulated spread of computers linked to storage devices, electronic bulletin boards, and private data banks has to be an existing threat to the party's monopoly on information. A computer linked to a printer is nothing more than a clandestine printing press—providing a more sophisticated way of publishing *samizdat* (prohibited) texts.

"We'll see," says Soviet computer expert Andrei P. Ershov, "but I see no principal difference between telephone communication lines, videotapes, audio tapes, books or other vehicles for exchange of information. Computers are only faster and more flexible."[16]

Another "vehicle for exchange of information" that is common in the West presents uncommon problems for a secret society like the Soviet Union—the office photocopier. Soviet sources produce approximately one thousand office copying machines a year, supplementing that number by buying several hundred imports. By contrast, Japan produces almost two million photocopying machines per year.

The problem is—photocopiers are considered top-secret equipment, and they are not available to the general public. With the exception of a few libraries and notaries' offices, legal photocopying is simply not available in Moscow or other large cities. In fact, even the Soviet scientific community complains of their inaccessibility to copiers.

Photocopiers are currently made by specially selected employees who are under the surveillance of a government department connected to the KGB. In addition to routine checks carried out within organizations, the work of photocopying equipment operators is periodically subjected to inspections by the Ministry of Internal Affairs and by the State Censorship Board (Glavit). Finally, the instructions for the use of duplicating and copying are regarded as state secrets and are carefully protected from unauthorized access.

The experts agree: one of the greatest challenges facing Moscow is the "information revolution" that is sweeping the West. Without a doubt, its consequences within the Soviet Union and its allies will have potentially far-reaching results.

Will such technology, coupled with video cassettes, shake the foundations of Soviet society? The answer remains to be seen. But one thing is certain: the economic demands are overwhelming—despite the ideological and social implications.

Industrial Espionage

The Soviet leaders find themselves in a bind. Being dependent upon the West, lacking hard currency, and facing Western computer export restrictions, the Soviets must urgently develop their own technology or obtain it some other way. Research and development, however, are not their only means of procuring computer systems.

The *New York Times,* in an article dated October 28, 1987, reported that Soviet technology may be obtained through their elaborate commerce unit, the U.S.S.R. Chamber of Commerce and Industry. This harmless sounding government department is headed by a KGB lieutenant general and systematically engaged in commercial espionage in the West. Branded as the center of industrial spying, according to classified CIA data, the Chamber employs 140 officials—one-third are known or suspected intelligence agents.

The intensity of such an operation was made known recently by the June 1988 expulsion of nineteen Soviet diplomats from Canada on charges of industrial espionage. That was one-fourth of the entire Soviet diplomatic complement in Canada.

This same *New York Times* article also reported:

> Hosting over 200 trade exhibitions and about 100 Western business delegations annually and inspecting thousands of goods each year give its employees extraordinary access to imported equipment and uncounted contacts with foreign companies.[17]

Despite the obvious lack of public access to computer technology, Soviet scientists insist they possess technological expertise in areas of greatest priority to them—military preparedness and space development.

Senior Soviet scientists, who recently visited the U.S., implied that Soviet military engineers have both the technical understanding, machinery, and software necessary for computer controlled manufacturing operations for even the most sophisticated military undertaking.

Dr. Andrei A. Kokoshin, deputy director of the politically powerful Soviet Institute for U.S.A. and Canada Studies, recently made the following statement:

> Washington's assertion that we had to buy foreign equipment to make quiet submarine propellers is merely a red herring . . . We know how to use computer control for milling extremely smooth, accurate surfaces of the kind needed for propellers.[18]

Such a statement lends credence to the comment of Richard N. Perle, a former U.S. assistant secretary of defense for international security policy. Perle strongly opposed the transfer of computer and other advanced technology to the Soviet Union. Any relaxation of computer exports, Perle felt, would eventually lead to setting up joint venture production facilities in the Soviet Union. Further, anything that makes it easier for the Soviets to acquire computer technology is a gift to their military effort.

Perle assessed the situation with the following statement: "There's a big difference between buying a few computers here and there and being able to plan to meet major requirements. They [the Soviet Union] cannot afford to have a computer revolution; on the other hand, they cannot afford not to."[19]

Revolution of another kind may be brewing in Eastern Europe. The Soviets demand of higher quality goods from its Eastern European trading partners will mean less hard currency for East-bloc countries. That, in turn, makes it harder for these countries to import new technology for their own efforts to modernize. The result will be a growing resentment toward the Soviet Union and a new wave of political unrest in the Eastern bloc.

"I'm very pessimistic about the future in Eastern Europe," says Alexander Alexiev, a senior analyst at the RAND Corporation. "Sooner or later, we'll have a political earthquake there."[20] "The political leadership knows they have to bring on board the information technology that has fueled the economic revitalization of the West," says a senior analyst with the CIA. "I don't think they know how to handle it."[21]

Waging the Economic War

When dealing with the Soviets, the basis of economics is always politics. Abel G. Abanbegyan, a top economic advisor to the Soviet leader and considered the chief architect of perestroika, said political reasons were at the root of trade agreements. "Now that political relations are improving, economic relations will improve in their time," he stated.[22]

In other words, in the Soviet Union there is no separation of politics and economics; in fact, economics is always subservient to the political aims of the Party. And who really benefits from the Soviets new economic policies? "The

Soviet military establishment becomes the main beneficiary of the economic dividends produced by the reforms," commented David G. Wigg, Deputy Assistant Secretary of Defense for policy analysis, "and the Western defense community will face a more powerful and dynamic adversary."[23]

Most of us in the West find our thinking dominated by the threat of military aggression by the Soviet Union. For now, though, the dominant war is being fought in the trenches of financial institutions, board rooms, factories, and through the media. While this second war appears harmless, it actually poses an even more serious threat to U.S. and European security than Russia's military might.

Although unpublicized in the United States, and perhaps even misunderstood by U.S. politicians, the economic war being waged out of Moscow is the one of paramount interest to Soviet leadership. Why? Because they're winning! Western capital, technology, and resources not only are streaming east, they're being sent, for the most part, with U.S. dollars, German marks, or Japanese yen.

Unfortunately, the United States cannot win this second war. Our government's policy of separating military and economic issues makes it almost impossible to counteract the carefully calculated Soviet policies of access to capital, markets, technology, and petroleum. What is the Soviet strategy? To lessen Soviet costs and responsibilities while driving a wedge between the U.S. and its allies. Few politicians and businessmen, however, care to confront or acknowledge that such well-defined, long-term Soviet plans even exist.

Perhaps the words of Lenin himself depict the dilemma facing the West: "Capitalists will sell the communists the rope with which the communists will hang them."[24] Unless the American government understands Soviet politics quickly, the United States is in danger of becoming an irrelevant player in the world community—the victim of its own inept design.

—Part Three—

Gateway to Power

13

Changes in the European Community

Nowhere have repercussions from Gorbachev's new policies been more powerfully felt than in Eastern Europe. Since the last quarter of 1987, all six of Moscow's Warsaw Pact allies have experienced dramatic political and economic events.

"Everywhere you look, something is happening. And that in itself is a real change," said a Western diplomat in Warsaw.[1] As a result, the stagnation of the then prevalent communist system has been shaken, and the Eastern bloc has been propelled toward the changes that Gorbachev seeks.

Consider the shake-up in Czechoslovakia. In December 1987, Gustav Husak, reform resistant leader of Czechoslovakia since the Soviet led invasion of 1968, resigned. Milos Jakes, a sixty-five-year-old central committee economic affairs specialist, replaced him.

The resignation of the premier and deputy followed shortly amid rumors of corruption and scandal involving numerous party officials. Jakes' first task in Czechoslovakia will be the direction of a "complex program" of economic reform that had slowly been taking shape in the final months of Husak's administration.

The broad generational turnover of communist leadership inaugurated by Husak can be expected to spread to five other East European countries within the next five years.

Other changes in leadership of Soviet Bloc countries seem inevitable:

East Germany's Erich Honecker is nearing his seventy-fifth birthday.

Hungary's Janos Kadar and Bulgaria's Todor Zhivkov are even older.

Romania's Nicolae Ceausescu is sixty-nine but rumored to be seriously ill.

Even Poland's General Wojciech Jaruzelski will be in serious political trouble should his economic reforms fail to respond adequately to the "descriptions and revolutionary explosions" of the past year.[2]

Radical Reformation

In spite of the political turmoil, Mr. Gorbachev has turned the Soviet Union into the Eastern bloc's most avid proponent of radical economic reform.

Now, both Hungary and Poland have prepared major programs to decentralize control over economic activity. In fact, their encouragement of private enterprise has gone even beyond Soviet suggestions. Such reformation of East-bloc economics is another crucial aspect of perestroika and is closely aligned to the Soviets' goal of rapid achievement of superpower greatness.

Hungary, the most progressive bloc country, is now the model rather than the maverick. The policy of allowing some freedom and diversity in the economic practices of its states indicates that Moscow feels it no longer has all the answers in relation to socialist economic practice. Changes have included price increases, implementation of an unprecedented personal income tax, and passage of legislation authorizing broader demonstrative privileges as well as multiple political parties.

A dramatic change in leadership has also taken place. Hungary's party chief, Janos Kadar, was replaced by Karoly Grosz, a Gorbachev imitator. Grosz subsequently selected a Harvard University educated 40-year-old economist Miklos Nemeth as government premier.

In other Eastern bloc countries, the transition to reform has been less smooth.

The trouble started in Poland when communist authorities announced a major economic and political reform plan, held a referendum on it, then made the unprecedented announcement that they had lost. Price increases were subsequently announced regardless. Out of desperation, Polish officials selected a new prime minister to try and stabilize Poland's worst labor unrest in seven years. Now the Polish Central Committee has been forced to legalize the labor union movement, Solidarity, in order to bring economic stability to the nation.

In Romania on November 15, 1987, over 10,000 protesters rioted. Enraged over pay cuts and shortages of food and fuel, they marched and shouted slogans against the communist regime of Ceausescu. Fliers printed in Hungarian and Romanian calling for silent protests have subsequently been distributed throughout Romania.

In keeping with the mood of the times, Bulgarian party leader Zhizkov announced his own radical reform plans, even claiming their overhaul of socialism goes back to 1956. *Radical* seems to be the word of the hour—radical change for desperate economic problems.

Dominated by Comecon

Why the sudden need for change among Russia's sister nations? The answer lies with *Comecon*.

Since the early 1940s, Comecon, as the Eastern bloc's economic community is known, has persisted as the trading system created by Stalin for its allies. Virtually unchanged since its inception, it has stifled economic exchanges among members both within and without the regions, slowing the introduction of new technology and holding down living standards. Forced to deal with the Soviets on their terms, Comecon represents for the East Europeans one of the chief instruments of Soviet domination of their region.

East bloc nations, because of their lack of convertible currencies, depend almost exclusively on the Soviet Union for supplies of energy and raw materials. These nations are blocked from significant economic integration, either with each other or with Western Europe. To get strategic supplies, East bloc nations are obliged to ship to the Soviet Union up to 75 percent of the total goods they produce. In addition, they must invest in often huge non-returnable projects inside the Soviet Union.

Yet the goods exchanged between the Soviet Union and Eastern Europe now tend to be the poorest these countries produce. Why? Each economy saves its best output for export to the West. Many Eastern European factories actually have separate production runs for East and West, with the East run typically receiving cheaper materials, technology, and packaging.

Such reality brought about this stern warning from Gorbachev on a June 1987 visit to Bucharest: "Socialist countries should cease to exchange shoddy goods among themselves and to consider [Comecon] a dustbin."[3]

Because each socialist country cannot easily determine either price or value of goods exchanged, bartering agreements form the basis of transactions by ministries between the community. Goods are exchanged, not money.

New Ways to do Business

One reason Eastern Eurpoean products are noncompetitive in the West lies with the fact that Comecon is so far behind technologically. In Romania, for example, 95 percent of the population of 23 million has never seen a computer.

In an effort to confront the lack of technology in Eastern countries and the humiliating failure of Stalinist economic policies in Romania, Poland, and Czechoslovakia, the Soviet government has proposed sweeping changes in the Comecon plan. First proposed in November 1986, the central element of reorganization is the creation of a convertible currency for use within Comecon. This would free each member from having to balance each product sold and received.

Convertible currency would put Comecon members in competition with each other, provide incentives for better products, and necessitate a realistic pricing system. For the Soviets, a convertible currency provides several very important benefits:

1. The Soviets are relieved of heavy subsidization of most Comecon member economies, freeing money, limited resources, and gained technology for Soviet use.

2. Each Comecon member is forced to initiate its own economic development, thus relieving Soviet ideological identification with existing failures.

3. Comecon members are required to produce better quality goods, assuring the Soviet Union they will get more of value when they do trade with members.

4. Existing regional ties—such as oil and gas pipeline networks, electric power grids, and energy sources—will continue to tie Comecon members to the Soviet Union more strongly than any existing political pacts.

5. The new plan allows Comecon members to look to Western resources for needed capital and technology.

6. The regional link-up of European nations (East and West) will establish strong economic and ethnic ties, making Europe less identifiable (and

dependent) on outside influences like the U.S.
7. Ideologically, Western pact nations will become
less defense oriented as economic relationships
expand.

Comecon officials finally agreed on only a partial and
gradual introduction of convertibility to be phased in over
a period of ten years beginning in 1991. Although this first
step would involve only four countries (Poland, Hungary,
Bulgaria, and the Soviet Union), the die is cast. The other
Comecon members won't have a choice.

Unemployment and Immigration

As all these changes take place in the Eastern bloc countries of the Soviet Union, Western Europe struggles to keep
its head above water. Faced with growing unemployment
and unprecedented immigration, France, Great Britain, and
West Germany look for new solutions to their economic
problems. With Western Europe's average jobless rate at 11
percent, with no net new jobs created in Europe since 1980,
European governments are well aware that unemployment
is a major political issue.

While the U.S. has created 14.5 million jobs since 1980,
Germany has lost 500,000. "We are stuck with an unemployment rate of around 11-12 percent, which is historically
unprecedented," said Stefan Lehner, an economist and unemployment expert with the European Community (EC) in
Brussels. "The rate has doubled since 1979 and quadrupled
since 1973."[4]

The 19.2 million unemployed Europeans—equal to the
combined population of Denmark, Ireland, Norway, and
Switzerland—compare with 7 million unemployed
Americans.[5]

Further unrest is stirring among white, northern Europeans who fear being swamped by waves of immigration

from the Third World. "We Europeans risk being like the Romans—invaded by the barbarians. The barbarians are the Arabs, the Moroccans, the Turks, and the Yugoslavs," stated Joseph Michel, Belgium's interim minister of the interior.[6]

Such apprehensions are present in Great Britain, where racial incidents between whites and immigrants from the Indian subcontinent are common. In France, the immigrant population helped to cause the collapse of the Communist Party and the rise of the National Front.

At the same time, West Germany has tightened rules on political asylum to prevent the escalation of current problems with immigrants. They want to keep a cap on places like Cologne, where 120,000 Turkish foreign workers and family members now reside, and Berlin where there are 200,000.[7]

With Gorbachev's new policy of glasnost, 39 percent of West Germany's immigrants in 1988 came from East Bloc countries.[8] That means more unemployed residents who are dependent on government support.

Wooing the European Community

How do all these changes affect Gorbachev's plan? What does he really hope to accomplish in Eastern Europe? To promote economic reform, Gorbachev hopes to capitalize on the Eastern bloc's religious and historical ties to their more prosperous Western European neighbors.

In his book, *Perestroika: New Thinking for Our Country and the World*, the words "We are Europeans" sends more than a geographical message. "The history of Russia is an organic part of the great European history." He even reminds his reader, "Old Russia was united with Europe by Christianity."[9]

Even Pope John Paul II, in an October 1988 speech to the European Parliament, echoed Gorbachev's call for European unity when he said: Europe extends "from the Atlantic to the Urals."[10]

Gorbachev's cultivation process is well under way to return mother Russia to the European family of nations. His openness overtures have been extended through various personal visits to European Community nations, resulting in reciprocal visits from their leaders. As a result Western Europeans stand in awe of this highly polished leader.

Gorbachev's overtures paid off, when on June 25, 1988, the European Community and Comecon signed a joint declaration of mutual recognition. This document will pave the way for the European Community to open diplomatic relations directly with individual Comecon members. After the signing ceremony in Luxembourg, West German Foreign Minister Hans Dietrich Genscher made this observation:

> We have embarked on a new chapter in the history of postwar Europe. The long overdue normalization of relations between the EC and Comecon is now a reality.[11]

Although only 7 percent of present European merchandise trade is with the ten Comecon countries, this figure does not include trading between the two Germanies. This figure is down from 10 percent in the 1970s.[12]

Viscount Etienne Davignon, a former vice-president of the twelve member EC's Brussels-based Executive Commission, said he did not believe that EC-Comecon relations would lead to a dramatic increase in this trade. He added, however, that relations between the blocs would bring "a great number of agreements."[13]

A United Europe?

These proposals are all well and good for Western Europe, but what about Europe's small neutral states? Will they face a similar challenge to their economic freedom and prosperity? Finland, Sweden, Switzerland, and Austria—

unaligned politically, militarily, or economically with either Eastern or Western alliances—fear commercial disaster as the EC moves toward political and economic integration.

"Our biggest foreign policy problems involve trade policy," a high-ranking Finnish diplomat says. "More than two-thirds of our exports go to the European economic space, so what happens in the EC is of vital importance to us."[14] The six member group calling themselves the European Free Trade Association (EFTA) now enjoys free access to Western European markets.

"You cannot have the benefits of an organization you do not want to join," declared Willy de Clercq, an EC Commissioner.[15] Under this pressure, some EFTA members are considering EC membership. Because of sensitive relations with the Soviet Union, several EFTA members, Finland and Sweden particularly, feel such a departure from neutrality would be ill-advised. EFTA is the Common Market's (EC) largest trading partner—even larger than the Unites States.

Since the solutions to Europe's economic problems obviously include all of Europe, the EC, Comecon, and EFTA will soon be aligned politically. The question to ask then is: Where does that leave the United States? As America is forced to ponder its relative decline in the world because its commitments have exceeded its means, the European continent looms large in the picture.

The EC's commitment to remove all trade and other barriers between member states by the year 1992 seems "irreversible."[16] Will a new balance be struck between all of Europe and the United States? Will European leaders find they have means that should precede commitments? Will the European Community, aligned through its commitment to unify its disparate markets in 1992, be forced to turn to the Soviet Union to motivate its staggering economic systems?

Moscow is skillfully moving into European markets with Eurobonds, long-term financing, expanded refugee policies, liberalization of border controls, kind words, and changed politics. Using every opportunity to bolster a strong West German mark over against the dollar, their efforts are paying off. The U.S.S.R. has the power and influence to initiate strong and lasting ties with its European neighbors—a relationship not possible with nations like Japan, which are separated by culture, history, and oceans.

A proposed unified Europe of the near future would involve: data base availability, satellite usage, the semiconductor industry, and consumer electronics. The design of European standards of products and services in areas such as videotex, satellite television programming, and high-density television (HD-TV), information technology, super computers, and automation confirms again that any decisions made will affect *all* of Europe. Limited segmentation of nations is no longer feasible.

If things fall into place quickly, will the European continent exclude the United States and turn to European Russia and Comecon? A switch to communist nations would allow Western Europe to deal with a region that is geographically accessible, ethnically consistent, and religiously and historically united.

Or, are there other alternatives? Regardless of the scenario, it is only a question of time. As economic ties develop, existing political and defense commitments will decrease in importance. And the United States may be left out in the cold.

14

U.S.A.—On the Outside Looking In

Only one new economic superpower has emerged in the world since World War II. Only one Asian nation has attained the rank of a modern industrial power and at the same time maintained a stable democratic government—Japan.

In the inevitable redefinition of economic prowess—even survival—what role will Japan play in Europe's future? The Japanese consider themselves the Westerners of Asia, and they are accepted within the group of seven leading industrial countries, collectively called the "Group of Seven," which join in annual economic summit conferences. Nevertheless the Japanese are still thought to be "Asian" and considered economically ruthless and emotionally rejected by Europe.[1]

Yet Japanese diplomacy, tied explicitly to its superior economic position in the world, is clearly in a period of transition. Newly elected Prime Minister Noboru Takeshita signaled the priority of Japan's relationship with the European Community and neutral European nations by meeting in May 1988 with leaders of major continental governments. At this meeting, he emphasized Japan's priority of expanded economic ties with Europe.

Significantly, the first European visit of Mr. Takeshita began at the Vatican when he presented Pope John Paul II with a Japanese doll. Was he saying to "Christian" Europe, just as another non-Christian, Mr. Gorbachev, has said—We can minimize our differences and be one, partners despite religious conflict? Perhaps religion is not even an issue.

"There has been a fundamental shift in attitude toward Japan recently," a West European diplomat said, "and it has been helped by the large jump in our exports to Japan in the past year."[2]

Such Japanese-European trade grew 16 percent in 1987 to $55 billion despite the $20 billion Japanese trade surplus with the EC. Both Europe and Japanese leaders acknowledge the profitability in dealing with each other's currencies as long as the dollar is still in a state of decline against the mark and yen. The Japanese enthusiasm for European trade stems as well from a "marked loss of faith" in the U.S. capabilities as an economic power.[3]

Japan's industrial overseas output abroad continues to grow, and sales of Japanese companies abroad rose 28.2 percent in the fiscal year ending March 31, 1988.[4] Reserves of yen held by countries outside of Japan reached over 10 percent of all gold and currency reserves for the first time.[5]

Japan itself is the world's number one gold owner, with 750 tons. An additional 1000 tons are in the hands of individuals. Caused largely by savings accounts reaching $2.3 trillion—an amount nearly equal to Japan's GNP—gold deposits total more than $11.3 billion.[6] As the Japanese make their way through the complexities of foreign relations, learning to deal with East-West and neutral nations, all of Europe is being forced to make a decision.

Money Talks

What binds nations together? Politics, military commitment, ideology, or economics? As a rule, economic ties have always been stronger.

The U.S. Congress found this out recently when it considered legislation imposing trade sanctions banning Toshiba, a Japanese manufacturing giant, from its $2.5 billion a year U.S. market. What had Toshiba done? Illegally sold submarine technology to the Soviet Union!

Ethics and national security fell by the wayside, however, as Congressmen were swamped with $100 million of lobbying efforts. American businessmen related directly or indirectly to Toshiba products went on the offensive. That's not to mention the political clout of tens of thousands of Americans who faced unemployment should maximum sanctions be allowed.[7]

Toshiba's plants were turning out computers in California, microwave ovens and television sets in Tennessee, television tubes in New York, copying machine parts in South Dakota, and engineering controls in Oklahoma. In addition, sales and service jobs in every state were also at risk. As a result, Congress put only minuscule sanctions into effect, proving once again that priorities of job and income displace even the strongest nationalistic issues.

Encouraged by such events, the Soviet Union, under the fashion of perestroika and glasnost, finds itself now in a position to be welcomed into the European Community with open arms. As world economic current events escalate tension and uncertainty around the world, particularly in the Middle East and Asia, the EC nations have an understanding new European ally waiting to come to their rescue.

What do the Soviets have that the Europeans need? Only one thing: a sophisticated space program.

The Soviets have chalked up impressive accomplishments in space, including a permanently manned space station, the world's largest booster, improved reliability and endurance of unmanned spacecraft, and the development of a space shuttle.

For European customers, this means services and opportunities no other country can match financially or technically. The Soviets offer quicker and less expensive orbit launches, better quality satellite pictures, the sale of launchers, and services of highly sophisticated research institutes. Why are they offering technology at such a bargain? The Soviets want to gain international prestige and hard currency.

A Modern Tower of Babel

Such high-tech Soviet superiority, once confined to obvious socialist priorities as military and defense, is now being adjusted to play a major role as a civilian component. By growing in size and openness, Soviets are increasingly finding Western cooperation.

If someone in Soviet authority determines that the development of satellite communication, television programming, or high-density television (HD-TV) is a socialist priority, the resources and facilities are in place to provide such services—at a lower cost. But where does that leave the United States?

In an April 1988 meeting in Geneva, Switzerland, an International Congress of Communication experts representing EC, U.S., Japan, and Comecon agreed to discontinue the current NTSC system now used in the U.S. and switch to a more sophisticated and advanced telecommunications system.

NTSC was first designed and operative in the U.S. but has since been replaced in all of Europe, Japan, and elsewhere with modified PAL systems. The current proposal, which would be in place by 2005, will force the U.S. to choose between the Japanese standard of PAL, or the incompatible European standard.

According to one participant, the U.S. shows no indication of rejecting the more sophisticated Japanese communications industry. If this happens, the U.S. will be further isolated from continental Europe and tied unequivocally to Japan. At the same time, the European continent will bond itself together in a unique system of total communication through satellite and communication dishes, a twenty-first century Tower of Babel.

The Iranian Connection

Other economic forces are lining up against the United States—alignments once considered impossible. More bizarre than the Soviet-European connection are Gorbachev's overtures toward nations in the Middle East.

With oil prices tumbling consistently during 1987, the price bottomed out on October 5, 1988, at $12.28 a barrel, the lowest price since August, 1986.[8] Most of the price fluctuation has been tied to the military conflict during the Iran-Iraq war rather than with OPEC (Organization of Petroleum Exporting Countries) efforts to curtail production.

It is obvious now, however, even after a cease-fire has been negotiated, that the eight and one-half years of fighting between the two OPEC nations continues to bring extreme disarray and nonconformance to existing OPEC agreements. Still desperately in need of hard cash from war efforts, both Iran and Iraq exceed desired OPEC quotas. Other Islamic nations are also in trouble, having economically extended themselves by supporting Iraq's war effort.

Now approaching depletion of its cash reserves, Iran faces difficult questions in regard to finding a benefactor. Should such an issue be resolved in favor of the Soviet Union, Iran's neighbor, it would be for a very significant reason.

Iran's minister of economic affairs and finance has said he expects ties with the Soviet Union to expand "remarkably." In fact, an agreement to resume Iranian gas exports to the Soviet Union was recently signed.[9] Even Khomeini himself stated he now wants strong relations to develop with Moscow.

Why this new desire for friendship? As usual, the answer revolves around Gorbachev's overall plan.

OPEC and Oil

At the start of 1987, verified oil reserves worldwide were estimated at 96 billion tons.[10] By 1996 the Soviet Union and the U.S., the world's two largest oil producers, will have exhausted their now known oil reserves if they keep consuming at their present rate.[11] Currently about 41 percent of the oil used in the U.S. is imported, and we continue to increase that amount.[12]

Britain, the world's fifth largest producer, will run dry even earlier. In fact, half of the oil pumped out of the ground in 1986 came from countries that in the year 2000 will have no oil at all.

If new speculation (unfeasible at today's low prices) does not find new reserves, or if alternative forms of energy are not developed, the U.S.S.R., the U.S., and Britain may not be major oil producers in ten years. Such a result turns the oil needs of the world over to the OPEC countries.

Speculation that OPEC will orchestrate a broad effort to constrict world supplies has already affected the market. In one day a huge jump in oil prices soared to the highest level in 1988.

What is OPEC's plan? To seek help from non-OPEC producers such as Mexico, China, Oman, Angola, Colombia, Egypt, Brunei, and Malaysia to restrain crude oil output to help combat weak prices and excessive supplies. Even the Soviet Union has joined OPEC's constriction program, announcing suddenly on March 4, 1989, its intention to cut its oil exports by 5 percent the first half of 1989.[13] That could have a tremendous impact on Europe and Japan since OPEC supplies much of their petroleum needs.

The Soviets, however, are not waiting for a worldwide oil crisis to take place. In fact, they have already turned to development of methane as a viable alternative to meet their energy needs. Now found experimentally in much of Europe, methane will surpass available oil in a year or two.

"The dominant energy source over the next fifty years will be neither solar nor fusion, but methane," insists Cesare Marchetti, a scientist at Austria's International Institute of Applied Systems, which is primarily financed by the U.S. and the Soviet Union, in conjunction with several other nations.[14]

According to Marchetti, in the next half-century, natural gas (methane) will play the same role that petroleum has played in the past fifty years. Heavily involved with its own methane digging, the Soviets intend to continue their dominance of natural gas supply to Western Europe through already established pipelines, regardless of the source of that gas, whether their own methane or Iranian oil. In either event, a dependent European continent cannot exist without Soviet supply.

A Recession for America?

As economic control of the world's markets shifts toward Japan, Europe, and the Soviet Union, where does that leave the United States? Are we on the brink of economic collapse?

"A recession is coming," many economists warn. 1987 U.S. figures exemplify gloom and doom for economists:

—Housing starts plunged 16 percent;[15]
—After tax incomes grew only 1.2 percent;
—Savings rates fell to a forty year low;[16]
—Consumer inflation climbed 4.4 percent;[17]
—The trade deficit soared 25 percent to a record $17.6 billion.[18]

Unfortunately, 1988 figures reflect little reason for optimism.

The fall of stock markets all over the world has made 100 to 200 million households in the West poorer than they had believed themselves to be before the crash. The loss is not just among private citizens; it also affects corporations, banks, and insurance companies.

Those who calculate their net worth according to the price of the stocks in their portfolios have experienced an unpleasant awakening. This does not mean that those who do not own stocks need not worry. The global stock market crash is a warning bell that alerts us to the dangers in today's world economy.

Overseas, the dollar fell to record lows. Despite our purchasing 40 percent of Japan's total exports, 20 percent of Europe's, and one-third of the Third World exports, U.S. trading partners, for the most part, denied similar access to American products, causing mammoth trade deficits.[19]

Foreign merchants from Japan and Europe began saying "No thanks" to the dollar in 1988. This makes Americans nervous. Polls show one out of every four Americans expects the U.S. to encounter another economic depression.

The big question, asked by some, is whether a recession can be kept from getting out of hand? "The present crisis is not just a stock market collapse," said David Calleo, a political science professor attending international discussions held in Bologna, Italy recently, but has "geopolitical dimensions." Building since the early 1960s, "the real problem," Mr. Calleo said, "has been the relative weakening of the U.S. in relationship to the rest of the world."[20]

Out of such a predicament, the European Community will be forced to take responsibility for the destiny of its own region influenced dramatically by Gorbachev's "unity-peace" overtures. Then, we will see a profound shift economically and politically from our present alignments and policies.

No wonder Mr. Gorbachev is growing impatient. He is on the verge of uniting all of Europe and simultaneously isolating the United States and Japan under the theme of "unity-peace."

To influence these allegiances, however, such "renewal" of the socialist dream will take more than kind words and feigned promises. To find those who identify with his goals and who know enough about western economics to implement them necessarily involves mutual relationships and generous gestures.

America can only watch and wonder what Gorbachev will do next.

15
Arms Control: A Balancing Act

Who is the enemy in the world today? According to Mikhail Gorbachev, it's certainly not the Soviet Union!

In an NBC interview on December 7, 1987, Gorbachev claimed the United States, now without an enemy, is no longer able to justify its military expenditures and dangerous adventures.

In fact, the keepers of one "doomsday clock" moved its hands backward for the first time in sixteen years, acknowledging the December 1987 Soviet-American summit as a long-awaited step toward peace. The clock now reads six minutes before the midnight hour that represents nuclear holocaust.

Gorbachev, in his book *Perestroika,* had this to say about the Soviet Union's goals in the world community:

> We want freedom to reign . . . everywhere in the world . . . We want peaceful competition; cooperation rather than confrontation; prosperity, welfare and happiness [in] a nuclear-free, non-violent world.[1]

Who is Mikhail Gorbachev? Is he a doomsday deliverer or a deceptionist? A hero or a master manipulator? Is he transforming the Soviet Union internally for domestic purposes or for a dynamic foreign relations power play?

If Gorbachev is "the most accomplished Leninist since Lenin" as some insist, in that he is totally flexible about means, yet unswerving in his goal, then one might reach one answer. If Gorbachev is compassionate, peace-loving, and nonconfrontational as some evidence indicates, one might arrive at a totally different conclusion.

Regardless of what "perestroika-glasnost" has changed, the ultimate test of restructuring centers on the issue of the Soviet military, its control by the party rather than the people, and its use as a power tool of foreign policy to expand Soviet influence.

A New Detente?

News of the U.S.-Soviet summit agreement, called the Intermediate-range Nuclear Forces or INF Treaty, quickly circled the globe on December 8, 1987. Most newspapers, magazines, and world politicians welcomed the treaty as if an age of peace and new detente had finally arrived.

Vladimir Bukovsky, a human rights activist who left the Soviet Union in 1976, was recently quoted as saying, "Personalities are not important in the Soviet Union. Functions are important." We must assess the ultimate purpose of Gorbachev as Soviet Communist Party General Secretary in no other light.

Certainly we can entertain hope that Gorbachev desires to reduce his arms spending and revise his bankrupt socialist economy. The West is scrutinizing new efforts to "democratize" the Soviet Union. Gorbachev must also show his good intentions to his people, thereby encouraging their faith and trust in his reconstructionist policies.

Yet some of us remember our hopes for Khrushchev were dashed in Hungary in 1956, and our hopes for Brezhnev were crushed in the Prague debacle in 1968. Even Afghanistan, now littered with an estimated 3 million Soviet-made anti-personnel mines and "booby-traps," has left tens of thousands dead and maimed.

History confirms that trust often brings greater risks than distrust. Trusting an aggressor nation without serious reflection invites hope for the best and, in reality, ill-preparation for the worst.

To understand the significance of the signing of the INF agreement that abolished certain short and medium range nuclear weapons, we must reflect on Soviet-U.S. relations since the end of World War II. The defense of Western Europe and the developments of postwar U.S. nuclear strategy are especially important.

The Worries of Western Europe

Two primary considerations have consistently been in the forefront of all American thinking concerning its defense policies of Western Europe.

1. The 1,200 mile border separating East from West includes 420 miles of topography suitable for armored invasion tactics. The threat of imminent armored invasion poses nightmarish impossibilities for defense strategists and unbelievable psychological trauma for all Europeans.

2. The European continent, occupied by aggressor forces during two world wars, found its patriotic resistance forces involved in bloody retaliatory acts. These acts were often excessive, even cover-up atrocities perpetrated outside the accepted rules of warfare. Such activities fostered negative feelings toward authority and disregard for law and order.[2]

Today these feelings are expressed in huge anti-nuclear movements, peace organizations, massive violence, and spiritual and moral disinterest. Europeans live under the imminent threat of invasion and war, and their worst fears are beyond the comprehension of most U.S. citizens.

Because continental Europe is the original homeland of most Americans, our country has invested personnel and military hardware to support European democracy during two world wars. The U.S. has consistently formulated its entire nuclear strategy around Western Europe with special emphasis on deterring an armored invasion by Soviet forces.

Because an anti-military attitude pervades Europe, and its long border is indefensible by conventional forces, the U.S. was compelled to explore other options in its defense of Western Europe after World War II.

The Cold War

After the administration of Franklin Roosevelt, which had encouraged the withdrawal of American troops from the continent in massive numbers, the East-West cold war began. At the same time, the Marshall Plan was implemented to rehabilitate war-torn Europe.

Then in 1948, the Soviets blockaded the roads leading to Berlin and also attacked the Baltic states of Estonia, Latvia, and Lithuania. Most Europeans were convinced the Soviet appetite for expansion had not yet been satisfied. A helpless and devastated Europe realized that Soviet troops could sweep over the entire continent and take control in only a matter of weeks.

At that time in history, the U.S. nuclear retaliatory power was centered on the atomic bomb (possessed only by us) to be delivered by long range bombers. This devastating weapon was the only means available to counter the Soviet threat.

Shortly after the trauma of 1948, the North Atlantic Treaty Organization (NATO) was formed. The U.S. supported the defense of Western Europe by taking action in three specific areas:

1. Requesting that NATO nations reinforce their conventional forces.[3]
2. Incorporating nuclear arms into its war plan.
3. Adopting the retaliatory strategy of bombing selected Soviet cities in response to any Soviet invasion of Western Europe.[4]

Complications soon developed, however, that rendered the U.S. massive retaliation strategy questionable.

In 1949 the Soviets succeeded in making an atomic test, and in 1953, a thermonuclear test. Through the exploitation of German rocket technology, which was brought to the Soviet Union from Germany after the war through espionage, the Soviets quickly overtook the U.S. in the development of nuclear weapons.

As early as 1951 many observers feared the end of U.S. nuclear supremacy was at hand. That fear only increased when the Soviet Union successfully launched Sputnik, the world's first artificial satellite, in 1957.

How did U.S. government agencies react to taking an unexpected backseat to the Soviets? Confusion was followed by reevaluation and change to improve U.S. nuclear development programs. But the doubt had been raised.

Would the U.S. risk the annihilation of its cities from comparable or superior Soviet nuclear power should the Soviets initiate its invasion of Europe? This doubt is still a crucial issue today, not resolved since the 1960s. A balance of Soviet-U.S. nuclear weapons capability might be the one circumstance to render such an issue theoretically dead.

Despite NATO promises to the contrary, the numerical inferiority of NATO conventional forces became woefully imbalanced. In some West European nations the concession, "better red than dead" began surfacing. Under these circumstances in 1955 NATO ordered:

1. The adoption of strategic nuclear weapons to offset its numerical inferiority.

2. The rearmament of West Germany and its participation in NATO.
3. The British and French possession of nuclear weapons for self-defense purposes.[5]

In response to tactical nuclear weapons being placed in the hands of Europeans, the Soviet forces quickly increased its nuclear capability to match its numerical superiority of personnel. Such developments forced Great Britain and France to build up their nuclear forces, hoping the consolidation of their nuclear capabilities with existing NATO armament would be enough to dismay further Soviet build-up.

A Balance of Terror

In the interim between the mid 1960s and the early 1980s, both the United States and the Soviet Union have developed and deployed:

1. ABMs (anti-ballistic missiles) capable of intercepting the enemy's incoming first strike missiles
2. SLBMs (submarine-launch ballistic missiles) that are not easily detected and destroyed
3. ICBMs (intercontinental ballistic missiles) with underground silos and mobility systems

Technology has also developed multiple warheads for the ICBMs and increased the precision of the missiles.

Current U.S. policies still center on "flexibility" and nuclear attack. Both U.S. and Soviet forces, however, claim the capacity to launch a second strike. The superpowers are trying to prevent nuclear war by maintaining an even greater balance of terror than before.

The participating nations seem to be reaching their limits in strategic nuclear weapons. How much of their GNP are these countries spending on nuclear forces?

United States	6.9 percent
Great Britain	5.2 percent
France	4.1 percent
West Germany	3.2 percent

The Soviet Union, however, is spending *four to five times the U.S. rate* on nuclear reinforcements, according to *U.S. News & World Report.*[6] The Soviets, despite a disastrous economic collapse and pledges made in January 1989 to reduce military spending by 14.2 percent, continue to make nuclear forces a priority.[7]

Since its inception, the Soviet Union has always been an empire. In order to survive, empires constantly must expand their boundaries or they die. Regardless of the nation and the person in leadership, the foreign affairs of empires were consistently tied to military aggression and terminated or controlled only in the same way.

Today the Soviet Union faces much more than an eroded world public image. The decline of revolutionary advances in Africa, Central America, and Afghanistan is embarrassing enough, but a possible shrinking of its own territories is humiliating. When Yugoslavia demanded and received freedom of national pursuit, the Soviets saw the handwriting on the wall.

Why has the Soviet Union been forced into other means of pursuing its goals? Three crucial areas stand out.

1. They have been unable to convert the world to socialism because of its well-documented history of failure.
2. They do not have the time to acquire needed technological superiority to break through the nuclear force impasse.
3. They have a failing domestic economy that cannot afford the cost of such research and development.

How will the Soviet Union expand its superpower image despite these setbacks? A series of carefully calculated European objectives were set in motion when Mikhail Gorbachev's administration began in April 1985. The Soviet Union has been making efforts to:

1. Eliminate and keep out of Europe all short and intermediate range American missiles.
2. Minimize the defense abilities of the U.S. against foreign nuclear attack.
3. Split and/or weaken the U.S. with its NATO relationships both economically and militarily.
4. Create an economic, ethnic dependence on the Soviet Union by Western and Eastern European countries.
5. Curtail U.S. and NATO military preparedness.
6. Control Middle East oil reserves.[8]

Reagan's Zero Option

In 1981 the U.S. supersonic ballistic missiles called Pershing IIs, capable of reaching Soviet targets in minutes, were set to be deployed in Western Europe. The presence of the Pershing IIs countered the strength of Soviet missiles that were armed with highly accurate warheads and had the capacity to strike anywhere in Europe.

Initially proposed by President Reagan in a speech delivered on November 18, 1981, the President said:

> The U.S. is prepared to cancel its deployment of Pershing II and ground-launched cruise missiles if the Soviets will dismantle their SS-20, SS-4, and SS-5 missiles.[9]

Reagan's "zero option" was an all-or-nothing package for Soviet response. Leonid Brezhnev and successors Andropov and Chernenko all denounced the offer in the strongest of terms as patently one-sided.

Brezhnev adamantly opposed the "zero option" alternative. Did the Soviet leader think that victory in a nuclear war was achievable? As early as January 1977, Brezhnev publicly proclaimed that nuclear superiority was "pointless" and was "dangerous madness." Further, the Soviets claimed they maintained nuclear forces that were only "sufficient" to hold the U.S. in check.[10]

Such a national policy inferring partial reduction in Soviet nuclear forces was nevertheless centered around the uncompromising goal that American nuclear weapons should never be present anywhere in Europe.

Yet such a goal was elusive. In a strikingly blazon counterproposal made only five days after President Reagan's "zero option," Chairman Brezhnev, on November 23, 1981, proposed the eventual elimination of all medium-range nuclear weapons "directed toward Europe," plus the elimination of all short-range missiles.[11]

The process of European denuclearization began, fueled initially by President Reagan's apparent obsession to be known in history as "the disarmer." Through a residual course of agonizing negotiations beginning in late 1981, Soviet and U.S. negotiators hammered away without progress. This forced the U.S. to go ahead with plans to place Pershing II missiles in Europe.

Now faced with counter strength to its SS-20s, Soviet leaders were forced to consider avenues of flexibility. They were convinced Brezhnev's failure to compromise forced the hand of the U.S. President and resulted in the European installation of the Pershings.

The Soviets seemed unable to make leadership decisions in the interim. When new Geneva negotiations began again in earnest in March 1985, the Soviets came to the bargaining table with two priorities in mind:

1. Get American Pershings out of Europe.
2. Stop Strategic Defense Initiative (SDI—called the Star Wars Defense System).

Both these goals were supported under the tutelage of a quick learner and spectacularly effective negotiator, the likes of whom the Soviet Union has never seen—Mikhail Gorbachev.

War is Big Business

Now after five years and four summit meetings, all U.S. missiles with an effective range capable of striking Soviet targets are out of Europe. Gorbachev severed the INF deal from SDI and START (Strategic Arms Reduction Talks), but any successes might prove to be temporary or illusory.

An INF agreement without a START agreement, which would curtail long-range missile deployment, gives the Soviets the advantage. Now nothing can stop Gorbachev from deploying his new ICBM—the SS-25—a mobile, three-stage intercontinental version of the two-stage intermediate range SS-20, which is just as capable of destroying every target in Europe.

The Soviets have spent an estimated $4.6 trillion for military purposes since 1960, or 20 percent more than the U.S. over the past decade.[12] With such an investment the Soviet Union boasts:

1. A civil defense system. (We have none.)
2. A deployed ABM system throughout the country. (We have none.)
3. A deployed, operational anti-satellite system. (We have none.)
4. Numerical superiority in conventional forces, ballistic missiles, and attack submarines.
5. Operational superiority in its space program, including military usage.[13]

The United States now faces a world of multipolar powers. Japan will soon have nuclear capability, and China might in fifteen years become second to the U.S. in Gross National Product.

In addition, U.S. interests are becoming increasingly harder to defend and decidedly more expensive. Why have defense costs skyrocketed? The U.S. forces have been called on for several reasons:

> 1. To provide massive security assistance in the Third World (Afghanistan, Nicaragua, the Persian Gulf, and Lebanon)
> 2. To defend its military allies from the constant threat of massive nuclear or non-nuclear attack
> 3. To deal with pockets of terrorism, subversion, and unrest all over the world

Whether the need is for fighting personnel, high-tech equipment, non-nuclear arms, or new "platforms" on which to mount them—ships, submarines, and aircraft—costs are now astronomical.

The America that reigned economically as king forty years ago is today's principle debtor. Many think that American allies overseas will inevitably have to bear more of their defense costs. That means more and more American troops will be coming home.

In 1986 the U.S. paid about 69 percent of NATO defense costs.[14] No wonder Congress and administrative agents constantly urge more financial participation from its allies. In 1987 global military spending increased $50 billion over 1986, which figured out to $1.8 million a minute or $930 billion overall. In anyone's books, war is big business.[15]

Where is the United States?

With the 1989 budget into law, the bottom line U.S. defense figure is still $8 billion more than the Pentagon was authorized to spend in 1988.[16] Pentagon planners expect Congress to slash more than $300 billion from Reagan's long-range defense-spending blueprint over the next five years.

Outright cuts of 2 to 3 percent face President Bush as real possibilities. Such a contingency will mean significant reductions in troop strength, training, weapons, and munitions.

"The system is broke," said Senate Armed Services Chairman, Sam Nunn (D-GA), "and it's got to be fixed."[17]

Although the Reagan administration spent more than $2 trillion during the past eight years, sloppy procurement, exaggerated budgets, inadequate testing of new weapons, and outright graft did not add the "bang for the buck" expected. Are we stronger than we were in 1980? "Yes," House Armed Services Chairman Les Aspin (D-WI) affirmed. "But did we get our money's worth? Absolutely not."[18]

No money. No weapons. No backbone. Where does that leave the United States in this most critical hour of world history?

16
NATO:
Caught in the Middle

West Germany is infatuated with Gorbachev. That nation's top periodical, *Spiegel Magazine,* named him 1988 Man of the Year.

At the beginning of the decade, 71 percent of West Germans saw the Soviets as a threat to peace. Now that figure is 11 percent. Eight out of ten West Germans want all nuclear weapons removed from Europe. Three-fourths say they trust the Soviet Union, yet over one-half hold negative attitudes toward U.S. policies. Sentiment in West Germany, the frontline NATO state, is shifting in waves toward a conviction that the Soviet military threat against Western Europe is diminishing.

Why are the West Germans changing their mind? In a country the size of Oregon, German citizens face universal conscription, and the threat of war plagues them continuously. They share their country with 400,000 American soldiers and other NATO troops who conduct 5,000 military exercises a year, flying over the countryside at tree-top levels. No wonder the Germans are capable of hasty political decisions contrary to NATO interests.

George Bush has said he expects relations with Europe to be his "preoccupying foreign policy issue of the next four years."[1] But Bush's European problems are not just with Gorbachev, who seems totally bent on removing all nuclear weapons and U.S. forces from Europe. President Bush must also be concerned about the NATO nations led by the West Germans.

Will West Germany succeed in diminishing support for NATO and even enter into separate agreements with the Soviets? Such an event would drastically affect defense line capabilities. Unilateral reductions of forces and funds in Europe would be a disaster for President Bush, who himself is facing strong military budget reductions from Congress.

Gorbachev, on the other hand, needs a notable foreign-policy achievement to deter domestic critics in his behind schedule economic reform program. He must be concerned about future Soviet capability to keep up technologically with development of new U.S. offensive and defensive weapon systems. How would he pay hard cash for such commitments? The key issue for both parties is Europe, and the key ingredient is money.

Peace at Any Price

Originating on April 4, 1949, NATO assumed the role of European protector. Now comprising sixteen member nations, the alliance is the benefactor of 620 million people: 352.8 million in Western Europe, 242.2 million in the United States, and 25.6 million Canadians.[2]

In a socialist response to NATO, The Warsaw Pact (WP) was formed in 1955 as a military alliance by the East European bloc of nations consisting of the Soviet Union, East Germany, Poland, Czechoslovakia, Hungary, Bulgaria, and Romania. The total population of the seven member nations of the Warsaw Pact is approximately 385 million, which amounts to approximately 62 percent of the population of NATO countries.[3]

Yet Warsaw Pact forces comparatively outnumber NATO forces two to one in deployed divisions, battle tanks, and artillery; five to one in anti-tank weapons and three to one in armed helicopters.[4] Nineteen Soviet divisions are stationed in East Germany alone. More than three million metric tons of ammunition are stockpiled in Eastern Europe.[5]

The major elements of any invasion force—troops, battle tanks, artillery, and anti-tank weapons—are controlled by Warsaw Pact forces with decided advantages. On the other hand, NATO forces lack mobility, unity in weapons and tactics, communication, readiness and have inadequate ammunition reserves for sustained combat. Any NATO conventional military effort, at present levels, would be short lived. That makes peace at any price attractive to most NATO members, especially West Germany.

Outspoken politicians in West Germany now complain openly that the Bundeswehr (the army) is costing too much. And with German Chancellor Helmut Kohl facing re-election in 1990, the offer proposed by Gorbachev to reduce short-range missiles puts added pressure on the coalition government to survive.

If such consensus is prevalent within our strongest continental ally, imagine the feelings of the Italians, the French, or the Greeks. Spain has already decided to remove U.S. F-16 war planes from the Torrejon air base near Madrid. The difficulty in finding a suitable replacement facility exemplifies the complexity of the times for European interests as we see them here in the United States.

"Just as with Spain," West German General Peter Haarhaus, chief of operations at NATO headquarters in Brussels, was quoted as saying, "[The U.S.] will have to negotiate with Greece, Portugal and Turkey to keep its bases in those countries. Nothing could be worse than a bad Spanish example."[6]

That makes U.S. officials wonder, Is anyone on our side?

The INF Treaty

The main purpose of the INF Treaty is to eliminate all U.S. and Soviet missiles having a range between 300 miles and 3,400 miles (all short and intermediate range ground based missiles),[7] including regrettably, conventionally armed missiles.

Soon after the INF Treaty, *Time* magazine reported that the U.S. deprived itself of 859 Pershing II ballistic missiles and its land based cruise missiles; the Soviet Union relinquished 1836 missiles of four types. Both sides are breathing a sigh of relief at some relaxation of tension.

The signing of the INF Treaty by Reagan and Gorbachev, however, has raised three basic questions:

> 1. Will the total abolition of INFs cause a drastic change in the NATO strategy to defend Western Europe through conventional weapons?
> 2. Will such a change, if any, accelerate the nuclear development of France and Great Britain?
> 3. Is the defense of the West by means of conventional forces possible?

Why didn't Soviet negotiators first propose a paring down of conventional forces? Only such a balance of conventional arm-cuts will prevent the outright armored assault through Germany, or the NATO flank diversions through Greece, Turkey, or even Norway.

Any trade-off of European based nuclear weapons that allows the nuclear material to be used to arm other weapons is of insignificant military advantage to the United States. To its allies in Western Europe, it could be devastating.

The rhetoric from Gorbachev is that Soviet unilateral reduction of forces, weapons, and funds equals good faith peace intentions. At a time when NATO foreign ministers were prepared to offer their own formula for troop reduction quotas, Gorbachev upstaged them and focused the entire world on his December 7, 1988 offer to eliminate 500,000 positions from the Soviet military, including 50,000 troops and 5,000 tanks from Eastern Europe by 1991. In addition, Gorbachev announced his intention:

1. To dismantle 24 short-range nuclear missile launchers from Eastern European use.
2. To terminate further production of chemical weapons.
3. To reduce his military budget by 14.2 percent.

These proposals suddenly left the U.S. at a decided political disadvantage.

"It's a very clever ploy by the Soviets," said a senior NATO official in Brussels, Belgium. "They get rid of old tactical nukes that they don't need anyway, and this puts heavy political pressure on Bonn."

A German senior defense analyst in Bonn said, "It is going to be much harder to push a nuclear modernization program through the [German parliament]. And I think that was the real purpose of the Soviet announcement."[8]

Closer inspection of the INF Treaty reveals that the Soviets gave up very little. Soviet manpower totals 5.5 million compared to 335,000 U.S. troops in Western Europe. Soviet forces number 380,000 in East Germany alone.

A reduction of 5,000 Soviet tanks (assumedly old, outdated models) would leave an imbalance in favor of Warsaw Pact forces of 48,000 to 22,200. At the same time, the Soviets will be producing 280 new tanks every month—or enough tanks to supply an entire tank division.[9]

The reduction of the 24 short-range nuclear rocket launchers would give Warsaw Pact forces a 1,355 to 91 edge. In addition, the Soviet Union currently stockpiles 300,000 tons of chemical agents with the U.S. stockpiling about 100,000 tons.

Even with a 14.2 percent reduction in funds, the Soviet military budget would be approximately *twice* the U.S. budget in percentage of Gross National Product.

The Waiting Game

Future reductions in defense spending by the Unites States makes the Europeans nervous. They fear that such cuts will lead to reductions in U.S. forces on their continent. This forces our European allies to seek other solutions to their problems.

Britain and France have been holding secret talks to more effectively coordinate their nuclear capabilities. At the same time, France has been talking with West Germany in an effort to combat eventual nuclear withdrawal in West Germany. A possible unification of the two Germanys could mean an eventual withdrawal from NATO, creating neutral status and separate accommodation with the Soviets.

In a further act of self-reliance, a defense forum of Britain, France, West Germany, Italy, Belgium, the Netherlands, and Luxembourg have begun meeting and pledging greater European defense cooperation through a pact called Western European Union.

Despite promises of new battlefield weapon systems to come, new strategies and fighting concepts to offset Soviet numerical superiority, and reassurances of the credibility of the American nuclear guarantee, Western Europe is in a waiting game. These countries are caught between the two world superpowers and held in an economic, ideological, and political vice. The pressure is on, and all of Europe feels the heat. Changes will have to come—perhaps before anyone is ready.

17

The Next Arms Race

The American public seemed to take a consistently "common sense" view of the December 1987 summit. Most were glad to see the superpowers talking and finding ways to eliminate weapons of mass destruction. Nevertheless, Americans need a "lot more tangible proof before they will believe that the communist leopard has changed its spots."[1]

With the advent of Mikhail Gorbachev to leadership within the Soviet Union and the signing of new weapons agreements, many Americans are confused. Some strategists assume that the Soviets seek military superiority in an effort to either blackmail the U.S. into submission or to unilaterally attack. Other political analysts are cautiously optimistic about arms control. But no one knows for sure.

In the past, communist objectives were made clear by their actions—the post-war suppression of Eastern Europe; Nikita Khrushchev's intent to "bury" the U.S.; and the extensive weapons build-up. Modern day "Commie bashers" like Ronald Reagan had no trouble identifying the problem—until recently.

Why did the U.S. President, who came to power calling the Soviet Union an "evil empire," change his mind? Seven years later Reagan signed a treaty that called for the destruction of medium and shorter range missiles and banned their future production. Why did such a proposal, initially propounded by President Ronald Reagan in November 1981, become reality in 1987? More importantly, what comes next?

What's Next?

Mikhail Gorbachev is a master politician and negotiator. Since coming to power he has made three especially noteworthy accomplishments:

1. Eliminating the only American nuclear weapons in Europe capable of striking Soviet territory.
2. Creating a drastic imbalance in NATO's conventional defense strategy.
3. Forcing upon European members the expense of its own huge conventional force build-up.

What far-reaching effects can this have on the rest of the world? The leaders of Western Europe find themselves left to make their own deal with the Soviets. In that case NATO will die, and the United States will be isolated.

Western Europe's only other option is to turn further toward its captive relationship with the U.S. defense establishment. By gambling on the rapid development and deployment of new super weapons, Europe hopes to temporarily ward off its current strategic dilemma.

The INF Treaty isolated only four percent of Soviet and U.S. nuclear stocks—totaling 11,786 warheads on the U.S. side and 10,986 on the Soviet side—all long-range weapons. So where does the United States go from here in its effort to protect Western Europe?

Post INF expansion possibilities center around improving the destructive power of current long-range missiles. The U.S. also hopes to devise new non-nuclear weapons to replace outmoded models and other nuclear weapons that could be banned by future treaties such as START.

1. One of the major strategic weapons in the new U.S. arsenal is the *cruise missile*—a small, unmanned aircraft that is suitable for equipping with nuclear warheads. Although the INF banned the ground launched version, it can be launched from aircraft, submarines, and ships.

The promise of developers to deliver such a nuclear tipped missile within three feet of its target from a distance of 1500 miles is still in question. Behind schedule and $2 billion over in costs, the nearly 1800 cruise missiles now in service are said not to work as designed.[2] One U.S. Congressman described the dilemma to be a "procurement disaster."[3]

2. *High-power microwave or HPM* is another scientist's dream not expected to become reality before the 1990s. This weapon is designed to be carried in space either by missiles from ground, sea, or air stations. Upon explosion, micro-wave emissions would be generated of either high or low intensity to disable ground targets, interdict flying missiles, or "blind, burn, or bake people to death."[4]

3. *Non-nuclear weapons* mentioned include "enhanced blast" techniques using existing fuel-air explosives that spray liquid mists into the air, then explode seconds later—devastating everything within a prescribed range.[5] Such explosive reactions could also create shock waves under water that could crush a submarine or split a ship.

With all these weapons at different stages of development, European leaders are asking themselves serious questions: Should we wait for these new weapons to be completed and hopefully provide the protection we need?

What about the United States? With the current financial deficit showing little abatement, will an American President or U.S. Congress sacrifice politically prudent domestic programs to save West Berlin or West Germany?

The Soviets March Ahead

While Europeans wait, the world acknowledges that Warsaw Pact forces are rapidly closing the gap in the quality of military hardware. The Soviets have acquired technology from Western computer, electronics, and submarine sources. Some were obtained through legal avenues, but others involved treason. U.S. Navy personnel convicted of selling secrets to the Soviets have seriously reduced our military edge.

The Pentagon, in an annual study entitled "Soviet Military Power," stated, "The technological advantages in military capabilities now enjoyed by the West have been threatened, if not eroded."[6]

But such a turnaround in the balance of power should come as no surprise to American politicians and military experts. In 1975, Leonid Brezhnev expressed concern over the development of what he termed new weapons of mass destruction "more frightful than the mind of man had ever imagined."[7] Unable to comprehend what the Soviets were talking about, the United Nations General Assembly showed little interest in a treaty proposal banning such weaponry.

Undeterred by world public opinion, Brezhnev embarked on a massive military build-up to prepare Soviet forces to take over the world beginning in 1985. Such a date had been established at a secret Prague meeting of Warsaw Pact leaders held in 1972.[8] The build-up has never been curtailed. The goal has been met.

Devastating New Weapons

The world is familiar with massed troops, mobile ICBMs, space supremacy, advanced bombers, ABM systems, anti-satellite systems, and even biological warfare threats. But the Soviets could be developing new weapons—*phase conjugate weapons* or weapons that use time-reversed electromagnetic waves (TR).

Unconfirmed estimates say that since the early 1950s the Soviets have amassed numerous such TR wave weapon systems with startlingly different weapon capabilities than the normal wave.[9] A TR wave is said to precisely retrace the path of the ordinary wave that stimulated it, neither deviating nor spreading its energy as do normal waves.

What if this concept is in place? Such "directed energy weapons" would have fantastic capacity to destroy personnel, facilities, and communications at appreciable distances. Practicing research scientists dispute this new weapons technology as "scientifically infeasible," and high ranking government officials downplay such advances as "imaginative."[10] Others, however, believe this weaponry actually exists. Why? Because the Soviets cannot help but boast of their superiority.

In January 1960, Nikita Khrushchev announced "fantastic weapon advancement." Even before Khrushchev's statement, the U.S. Embassy in Moscow had been bombarded by scalar electromagnetic (EM) waves and phase conjugate energy modulated upon weak microwave carrier beams, later causing illnesses and blood changes in targeted Embassy personnel.[11]

Yet the microwave radiation of the U.S. Embassy in Moscow is nothing compared to the potential of Soviet transmitters capable of producing similar conditions in distant target populations. At the whim of a Soviet official, large numbers of people can even be killed through the transmission of some lethal biological warfare (BW) virus. U.S. authorities acknowledge that destructive biological experiments are conducted in Soviet research institutes.[12]

Such warfare may have already begun. But how will a killer virus be recognized in the West? Will it be slow, highly infectious, quick-acting like influenza, or transmitted by insect vectors such as mosquitoes? The possibilities are unending. The transmission of biological warfare most likely will never involve the Soviets but some fanatical terrorist

group or inadvertent private contamination. What better way
to take over a continent than by killing off masses of people before your troops arrive?

Electromagnetic Warfare

After Brezhnev's boast to attain military superiority,
strange things began to happen. December 1985 saw the
beginning of a mysterious wave of actual destruction of
selected U.S. missiles and aircraft, involving at least three
NASA shuttle launches.[13] In 1986 and 1987, the U.S. suffered
the unexplained loss of two highly classified Stealth aircraft,
which are supposedly immune to normal radar waves.

Those losses are thought to be associated with a highly
sophisticated weapon of the kind used to down Gary
Powers' high flying U-2 aircraft over the Soviet Union in May
1960. This technology may also explain how the electrical
controls of the atomic submarine U.S.S. Thresher became
electromagnetically dead on April 10, 1963. The next day
a huge underwater electromagnetic blast occurred one hundred miles north of Puerto Rico.[14]

Thomas E. Bearden, a nuclear engineer who has spent a
lifetime involved in development of U.S. Army weapons system requirements, makes these shocking conclusions:

> We are referring to a new kind of blitz-krieg war:
> war conducted by powerful beams and destruc-
> tion engendered at the speed of light. War in
> which electromagnetic radiators are the primary
> decisive weapons. War in which new kinds of
> directed energy weapons play the major role. War
> which renders all our present defensive armada
> of weapons archaic and useless. War in which the
> material and personnel loss rates are so incredi-
> bly high that they boggle the mind of the more
> conventional military tactician and planner.

War in which even a small nation with TR wave weapons can strike and devastate a major power, and possess a first-strike capability unparalleled in human history. War which could be triggered by radical splinter groups and terrorist groups that acquire the technology. War in which the slightest miscalculation or the misuse of the weaponry can completely destroy the earth.

War which places extreme emphasis on finding "other ways"—such as surreptitious biological strikes and insidious electropsychological attack and control—to decimate a foe. War that Western governments, populaces, and Armed Forces are completely unprepared—militarily and psychologically—to face. NATO can be defeated in two hours or less, and the entire war—mop up and all—would last perhaps three days.[15]

A horrible scenario. But one we must consider in light of the facts and the opinions of those with access to classified information.

The geographical proximity of the Western theatre of war to the Soviet Union puts Europe in a dangerous and vulnerable position. Any powerful TR weapon, if used without restraint, would cause nuclear warheads and nuclear material to explode as surface bursts in the dirtiest fashion possible. As Chernobyl exemplified, the resulting radioactive fallout would indiscriminately wipe out—or at least detrimentally affect—all of Europe and the Soviets themselves.

How can this threat be minimized? By continuing to store nuclear weapons in NATO arsenals and deploying Pershing IIs and cruise missiles. This would greatly reduce the European continent's risk against substantial Soviet usage of any powerful TR wave weapons in their arsenal. The Soviets don't want to contaminate their own land mass by blowing up NATO's weapons. Could that be why Gorbachev reversed his position and agreed to President Reagan's zero option overture at the Reykjavik summit?

To sweeten such a response, Gorbachev, through INF and perhaps START in the future, could readily acquiesce to on-site inspections to assure the dismantling of missiles and their destruction. Once NATO is disarmed, the Soviets can use their new weaponry without fear of destroying themselves.

An Ace Up Their Sleeve

If Soviet strategic superweapons are in place and operational, only two obstacles may remain in the way of Mikhail Gorbachev's ascension to the role of undisputed world leader:

> 1. The need to "thin out" stockpiled and deployed West European based nuclear weapons.
> 2. The elimination of the United States' Strategic Defense Initiative (SDI).[16]

As a possible breakthrough in the nuclear stalemate, Ronald Reagan proposed SDI (Strategic Defense Initiative). George Bush is anticipated to continue the program, at least on a research and development level, until it is determined to be feasible.

How does SDI work? U.S. scientists envision a high energy laser in orbit, pumped perhaps by means of a nuclear explosion. The pulsed beam from this laser would have sufficient power to destroy any ICBM 10,000 miles away. Converted to a scalar electromagnetic laser (one that turns much of its electromagnetic energy into gravitational energy), however, it could destroy perhaps one-fourth of the Soviet Union in a single shot.[17]

Future testing and conversion through SDI could provide the United States with a very real strategic retaliation capability or mutual assured destruction. What has been endorsed as a purely defensive deterrent, however, is seen by socialist authorities as retaliatory power. No wonder Gorbachev is adamant that SDI must not be developed and tested in space.

Perhaps every American should take to heart the strong warning of former Soviet Chief of Staff Sergei Akhromeyev. On August 26, 1986, he warned:

> If the U.S. deploys a shield in space, the Soviet Union will have several options, none of what Washington would wish . . . The Soviet Union will very quickly find a response of which the U.S. has no inkling as yet.[18]

Do the Soviets have an ace up their sleeve? How will the Soviets respond to a U.S. deterrent in space? Soviet policy makers, wary of SDI, are tempted by two options:

> 1. Mounting a pre-emptive nuclear strike against the West.
> 2. Deploying its superior conventional forces to take advantage of the current European political, economic, and ideological vacuum.

How do the Soviets hope to achieve either goal? Mikhail Gorbachev is the policy maker whom the whole world is watching. His next move could set the stage for World War III.

18

Communism: No Longer a Threat?

Most Americans no longer see the Russians as the greatest threat to world peace. The generation of the 1980s, whose current political outlook has been shaped more by Vietnam than the Berlin Wall, regard the Soviets as less dangerous than China, Third World violence, the Middle East, and the Persian Gulf.

While visiting in Moscow, President Reagan tried to assure the world on June 1, 1988, that the Soviet Union is no longer an "evil empire." But there still exists some doubt.

Can we really believe they are changing from an offensive to a defensive military posture? If they have changed their tune, why are the Soviets:

1. Constructing an "enormously expensive" system of underground shelters and command facilities capable of allowing Soviet leaders to wage a protracted nuclear war;[1]

2. Increasing Soviet military expenditures;[2]

3. Aggressively deploying thousands of Warsaw Pact commando units to penetrate Western Europe for military intelligence gathering purposes?[3]

The Soviets have as recently as January 1989 refused Washington requests to disband paramilitary camps that have trained as many as 6,000 guerrillas and terrorists a year. "We're disappointed but not altogether surprised," said a U.S. expert on counter-terrorism.[4]

Now comprising fifty-six countries (36 percent of the world's population and 33 percent of its land mass), the empire of Marxism has allowed no free elections within its history, and every hint of political dissension has been stamped out with military force. Since 1945, forty-one countries have fallen prey to communist domination.

In his book, *Perestroika,* Gorbachev states that "communism originated and exists in the interests of man and his freedom, in order to defend his genuine rights, and justice on earth."[5] He also emphasizes that "we have no intention whatsoever of converting everyone to Marxism."[6] Yet, when we look at several strategic areas of Soviet interest, we see a different picture.

A tremendous build-up of conventional arms is occurring all over the world.

Building Bases in the Pacific

The Soviets have amassed 830 ships in the western Pacific while the U.S. has approximately 70 ships in the same region. Employing modern Kiev-class aircraft carriers as well as 130 submarines (the entire U.S. Navy has 130 submarines), the Soviets operate a safe haven for its 32 ballistic-missile submarines whose missiles can reach U.S. targets from Russian waters.[7]

Cam Ranh Bay, Vietnam, now the Soviets' only warm water port in the Pacific, has expanded three times since 1975 to become their largest base outside Soviet territory. Only seven years ago, Cam Ranh was primarily a liberty port for Soviet sailors. Today this strategic base provides air strike capabilities against China, Australia, and the Philippines. In addition, it serves as a staging facility to blockade the vital southern straits of Malacca, Sunda, and Lombok through which much of the West's oil and other important materials pass.[8]

While the Soviets gain strength in Asia, the U.S. finds itself on the defensive in the Pacific. In the Philippines, the threat of losing access to Clark Air Force Base and Subic Naval Base in 1991 remains serious. In addition, when the Anzus nation of New Zealand declared their area a nuclear free zone, the United States experienced an embarrassing setback.

Having spent $140 billion more than the U.S. on strategic force procurement over the past twenty years, the Soviets have established new base access to:

1. Australia, through Cam Ranh Bay in Vietnam
2. The Persian Gulf, the Indian Ocean, and Southeast Asia through bases in Afghanistan
3. The island of Socotra at the entrance to the Gulf of Aden
4. The Former British base at Aden
5. The Ethiopian island of Dahlak Kebir in the Red Sea.[9]

Not bashful about seeking inroads in the Pacific Ocean, an area previously dominated by U.S. influence, Moscow has gone from one island state to another, extending offers of economic assistance. The Soviet Union has sent trade delegations to Southeast Asia nations, signed friendship agreements with Vietnam, and inked military and economic support pacts with North Korea, Cambodia, and Laos. Moscow has also extended commercial overtures to Japan and the South Pacific Island nations.

What is motivating their sudden friendliness? The Soviets hope to attain with expanded military influence an acceptance and prestige that traditional diplomacy has failed to gain.

Even Japan and China are not immune from the Soviet military presence. The Kurile Islands north of Japan, which Japan claims as its "Northern Territories," now contains 10,000 Soviet troops and 40 Mig-23s. The Chinese border has amassed 500,000 troops, one-fourth of the total Soviet ground force strength. These forces man 80 backfire bombers capable of firing cruise missiles and 165 SS-20 intermediate range land based nuclear missiles—many more than they deployed three years ago. Each bomber is capable of delivering three independently targetable nuclear warheads all over China, Japan, South Korea, and Okinawa.[10]

The South Pacific Islands of Kiribate (formerly the Gilbert Islands) and Vanuatu (formerly the New Hebrides) lie in strategic positions. Through newly established commercial and diplomatic agreements with Moscow, these island governments have recently provided potential access for Soviet military operations all the way to Australia.

The Northern Pacific is also not without military activity. New reports from Alaska Army National Guard scouts tell of unidentified aircraft, submarines, swimmers in scuba gear, and discarded Soviet military equipment. Such reports have stimulated an increase in operations of the U.S. Third Fleet near Alaska and the Aleutian Islands.[11]

The Atlantic Expansion

Not limited to the Pacific, the Soviets are also extending their presence in the Atlantic Ocean. The *Wall Street Journal,* in its European edition dated May 2, 1988, made several interesting observations of the Soviet expansion into the Atlantic.

Now the home of the Soviet Northern Fleet, the Soviet port of Murmansk off the Barents Sea contains the most powerful of Moscow's four regional naval forces. Measured in sheer nuclear-strike capacity, the Northern Fleet is the equivalent of the Soviet Pacific, Black Sea, and Baltic Sea fleets combined.

The ice-free southern portion of the Barents Sea provides year round access to naval fleets. "One cannot overestimate the importance of the Murmansk area as a naval asset to the Russians," a Western diplomat was quoted as saying.[12] The Barents Sea is a strategic key to Soviet naval access to the entire Atlantic.

The Soviets are determined not to allow future exploration and development of contested oil and gas deposits by Norway, a NATO member. As a deterrent, the Soviets have repositioned their newest Typhoon-class submarines along with subs from U.S. coastal patrol assignments in the Barents Sea.

With continental Europe within easy range of the nuclear submarine missiles, the Soviets have permanently staked their claim despite increased activity from NATO trailing vessels. "There wasn't a single strategist in the West who thought of this before the INF treaty was signed," claims Finn Sollie, a former Norwegian diplomat and northern security analyst.[13]

The Soviets, however, knew exactly what they were doing by manipulating the INF treaty to fit into their plan for global expansion. And all the while, Gorbachev continues to trumpet peace and goodwill, hoping no one would notice what he is really up to.

The Mediterranean: A Sea of Peace?

Recent proposals by Mikhail Gorbachev on March 16, 1988, in Belgrade, Yugoslavia, asked for a "sea of peace" to be created. The Soviet leader recommended the withdrawal of U.S. forces and nuclear weapons from the Mediterranean-Balkan areas of Greece and Turkey (NATO member countries) as well as Spain and Italy. In turn, the Soviets would respond accordingly. The catch is that the Soviets base no troops or nuclear weapons in either Romania or Bulgaria, the only Balkan area within the Warsaw Pact alignment.

The Mediterranean Sea, long a naval stronghold of U.S. forces, now finds its superiority not just diminished but equated by recent Soviet expansion. The U.S. Sixth Fleet has an average of fifty ships permanently stationed in the Mediterranean, opposing some forty to forty-five Soviet warships.[14]

The Soviets know that Western Europe has highly vulnerable southern flanks. Sea and air launched missile systems, necessary in NATO's defense of Western Europe, would be drastically curtailed should naval vessels be reduced. And if aircraft bases were eliminated, through either local hostility or created nuclear free zones, Europe's lower parts would be embarrassingly exposed.[15]

Mr. Gorbachev would like to deny U.S. aircraft the privilege of basing anywhere in the Mediterranean theatre. He hopes Spain's recent hostility to its American F-16 fighter squadron will spread to Portugal, Italy (which has agreed to receive the displaced Torrejon unit), Greece, or Turkey.

Soviet tactics, however, are not limited to the European continent and Asia. In fact, their strongest ally sits perched on the fence in America's own backyard.

Cuba: The Bear in Our Backyard

The strangest phenomenon of all Soviet military accomplishments took place only ninety miles from Florida—in Cuba. This "unsinkable aircraft carrier" built in the very backyard of American presence and influence, holds the key to a deliberate and sophisticated Soviet strategy.

Wanting to avoid military confrontation with the West, Soviet expansion has always taken place with extreme caution. The Soviets are experts at using indirect means such as military assistance, employment of surrogates, covert action, and other low risk tactics. In no other country has success been as obvious as in Cuba.

Fidel Castro knows the U.S.S.R. would never sacrifice its own self-sufficiency to come to the aid of Cuba in the event of a Cuban military attack by the United States. But he also knows that such a U.S. victory would come at extremely costly results solely because of the extensive build-up of Cuban defense forces.

Cuba has become a major Soviet facility involved in intelligence gathering, military training, and disseminating propaganda. Today the Soviets consider the Cuban intelligence forces second only to the KGB in furthering Soviet global ambitions.

How did we allow such a military stronghold to develop right under our noses? Timothy Ashby, in his book *The Bear in the Back Yard,* maintains that without the help of Presidents Kennedy and Carter, the Soviets would not be using Cuba as a military bastion and a military surrogate.

John Kennedy in 1963 handed the Soviets a major victory when he recognized the right of the Soviets to maintain military forces in Cuba. President Jimmy Carter, in 1979, allowed the accidental discovery of a 2,600 man Soviet combat brigade photographed on maneuvers to remain in place as "no direct threat to the U.S."[16]

This sanctioning of Soviet combat forces in Cuba bolstered Moscow's theory that U.S.-U.S.S.R. "crisis" situations would not be met "head-on" by U.S. policy makers but circumvented in the most expedient fashion possible.

As early as 1970, U.S.-Soviet detente only solidified the role Cuba was to play in increased opportunity to influence not only the Caribbean area, but all of South America. Today U.S. policy is clearly not to expel "extracontinental communist powers" from the Americas, but only to contain such activities within Cuba.

Cuban Military Build-Up

Cuba's military airfields serve as permanent facilities for TU-95 Bear Ds, TU-142 Bear Fs, and Mig-23BNs that routinely fly America's eastern and southern coastlines.

Such aircraft also provide anti-submarine warfare capabilities and are capable of delivering nuclear payloads within the entire Caribbean basin.[17] Using bases in Nicaragua, similar capabilities extending north to Seattle would cover the Pacific coastline just as effectively as the Gulf and Atlantic coastlines are now covered.

The Cuban air defense system includes:

—28 surface-to-air missile (SAM) battalions equipped with Soviet missiles
—50 Frog-4 surface-to-surface missiles, each of which is capable of carrying a two-hundred kiloton nuclear warhead.

In addition, the Soviets have supplied 2,800 military advisors who provide partial support for these systems.[18]

Because of commitments in Grenada and Nicaragua, the Soviets have been amassing a gigantic war inventory in Cuba, tripling in quantity since 1980. The Soviets supply nine active and eighteen reserve Cuban army divisions. With sixteen thousand Soviet personnel, such troops include an armored brigade with forty T-72 tanks, mechanized infantry units, artillery, helicopters, engineers, support troops, and commandos.[19]

With an island arsenal in our backyard, a slipping grip on Central America, and a compromising Congress, our nation is already behind on our own turf. Without major changes in our foreign policy toward communist aggression, we may awake someday to find Cuban insurgents no longer content to stay in the backyard.

Losing on Our Own Turf

Rest assured that the Soviets have never been dissuaded from accomplishing their goals in any way possible. The Soviet plan? To penetrate and utilize the entire Caribbean region—including Central America—for Soviet military purposes.

Soviet aims were expressed by Anatoly Gromyko, chief of the Africa Institute of the U.S.S.R. Academy of Sciences and son of the Soviet President. Their goal in South America, he said, is to "sap and undermine U.S. positions" and "inflict significant damage to the U.S. power position not only in the region but in the world at large."[20]

Why is Soviet influence in Cuba an advantage to any conflict in Western Europe?

Ashby maintains that, in the event of any NATO-Warsaw Pact confrontation, more than half of all NATO resupply materiel would be shipped from U.S. Gulf Coast ports using shipping lanes that pass within easy striking distance of Cuba. Any subsequent confrontation with Soviet forces means the U.S. Navy would have its own war to fight, diverting necessary and strategic forces away from areas of strongest Soviet naval influence such as the North Atlantic.

The growth of Soviet nuclear and non-nuclear capabilities emanating from the island fortress of Cuba repeatedly point to a pattern of strategic planning. What is their goal? To exploit both "peacefully" and militarily, if necessary, "wars of national liberation." The Soviets sent $515 million worth of military equipment to Nicaraqua alone in 1988—the second highest total since the Kremlin began weapons deliveries to that tiny, war-torn nation in 1980.[21]

Mikhail Gorbachev's "new political thinking," however, may force him to consider the economic realities of huge military expenditures in Central America. Nonetheless Gorbachev will make concessions on regional expansion only when pressure from the United States forces the Soviet leader to save face and maintain his image as a world peacemaker. Until then, no nation is safe.

──Part Four──

Gateway to Revival

19

On the Path to Destruction

"Israel's next war will not be with the Arabs, but with the Russians," stated Israeli General Moshe Dayan in 1968.[1] Putting his finger on a fact that most of us believe but don't want to face, Dayan has verbalized the fear of many all over the world.

No matter who you ask—the Soviet recruit in Afghanistan, the Jewish cabby in New York City, the Jewish diplomat in Tel Aviv, evangelical American believers, or the Arab refugee—each looks to an inevitable world war involving the Soviet Union and Israel.

That doesn't mean the Arabs won't play a part. It's common to see news reports showing Palestinian youths throwing rocks at rifle-toting Israeli soldiers. In fact, conflict between Arabs and Jews erupts almost daily within and without the borders of Israel.

"There is nothing new in this," said Israel's Prime Minister Yitzhak Shamir recently speaking of the Israeli-Arab conflict. He continued,

> Our people fought for 3,000 years for its land, for its freedom, for the right to observe its culture and heritage, and it is certainly continuing to fight.

> There is no end to this war, and it is a war in which
> we must triumph, in each and every generation."[2]

"Jews are subhuman (to Arabs) and the Arabs are subhuman (to Jews) . . . it is not new," added Meron Benvenisti, the director of a West Bank Israeli research group.[3]

Past Islamic attacks (they've had five) fueled with Soviet arms and equipment have proved futile for the Soviet proxies. That means ultimately the Soviet Union itself will have to do the job. But when? And how can one know for sure?

Surrounded on three sides by Islamic forces, Israeli troops are outnumbered by as much as seven to one. In the face of such odds, Israel has always counted on the quality of its military hardware to override the quantitative advantage of the Islamic coalition. But the gap is decisively closing.

The number of missiles targeted on Israel from five surrounding countries has increased from 200 in 1982 to 340 in 1986.[4] Syria has Soviet SS-21 missiles and Saudi Arabia has Chinese East Wind missiles with a range of over 1000 miles. Egypt and Libya can bombard Israel with nuclear or conventional warheads or use chemical warfare if necessary.[5]

This puts the tiny country under constant siege and on continued military alert. With Islamic airfields minutes away by jet aircraft and only hours away from Jordanian tanks, every inch of the Israeli territory has to be protected.

The Mediterranean, once considered the private lake of America, is now being fiercely contested by an increased Soviet naval presence, bringing to bear the old saying, "He who controls the Mediterranean Sea rules the World."

Yet the key to the peace and tranquillity of Israel begins not with the Mediterranean but with the Islamic world.

Islam's Blind and Costly Allegiance

Although the term "Arabic" and "Muslim" are often used interchangeably, not all adherents to Islam are Arabic. Although not all Arabs are Muslim, 99 percent are.

In addition, not all of the Islamic peoples of the mid-east are Arabic. The Iranians are Persian and speak Farsi, not Arabic. The solidifying force of all these people, regardless of geographical location and nationality, is their religion. Whether Arabic, Persian, Indonesian, or American, the Muslim is bound to the same principles of ideology as taught by Muhammad.

The religion of Islam recognizes no distinction between religious and temporal power. Since all Muslims are of one faith, the religion is hostile to nationalism as well. Supposedly united under one common community of believers, held together by the same sacred law of Islam, in theory at least, the Islamic world is devoid of national jurisdictions.

Authorities in every Muslim country fight an increased erosive attempt from Islamic extremists to undermine loyalties to national regimes. This motivation—to rise up and rediscover their former greatness as Muslims—comes from the Ayatollah Khomeini. With the Iranian overthrow of the Shah in 1979 and their defiance of the "Great Satan" by the taking of American embassy hostages, the Islamic movement gained new boldness.

The religion of the prophet Muhammad, to whom the words of Allah were dictated and written down in the Koran, has now been altered by the Ayatollah Ruhollah Khomeini. In a lengthy exposition, he has proclaimed that the government of Iran has supreme validity, overriding even the Koran.

The government has the power to stop any religious law, close or destroy mosques as it sees fit, even "prohibit anything having to do with worship if these things would be against the interests of the country."[6]

In Khomeini's words, God's absolute authority vests in the legally trained cleric—himself—or his appointed successor. The streets of Tehran are filled with students shouting, "Khomeini's command is as good as that of the Prophet!" as they blindly follow the call to Islamic martyrdom against other "cousins" who disagree with them.

Throughout the Islamic world, battles rage between local governments and Islamic extremists who want to supplant secular governments with a complete Islamic theocracy. Such conflicts are necessarily violent and expensive.

Westerners, taught the importance of separation of church and state, can't imagine a nation basing its entire domestic and foreign policies and programs on Islamic theology. Countries such as Libya, Iran, and Saudi Arabia are obsessed with the teachings of Mohammed and Khomeini.

An example of religious factions dominating national policy is the Iran-Iraq war. Raging since September 1980, having inflicted 20,000 Iranian casualties in only two days of fighting[7] and over one million during the course of the conflict,[8] these two enemies have almost destroyed one another.

In the past plenty of cash was available for purchasing weapons and supporting troops—$1.5 trillion in the Mid-Eastern states since the 1973 oil shock. Now, however, the situation is different. In 1981 Saudi Arabia earned nearly $120 billion from oil; in 1987, only $22 billion.[9]

Today the Mid-Eastern countries export their people, sending transient work forces to bring home necessary capital to shore up cash deficient economies. In Jordan 50 percent of the work force is overseas; Egypt has 2 million away.[10]

The very survival of these same political regimes is tied to unfamiliar economic forces beset by foreign exchange, famine, and inability to provide required services at home. Faced with a delicate balancing act to combine economic stability with a degree of social and religious moderation, many mid-East nations are losing support from the people.

Iran's New Foreign Policy

Not all Arabic nations support the Ayatollah's radical tactics. In fact, the fear of the moderate Arabic nations, which sided consistently with Iraq in the Iran-Iraq conflict, was that Iraq would be overthrown. They knew if Iran won the war, the dominant radicalism of the Ayatollah would take over the Arab world.

Iran, however, was forced to capitulate in its war efforts. It was the policies of the United States through its Persian Gulf fleet that brought Iran to the bargaining table. The Soviet Union's consistent supply of arms to the Iraqi army also contributed to Iran's new peace moves. Few people realize that the Soviets have escorted Kuwaiti oil tankers through the Persian Gulf for about as long as the United States has.

Now the Ayatollah faces losses on all fronts, militarily, diplomatically, and at home through political conflict and civil disorders. Iran now finds itself devoid of a world market for its oil, without weapons, and disgraced in the eyes of the entire Muslim world. In addition, the Salman Rushdie debacle brought an end to Iran's relationship with Great Britain and reminded the West that the Ayatollah marches to the beat of a different drummer.

In spite of these setbacks, Iran is no longer burdened with its major war effort with Iraq and can now pursue new alignments with new directions. Having previously entered into friendship pacts with Iraq and Syria, two of the Soviet's closest allies in the Arab world, Iran has lifted the last hurdle.

Now a pact between the Soviet Union and Iran is only a matter of time. With the withdrawal of Soviet troops from Afghani soil, the predictions of Eastern European diplomats that such a treaty has been negotiated is a first step to a world-changing alliance.

The Soviet-Iranian Connection

The Soviet-Iranian connection, however, is nothing new. As far back as 1960, the Ayatollah Khomeini was fingered by a high ranking Polish defector as Russia's top secret agent in Iran during the mid 1950s.[11]

Today with the Ayatollah's power in question and Iranian fundamentalism running rampant in Iran, Teheran's fractionalized leadership after Khomeini will likely prove to be even more radical. Increased terrorism will only be the beginning as the Iranians look to expand their religious commitments, first against the more moderate Arabic sheikdoms, then against Israel, then the ''Great Satan'' itself. Who will assist Iran in these ventures? Its new partner: the U.S.S.R.

What can the Soviets offer? Military and economic aid to Iran as well as a railroad, an oil pipeline, and a ready customer for its petroleum products. What will the Soviets gain in return? Access to major intelligence gathering installations on the Persian Gulf, and eventually access to a warm water port on the Gulf—something that Iran had previously denied Moscow.

By helping to bring peace to the Iran-Iraq conflict, the United States actually played into the hands of the Iranian-Soviet scenario adopted in the mid-1950s by Khomeini and Soviet security forces. Their objective? To accomplish the age-old purpose of culminating a march all the way to the Mediterranean Sea, devastating the Jewish people in the process.

Such a scenario was planned as far back as 1930 when the Soviet Union produced a 14 kopek postage stamp showing an usual picture. The background represents the Soviet Union. In the foreground the red cavalry, depicted by four horsemen with swords drawn, are riding out of Russia on a path leading directly southward across the Tigris-Euphrates Rivers into what is today Israel. The map indicates the path of the army to be around the Black Sea through Iran, directly into Israel. An ominous cloud forms the background for this prophetic stamp.

Strange Bedfellows

The Jewish nation with Jewish leadership and military resources remains the greatest obscenity possible in the eyes of Muhammad's followers. Without pretense, they seek the total destruction of Israel.

For centuries, the Muslim nations have determined to decimate the Jewish people. In the past they have recruited formidable assistance from the Greeks, Romans, Mongols, Asiatics, and Africans. In the last world war, Benito Mussolini of Italy and Adolf Hitler of Germany joined together in seemingly untenable alliances—not ideological ones—but theological. Their goal—to eliminate the Jewish population.

Now with new partners comprised of the Soviet Union and its allies, an even stranger theological coalition has been formed within the Islamic world. Yet, their alliance makes sense. Muslims and Marxists use the same techniques to accomplish their goals: repression of the people and conquest of other nations—especially their enemies.

In support of their theological mandate, Muslims believe Allah has generously bestowed oil as their assurance of victory. This explains why the coalition between the Soviet Union and the Islamic nations is sealed by their economic necessity of supply and demand of petroleum.

Muslims and communists also share a mutual hatred of Israel. Their vehement loathing of Jews goes beyond economic and political rationale and can only be explained in light of a much greater spiritual battle being waged in the heavenlies. The Islamic-Jewish conflict is historically documented in the Old Testament. Traced back to the family disunity between Jacob and Esau, the Arabs and Jews have been at odds for thousands of years.

Similarly, the origins of the Marxism-Jewish-Christian conflict germinated through a disgruntled Jew (Karl Marx) and a Judas Christian (Joseph Stalin). These men, seeking to find a scapegoat for their failures and sin, blamed God. Because they could not touch the Almighty, they sought to destroy that which is most precious to Him—His people.

Men whose hearts were filled with hatred and obsessed with revenge spawned the ideologies of Islam and communism. Because the origins are spiritual, their goals, while seeming to be political, are motivated by spiritually evil forces intent on the destruction of all that pertains to the God of the Jew and Christian.

When the Government is God

Communism has replaced the religion of the Russian people with the statutes of atheism.

Arkady Polishchuk, formerly an avowed communist, explains his allegiance.

> Communism was my religion. [As a child] my first song was about Lenin, my first poem was about Stalin, and my dream was to become a Communist [Party] member. I was one for nearly fifteen years. That's why it was so difficult for me to get rid of my Marxist ideology, because it was my religion.[12]

What happens when the government is god? The final authority becomes communism, and the people must submit or be crushed. History records no other nation on the face of the earth responsible for more deaths, more blood, and more devastation than the followers of Lenin. Their hate for organized religion, especially Christianity, makes communism as fanatical as Islam.

Commissar Lunarsky, an early Soviet Commissar of Public Instruction, tells why Christianity is feared and hated:

> You must remember this, that we hate Christianity and the Christians. Even the best of them must be regarded as our worst enemies. They preach love to one's neighbors and pity [mercy] which is contrary to our principles. Christian love is a hindrance to the development of the revolution. Down with love of one's neighbor! What we need

is hatred. We must know how to hate, for only at this price can we conquer the universe.[13]

When Joseph Stalin left his studies at Tbilisi Theological Seminary to become an Octoberist revolutionary, he had to change his theology to agree with his goals. This "backslidden" disciple of the Russian Orthodox Church established a counter spiritualist movement ironically taken directly from Scripture. Yet, in practice, no human being has been responsible for more deaths than this one man.

Let's examine four parallel points between Christianity and Marxism.

1. Marxism, like Christianity, demands blood. Yet in the Christian faith, the blood of the new covenant was shed once and for all in the person of Jesus Christ for the remission of one's sins and right standing with God. (See Hebrews 9:14.) Marxism, however, demands the death and blood of anyone who dares to disagree with their objectives.

2. Marxism, like Christianity, relies heavily on confession. Christians are encouraged to confess publicly their faith in Christ and their love for God. Marxism, however, obtains confessions of allegiance in dungeons of torture or psychiatric wards of Soviet hospitals.

3. Marxism, like Christianity, sends forth its emissaries. No place on earth is too distant, too desolate, too gentle, or too violent for the Marxist propagandist. Christians have also received their marching orders to "go into all the world and preach the gospel" (Mark 16:15).

4. Marxism, like Christianity, sends forth the call of repentance and acceptance. Marxism, however, issues an obligatory call to all, with no respect for personal liberties or freedom of choice. Christianity is offered to those who freely choose to follow the Savior. Only volunteers will qualify for eternal life.

All false ideologies base their principles on some teachings of Scripture. Satan has no new ideas. His best tactic is deception, mixing lies with the truth, thus appealing to man's lower nature and giving man an excuse for his sin and his cruelty.

When Marxism is not at war with a stranger, it is clearly at war with itself. During the bloody purges of the 1930s, an estimated 120 million Soviet people died or suffered directly or indirectly from civil unrest.[14] A more recent purge occurred in Mao's Red China during the Cultural Revolution of the 1960s.

Referred to as "Marx's Tapestry," the motives and objectives of the October Revolution have consistently been confirmed with exceeding clarity over the decades. For untold millions, Marx's tapestry became a death shroud.

We'll Tell You What to Believe

Although Stalin and his crimes have been officially disavowed in the Soviet Union, his theological positions have not. In practice and in law, the Soviet state remains diametrically opposed to any religion other than scientific materialism.

In the recent words of General Secretary Gorbachev at the June 1988 Communist Party Conference in Moscow: "We do not conceal our attitude to the religious world view as an unmaterialistic and unscientific one."[15]

Despite his rhetoric of "full rights" for believers, Gorbachev still affirms the Marxist principle. The Communist Party itself considers such freedoms to be "abuses of democratization" that "run fundamentally counter to the tasks of restructuring and are contrary to the interests of the people."[16] Gorbachev himself denied that human rights were "a gift from the state," suggesting that they were "an inalienable characteristic of socialism."[17]

In other words, religion as a fundamental inalienable right of man is structured within the ideology or theology of

Marxism-Leninism. And what religion are Soviet citizens to follow? Whatever the Communist Party tells them to. Therefore, any freedoms as well as abuses will be determined and defined only by the Party. Soviet theology is what the Party or its appointed ideologue says it is. Period.

Such a position is no different from Iran in principle. This is why both countries will one day compromise their intense dislike for each other and join hands in a common bond and purpose to eliminate their mutual religious enemies— Israel and the ''Great Satan'' itself, the United States of America.

An enmity exists between the Marxist and the Christian as significant as the enmity that exists between the Jew and the Muslim.

Worldwide Anti-Semitism

Like the Muslim, the Marxist's obsession with his hatred of Christians and Jews dominates national policies and defies explanation.

Arkady Polishchuk, a Russian Jew who was educated at Moscow University and majored in Marxist philosophy, became a leading Soviet journalist, party member, and radio and TV commentator. Disillusioned with Marxism, he became an active dissident, later immigrating to the United States. He shares his testimony of Soviet prejudice and hatred of Jews:

> As a boy in the streets of Moscow, I was beaten many times for being Jewish. There is real anti-Semitism there. I only got into Moscow University through unusual circumstances.
>
> The Soviet Union is the most powerful empire in history. Like any other empire, it must keep growing. That's why they always try to expand, into Africa, the Middle East . . .

> The Middle East is a very special place for the
> Soviets. Not just because of oil . . . and [military]
> strategy, but because of Soviet hatred of Jews.
> Soviet officials just hate Jews. They want to destroy
> the state of Israel. There's a certain demonic
> dimension about this that's impossible to explain.[18]

With anti-Semitism on the rise all over Europe, in the U.S.,
and even in Japan, Jews continue to be the scapegoat of society. Former Nazis are still active in post-war Germany, and
American "skin-heads" spew out their message of hatred
and violence on television talk shows.

The real surprise of the resurgence of anti-Semitism, however, is in post war Japan—a country of 120 million people
with less than 500 Jewish inhabitants.[19] An outpouring of
hate has brought threats, discrimination, and violence on
the small Jewish remnant in Japan. In the future, such an
attitude could affect Japan's foreign policy decisions and
forge an alliance with the Soviet Union based on their mutual
hatred of Israel.

Anti-Semitism abounds in the Soviet Union where the second largest Jewish population outside Israel resides. Yet, for
economic reasons, the Soviets are careful about bringing
stringent reprisals against the Jews in their country. In fact,
they are using the Jews to woo the Common Market countries and others eastward. To foster positive world opinion,
the Soviets will not only be forced to let the Jews emigrate
to Israel but to become a viable part of the Mid-East peace
process.

The Soviets have maintained no diplomatic relations with
Israel since 1967 and have consistently opposed the policies of Israel and its aggressive posture of defense against
its Muslim neighbors. Under Mikhail Gorbachev, however,
diplomatic overtures express hope for a change. Now, for
the first time since the Six-Day War, a Soviet leader is working diligently to influence the Middle East peace process.[20]

This may force the United States, as Israel's foremost ally and friend, to take an unusual position. Adding to the dilemma is the fact that only one-fourth of last year's Soviet Jewish emigrants chose Israel over the U.S. for their ultimate destination. Both superpowers are now inexplicably intertwined in whatever solutions affect Soviet-Israeli relations.

The world waits with apprehension to resolve an issue that reflects more than racial prejudice and more than politics.

The Final Battle

Neither the Muslims nor the Soviets take lightly the position of Israel in the world today. Without a doubt this small remnant of 2.5 million people is destined to be the catalyst that will bring the superpowers to battle—a conflict of devastating proportions.

The final fulfillment of Scripture centers on the Second Coming of the Messiah. Satan knows that the Bible predicts the subsequent return of a resurrected, glorified Savior to rescue His people from the enemy's armies. This will be a moment of ultimate and final victory over the satanic forces of the world—an event every contrary spirit will fight to its last existence.

In the end, God desires to use Israel for even greater displays of His power and glory than ever before. His purpose? To bring all the world, including Israelis today, to a saving knowledge of the glorified Messiah.

If anyone in history had been able, or is now able, to interdict such a scenario, it would literally disprove Scripture and make God a liar—even prove Him non-existent. That is Satan's objective, and his pawns are the Soviet Union, its Islamic allies, and other anti-Semitic nations.

At the same time, God will use Russia, Israel, and their leaders in the developing end-times scenario that will bring about the next world war, the battle of Armageddon, and ultimately the return of Jesus Christ.

20

World War III or Armageddon?

One cannot talk of Russia and Israel without the issue of "end times" becoming the topic of concern. Are we living in the "last days"?

According to the New Testament, the last days began with the birth of Jesus Christ. Every generation, including the generation of Christ's birth, thought they were in the last days. New Testament writers penned their words with the impression that the last days or end of the world was imminent.

The question we are asking in this book is: To what extent will the Soviet Union of today be involved in the end-time scenario, and how will the rest of the world be affected?

Three factors are interrelated in God's timetable:

1. Mid-East events
2. Biblical prophecy
3. The U.S. Church

In this and the next few chapters, we will look at how these key elements relate to one another.

Spiritual Judgment of the Nations

End times is explained scripturally in terms of spiritual judgment not physical calamity as you and I would normally think. Because ''God is spirit'' (John 4:24), He deals primarily in spiritual matters, using physical means to accomplish spiritual ends.

To our human thinking, end times, judgment—''Armageddon''—means war, devastation, and physical destruction. Yet God uses such physical occurrences as a means to bring about an end result—an end more awesome and eternal than is humanly possible to contemplate—spiritual judgment.

Religious prophets thousands of years ago prophesied of spiritual judgment, resurrection, or an accounting of good and evil. Moses, Jacob, Zechariah, Daniel, Ezekiel, Joel, and other Old Testament Bible writers looked to a future event they deemed to be so significant that not only would future generations be impacted but their eternal destiny as well. Much of the world scoffed and ridiculed such predictions as fantasy or Jewish fable until 1948 when Israel became a nation.

Now tenaciously gripping an area of reclaimed desert and swampland the size of New Jersey, the small nation of Israel has survived five wars within its recent history and seen numerous Old Testament prophecies fulfilled. As the world watches the hand of God at work in Israel, even the skeptics are forced to take note of the existence of such prophetic writings.

Both Old and New Testament writers were concerned with end times, the resurrection, and judgment day. Even today such topics are the second most popular issue of religious inquiry. Such a wealth of historically factual and accurate Scripture must be considered in any complete analysis of the Soviet Union.

Old Testament Scripture pointed to a man, a Mesuash or Messiah, who would save the world from its sins and bring each individual to a right relationship with God. Although many have come in such a name, only one man was confirmed by God Himself in that office—Jesus Christ of Nazareth, who was born of a virgin, crucified, resurrected, and ascended to the right hand of God Almighty.

This same man—the Son of God—will come again to judge the living and the dead. (See Revelation 19:11-21.) Since 332 Old Testament predictions were fulfilled through the existence and ministry of this Jewish man, one must historically acknowledge His claim to be God incarnate.[1]

The fact is: Jesus Christ is coming again. But when?

Signs of His Coming

Jesus' disciples asked Him, "Tell us," they said, "when will this happen, and what will be the sign of your coming and of the end of the age?" (Matthew 24:3). Every generation asks that question.

As part of His answer, Jesus predicted the complete destruction of the city of Jerusalem (realized in 70 AD), then He talked about the end of the age.

> "Watch out that no one deceives you. For many will come in my name, claiming, 'I am the Christ,' and will deceive many. You will hear of wars and rumors of wars, but see to it that you are not alarmed. Such things must happen, but the end is still to come. Nation will rise against nation, and kingdom against kingdom. There will be famines and earthquakes in various places. All these are the beginning of birth pains.
> "Then you will be handed over to be persecuted and put to death, and you will be hated by all nations because of me. At that time many will turn away from the faith and will betray and hate each other, and many false prophets will appear and

deceive many people. Because of the increase of wickedness, the love of most will grow cold, but he who stands firm to the end will be saved. And this gospel of the kingdom will be preached to the whole world as a testimony to all nations, and then the end will come''—Matthew 24:4-14.

In this passage, Jesus emphasized three main topics: nationalities, missionaries, and mission.

1. *Nationalities.* The world of the end times will be a politically structured amalgamation of nations. Pacts, alliances, treaties, and commitments between sovereigns will depict reliance on man not God. The very existence of such alliances will be an abomination to the people of God (the Church) in this day. Such analogy might be stretched to include the politicized religious structures of today to which the church leans for support and influence rather than God.

Remember, Jesus is talking about spiritual judgment. Therefore, everything He says about specific physical happenings (i.e. wars, rumors of wars, famines, religious systems, etc.) are only symptoms of spiritual movement.

2. *Missionaries.* Another characteristic of the end of the age is reflected by the rejection of the gospel message proclaimed through messengers who are fulfilling the great commission. In fact, such ambassadors will be physically persecuted and hated all over the world.

The apostate church will succumb to such pressure and rescind its world evangelism measures, restricting the effectiveness of true believers drastically around the world. This worldly church will be full of apostate teaching and improper emphases. Because of its unwillingness to suffer persecution and forfeit its comfortable lifestyle, many will question the credibility and compassion of this religious system.

3. *Mission.* The remnant, the true Church, will nonetheless preach the gospel to every people group, enduring great hardships. This effort will be different from the traditional, conventional actions of the past by distinguishing mission from missionary. They will reflect mission as a sense of purpose, goal, or vision at all cost. As such, these examples of mission will be a testimony to the true Church and reveal the deceptive nature of the apostate church.

In conclusion, Jesus challenged the disciples to watch the fig tree, an expression referring to the true Church. "As soon as its twigs get tender and its leaves come out," Jesus said, "you know that summer is near. Even so, when you see all these things, you know that it [the end of the age] is near, right at the door" (Matthew 24:32,33).

Only three events stand in the way of the end of the age:

1. Jesus' promise that Jerusalem would not see Him again until the Jews say, "Blessed is he who comes in the name of the Lord" (Matthew 23:39).

2. Jesus' prediction that "Jerusalem will be trampled on by the Gentiles until the times of the Gentiles are fulfilled" (Luke 21:24).

3. The apostle Paul's insight that "Israel has experienced a hardening in part until the full number of the Gentiles has come in" (Romans 11:25).

All three of the "untils" relate to fulfillment of spiritual conditions. The church age, a period of grace or unmerited favor, could be terminated abruptly. Who is to say when the last elect of the Gentiles will be brought in?

How will God bring to pass the requirements of Matthew 23:39? Perhaps this has already been fulfilled. Or it may be symbolic and should not be taken literally. If so, all that remains is for the Gentile world power to attack Jerusalem.

The Soviet Union in Prophecy

As we have seen, religious issues motivate the Marxist and Islamic nations, and a devastating war may result from their actions. For these reasons, the Bible must be considered as a reference in evaluating future events of the Mid-East and ultimately the world.

What is God trying to tell the Church in relation to the Soviet Union? Let's look at a familiar Old Testament passage that describes how an enemy from the north will attack God's people.

Ezekiel chapters 38 and 39 have consistently been interpreted to apply to some future event involving the Soviet Union. Although written 2500 years ago, Ezekiel's account reads like tomorrow's newspaper:

> The word of the Lord came to me: "Son of man, set your face against Gog, of the land of Magog, the chief prince of Meshech and Tubal; prophesy against him and say: 'This is what the Sovereign Lord says: I am against you, O Gog, chief prince of Meshech and Tubal. I will turn you around, put hooks in your jaws and bring you out with your whole army—your horses, your horsemen fully armed, and a great horde with large and small shields, all of them brandishing their swords. Persia, Cush and Put will be with them, all with shields and helmets, also Gomer with all its troops, and Beth Togarmah from the far north with all its troops—the many nations with you'"—Ezekiel 38:1-6.

An Anglican priest in England writing in 1815 developed the following scenario from Ezekiel's prophecy.

> The prophecy without question relates to the latter ages of the world, when . . . Israel shall

return into their own land. Rosh signifies those inhabitants of Scythia, from whence the Russians derive their name . . . this formidable invasion of the land of Israel . . . God will defeat it. . . .

The Persians [Iran and Afghanistan] from the East, the Ethiopians from the South, the Moors [Libyans] from the West . . . shall join with them in this onset . . . towards the end of the world . . . (after) the general restoration of the Jewish nation.[2]

Several identifications of persons (Gog) and countries (the land of Magog) seem purposely vague, depicting an as yet unknown enemy of God's people. Yet tradition has consistently held *Gog* to be the military ruler of *Magog* or the Soviet Union of today, being the land of Meshech and Tubal (Moscow and Tubolsk of the U.S.S.R.).[3]

Ancient historical writings trace these tribal families from the creation period to northern Asia Minor or more specifically northern regions above the Caucasus Mountains— today's Soviet Union.[4]

The Hebrew word *Tubal* is said to relate to the son of the founder of the Tibereni people dwelling today on the Black Sea.

Rosh designates the tribes living north of the Taurus Mountains in the vicinity of the Volga deep within the Soviet Union.[5] An alternate translation of *Rosh* in Hebrew is *bear,* the international symbol of the Soviet Union, including "Mischa," the 1980 Olympic symbol.

Due north of Israel, the Soviets still maintain the largest horse cavalry of any army in the world.

Persia is the ancient Persian Empire area from West Pakistan to Turkey, predominately Iran and Afghanistan all the way to Egypt, excluding Saudi Arabia.

Cush is Ethiopia, Somalia, and Sudan of today.

Put or Libya is the North African nations of today.

Gomer and his bands is the Warsaw Pact area of Eastern Europe.

Togarmah of the north quarters is the Baltic states area of the U.S.S.R. now called Estonia, Lithuania, and Latvia. Togarmah was a son of Gomer who was a grandson of Noah. Part of his family settled in Turkey and part went north to the Baltic region, this being the reason Togarmah is referred to as belonging to "the north quarters."

Of the principle nations identified, only Iran is presently outside the control of Soviet influence. Ethiopia, formerly a Christian nation, succumbed to Soviet domination in 1974. Prior to 1970, such a configuration of nations was impossible since Afghanistan, Iran, Libya, and Ethiopia experienced strong western influences. Today, however, the stage is set for Ezekiel's prophecy to take place.

America and the Mission of the Church

How soon the next great armed conflict occurs is an open question, subject to many variables including the political decisions of the President of the United States.

Politics and religion go hand in hand, and are inseparable and necessary for the survival of the Church. The Scriptures plainly tell of military resources in the hands of ungodly leaders used to further the purposes of Almighty God.

When secular armies liberate certain areas of the world, the Church survives and prospers. Recent examples include the Ukraine that was liberated from Stalin's devastating persecution by, of all people, the Nazis. And who can forget Korea? Because the Korean War was fought, the largest evangelical church in the world exists, with over 500,000 members in Seoul, South Korea.[6]

The United States, in particular, stands as a beacon of religious liberty throughout the world. Our forefathers came to North America seeking religious and political freedom.

Few of us comprehend the spiritual destiny placed upon the United States of America at its birth. Fewer still understand the vast importance of a correct secular posture this nation must maintain to fulfill God's purposes in the world.

The U.S. Constitution says more about the freedom of religion than the freedom of the press. Yet many believe the document accommodates ABC, CBS, and NBC rather than Almighty God. Benjamin Franklin stated to Constitutional framers in 1787:

> God governs in the affairs of man. And if a sparrow cannot fall to the ground without His notice, is it probable that an empire can rise without His aid? We have been assured, Sir, in the Sacred Writings that except the Lord build the house, they labor in vain that build it. I firmly believe this.[7]

Thomas Jefferson in a letter to Moses Robinson, March 23, 1801 wrote:

> [The] Christian religion, when divested of the rags in which [the clergy] have enveloped it, is a religion of all others most friendly to liberty, science and the freest expansions of the human mind.[8]

George Washington in his farewell address of September 17, 1796, said: "Of all the dispositions and habits which lead to political prosperity, Religion and Morality are indispensable supports."[9]

Finally, John Quincy Adams summarized it all when he said, "Our constitution was made only for a religious and moral people. It is wholly inadequate for the government of any other."

Even obscure Scripture passages have been interpreted by some to relate to the role America would play in the molding of the spiritual destiny of mankind. One of Daniel's visions describes four great beasts. "The first was like a lion [England], and it had the wings of an eagle [the United States]" (Daniel 7:4).

Yet time and time again, the political blunders of this nation, especially in international affairs, have come in direct conflict with the propagation of the gospel around the world and the American Church's accessibility to such a task. From World War I, which saw international communism birthed, to World War II, which saw international communism firmly established, the scenario has consistently been the same: the *closing* of doors to the evangelizing of the nations of the world.

History proves that political parties of the U.S. and politicians themselves play a prominent role in the development of "end times." The decisions of our president and the U.S. Congress affect more than world events and the people of our nation. They may determine the very pace at which the final clock is ticking.

One World: The Ultimate Rebellion

Wherever we are in God's timetable, one thing has never changed: Man's desire to be God.

From the beginning of creation, mankind has been at enmity with God, striving continually to rebel against His Law and His Word. In fact, it didn't take man long to completely turn against God and His ways.

> The Lord saw how great man's wickedness on the earth had become, and that every inclination of the thoughts of his heart was only evil all the time. The Lord was grieved that he had made man on the earth, and his heart was filled with pain— Genesis 6:5,6.

Because of man's wickedness, God destroyed the first world with a flood, sparing only Noah and his family.

(See Genesis 7:23.) Yet no sooner had the children of man multiplied and the terror of the flood receded from their memory, than they forgot the Lord God. This time they decided to take matters into their own hands.

> Now the whole world had one language and a common speech. . . . Then they said, "Come, let us build ourselves a city, with a tower that reaches to the heavens, so that we may make a name for ourselves and not be scattered over the face of the whole earth"—Genesis 11:4.

Today, thousands of years later, man still wants to control the world and his own destiny. Although the "tower" of today has changed in design, the purpose remains the same. The human race, in the twentieth century, is united in one proud attempt to seize the reins of history in unrestrained rebellion against God. The kingdom of man still attempts to displace the kingdom of God.

The self-centeredness of man focuses on ideas of one-world government, army, language, monetary system, and religion. Such humanistic thinking dominates the pursuits of national leaders, the secular media, and educational systems throughout the world.

The stage is set for a one world government. But the leadership and the motivation to bring these worldwide systems together effectively is still missing.

The backdrop, however, has been in place since 1940. With World War II and the actions of Democratic President Franklin D. Roosevelt, history took a different turn. He ultimately approved the sins of Soviet communism, selling Eastern Europe into the hands of a psychopath. Going a step further, Roosevelt approved a plan calling for an international conference at San Francisco to draft a charter for world peace.

After over forty years of United Nations efforts, however, Roosevelt's plan remains incomplete. Despite the world economic systems that are in place, universal adoption by all nations remains far from being consummated. Why? Because the world is not ready for the traumatic and far reaching experience of world government.

What would it take to bring about a world peace organization? Only a war of horrendous magnitude will be adequate to remove the barriers of nationalistic pride, racial and ethnic animosities, and monetary securities that rule the world of today.

Soon, however, the nations of the world will find themselves in a perfect unison to relinquish their sovereignty without tears or regret. Following a devastating war experience, (probably called World War III), a common denominator will bind mankind together. What is that common bond? Fear and a desire for world peace.

Fear of extinction will overcome many obstacles and will move the people of the world (including the Church) to do the unthinkable at this crucial hour in the history of mankind.

World War III then Armageddon

World War III is not the battle of Armageddon. But a third world war will precede the latter by at least seven years. A certain alignment of nations will be involved in World War III, but the battle of Armageddon will include *all* nations of the world. (See Revelation 19:17,18.)

The reason for World War III is to be found in Scripture.

> You [Gog] will say . . . "I will plunder and loot and turn my hand against the resettled ruins and the people gathered from the nations, rich in livestock and goods, living at the center of the land"— Ezekiel 38:12.

World War III will be fought for political and economic reasons as certain nations try to establish world domination.

The battle of Armageddon, however, will be fought for different reasons.

> Then I saw three evil spirits that looked like frogs; they came out of the mouth of the dragon, out of the mouth of the beast and out of the mouth of the false prophet. They are spirits of demons performing miraculous signs, and they go out to the kings of the whole world, to gather them for the battle on the great day of God Almighty—Revelation 16:14.

The battle of Armageddon is purely a spiritual battle. "The rest of them were killed with the sword that came out of the mouth of the rider on the horse, and all the birds gorged themselves on their flesh" (Revelation 19:21). This "sword," the Word of God, is "living and active. Sharper than any double-edged sword, it penetrates even to dividing soul and spirit, joints and marrow; it judges the thoughts and attitudes of the heart" (Hebrews 4:12).

Again, Armageddon is described as a spiritual battle.

> Satan will be released from his prison and will go out to deceive the nations in the four corners of the earth—Gog and Magog—to gather them for battle. In number they are like the sand on the seashore. They marched across the breadth of the earth and surrounded the camp of God's people, the city he loves. But fire came down from heaven and devoured them—Revelation 20:8,9.

The "city he loves" is the spiritual Jerusalem (described by the apostle Paul) rather than the present day Jerusalem. (See Galatians 4:25,26.) Modern Jerusalem, presently claimed by three faiths, will ultimately become a center for one world government and thus the religious center of the world religions (and apostate church as well) after World War III.

The Bible obligates certain events to take place in Israel and the city of Jerusalem. It's important to recognize, however, that God has no spiritual identification with the present day Jerusalem because of its apostasy. Scripture predicts and confirms this fact when Revelation 11:8 describes the city of Jerusalem to be in Egypt, symbolic of "bondage to damnation." In fact, God recognizes present day Jerusalem only by the name of "Sodom," which means "spiritually defiled by religious perversion."

Ezekiel's prophecy, written 2500 years ago, talked of 50,000 Jews returning to Jerusalem after twenty-one years in exile to build a massive temple of gigantic proportions. Yet the temple was never allowed to be restored.

Today, God's temple is His Church—the Body of Christ— and His purposes in the world revolve solely around what the Church is called to do and fulfill in these last days before Jesus returns.

Blow the Trumpet in Zion

Few Christian leaders today feel the necessity to warn the Church of the terrible days ahead.

> Blow the trumpet in Zion [God's church]; sound
> the alarm on my holy hill. Let all who live in the
> land tremble, for the day of the Lord is coming.
> It is close at hand—Joel 2:1.

Despite consoling interpretations that the church will be "whisked away" (raptured) in smiles and laughter, the prophet Joel apparently didn't think so.

> Blow the trumpet in Zion [a call to religious
> assembly, not a warning], declare a holy fast, call
> a sacred assembly. Gather the people, consecrate
> the assembly; bring together the elders, gather the

children, those nursing at the breast. Let the bride-groom leave his room and the bride her chamber.

Let the priests, who minister before the Lord, weep between the temple porch and the altar. Let them say, "Spare your people, O Lord. Do not make your inheritance an object of scorn, a byword among the nations"—Joel 2:15-17.

In the same chapter of Joel, Israel has this promise from the Lord God Almighty concerning the outcome of World War III:

"I will drive the northern army far from you, pushing it into a parched and barren land, with its front columns going into the eastern sea and those in the rear into the western sea. And its stench will go up; its smell will rise"—Joel 2:20.

In the book of Ezekiel the Lord promises the Soviet army what He will accomplish with them when they come against Israel:

"I am against you, O Gog, chief prince of Meshech and Tubal. I will turn you around and drag you along. I will bring you from the far north and send you against the mountains of Israel—Ezekiel 39:2.

In the "end-time" battle of Armageddon we find a graphic account given when the Lord Himself comes with His armies to fight the last war:

And I saw an angel standing in the sun, who cried in a loud voice to all the birds flying in midair, "Come, gather together for the great sup-per of God, so that you may eat the flesh of kings, generals, and mighty men, of horses and their riders, and the flesh of all people, free and slave, small and great. . . ."

The rest of them were killed with the sword that came out of the mouth of the rider on the horse, and all the birds gorged themselves on their flesh—Revelation 19:17,18,21.

The Day of the Lord

Not all are killed in World War III, but all are slain in the battle of Armageddon; there is a difference. Armageddon translated from the Hebrew means a "gathering" or "assembling," and the prophet Joel speaks plainly concerning the "Last Battle," which is also called the "Day of the Lord."

> Come quickly, all you nations from every side, and assemble there. Bring down your warriors, O Lord! Let the nations be roused; let them advance into the Valley of Jehoshaphat, for there I will sit to judge all the nations on every side.
> Swing the sickle, for the harvest is ripe. Come trample the grapes, for the winepress is full and the vats overflow—so great is their wickedness! Multitudes, multitudes in the valley of decision! For the day of the Lord is near in the valley of decision—Joel 3:11- 14.

Jehoshaphat means "the Lord judges," and the battle of Armageddon is a spiritual war where the Lord will judge the heathen. No doubt it will take place in some topographical location of renown, but it is unnamed in Scripture.

As the battle of Ezekiel 38 and 39 prepares the world for judgment and is fought in the mountains of Israel, nothing short of a horrendous war will bring to pass the predictions of "what must take place" (Revelation 4:1).

Without a war to shake the very foundations of mankind's age-old traditions and beliefs, the "Red Dragon" will never rule over the "Bear," the "Lion," and the "Leopard" and just as surely one-world government will never receive the breath of life.

World War III is inevitable. Only a devastating war of global proportions can prepare the world for the leadership of the anti-Christ and set the stage for the final battle—Armageddon.

21

While the World Waits

Is Gorbachev the global leader for whom the world waits? While only time will provide the answer, one thing is sure: Gorbachev is in trouble. Hope for a peaceful transition to democracy under Gorbachev's leadership is fading daily.

Politically, Gorbachev's pre-emptive coup against Yegor Ligachev and his anti-reform colleagues firmly secured Gorbachev's position as a dictator. But he must maintain this position in order to implement his reforms, especially as Soviet economic turbulence increases.

The crisis in the Baltic area republics is forcing Gorbachev to make concessions or risk the devastation of the local Communist Party. As long as this economically stable region continues to work, pay taxes, and help hold together the rest of the country economically, Gorbachev most likely will allow more social and political concessions.

Yet, the days of glasnost, such as they were, may be drawing to a close.

Party directives indicate that 1989 will be a year of tightening the grip on all unofficial grassroots activities. A muzzle may be clamped on glasnost. We can expect new controls on the Soviet official media—Tass, Pravda, etc.—followed by criminal charges against independent publishing activities.

Particular targets will be ethnic/nationalistic groups (other than the Baltic area), such as Armenians, Ukrainians, and Jews. Gorbachev himself has denounced Armenian activists and ordered the detention and prosecution of hundreds.

Independent labor union participants, human rights activists, and publishers/distributors of "samizdat" (unofficial writings) have had literature confiscated along with typewriters, books, and clandestine presses through unannounced house searches.

Even Sergei Grigoryants of the *Glasnost* newspaper was jailed, then released. The KGB seems back in charge, denouncing through official news sources various "provocateurs," "irresponsible extremists," and those "hostile to the people." In a barrage of verbal garbage, the tone is consistent with past KGB practices. We can expect to see more arrests and prosecutions of those who risked speaking out during the brief period of glasnost.

In Moscow, a sense of apathy and disappointment can be felt among the people. The completely fraudulent nature of local elections is clear to everyone. Although four years have passed since he came to power, Gorbachev still has not established any significant social basis for democracy. 1989 will probably bring Gorbachev's first acts of political terrorism against his opponents.

Perestroika: Failing Badly

Yet the real sense of concern in every Soviet home is the economy. Even Gorbachev publicly admits the failure of perestroika to reach its simple goals of providing basic necessities. Soviet reformers are beginning to acknowledge Gorbachev's perestroika is no different than Lenin's New Economic Policy (NEP) of 1921-27.

Stalinism was the answer to that ill-conceived plan and looms gigantic in the minds of many as the solution to this dilemma. Uncontrolled private enterprise can be expected to be the culprit necessitating "accelerated administrative intervention."

The imminent failure of perestroika can best be confirmed by the enormous Soviet deficit and the hyper-inflation consuming the country. Soviet economists now estimate (no one is sure) the deficit to be "between 15-17 percent of the national income" or 100 billion rubles. This is three times the U.S. budget deficit. Many regions in the Soviet Union have no cash to pay workers.

What makes up this huge deficit? How did the Soviets get so far behind economically?

1. Drop in world oil prices—15 billion rubles
2. The Chernobyl tragedy—8 billion rubles
3. Gorbachev's anti-alcohol campaign—19 billion rubles
4. Unsold, worthless manufactured goods—470 billion rubles

In addition, Gorbachev faces the tremendous damage caused by the earthquake in Armenia, estimated by some to cost several times more than Chernobyl.

Nor are foreign credits such as loans, grants, or benefits a solution to the Soviet problem. Without the necessary changes in economic structure, vast sums—which have accelerated the Soviet hard-currency debt to the West of over $40 billion—provide little economic relief.

With the debt more than doubling since Gorbachev came to power, the debt service alone will consume roughly one-third of all hard currency export earnings in three years at its present rate. The only consistent aspect of the Soviet economy is its defense spending, which continues to demand 20 percent of the Soviet economic output.

Shortages and High Prices

One past solution to Soviet needs for more money has always been simply to raise prices. Now, however, prices for goods and services have risen 43 percent between 1971-83. Today's ruble is worth only 42 kopeks of the 1960 ruble.

Some prices increased 400 percent in the past fifteen years, perhaps half of that increase coming during Gorbachev's tenure. Price increases have affected practically everything people need on a daily basis.

Today, a woman would pay 260 rubles for a winter coat or 135 percent of the current average monthly wage. This is up 30 percent since 1980 and 45 percent since 1970. But coats aren't easy to come by. The same coat outside Moscow, if available, would be 400-600 rubles.

Bread is up 20 percent, and other food products have risen 15 percent in only two years. But the chief problem is unavailability of cheaper goods or non-existent goods. Dramatic shortages exist for children's items, affordable clothing for adults, and medicinal items.

Because of the limited availability of some products, many Soviet regions require ration-cards for citizens to purchase the most widely used agricultural products. One-fourth of the Soviet population is under food rationing. Food riots are a definite possibility.

Forty-five per cent of the Soviet population is living in poverty if a level of 100 rubles per month is accepted. These include single parent households, pensioners, most young Soviet families, and others who cannot afford even the barest necessities. Malnutrition is becoming clearly visible among children from large families and retired people.

Gorbachev's reforms are causing great problems, and the disdain for him among ordinary people is growing. "Empty counters make people nostalgic for the days of strictness and order"—that feeling is expressed by millions within the Soviet Union today.

This puts Gorbachev's opponents in a favorable position, guaranteeing them a ready support group. Tragic consequences could result, either through new administrative changes or in new leadership. Gorbachev's days may be numbered.

The western Church, however, fails to see the significance of Gorbachev's position. What lies ahead for the people of the Soviet Union and the world if Gorbachev's policies fail? Does the Church have a role to play in preventing global disaster? Will Gorbachev be the world leader who will usher in peace? Only time will tell.

Controlling the Minds of Men

Two technological advances will hasten the development of a new-age leader. These powerful communication tools—television and computers—will be used to dominate the world. What is Gorbachev's goal? Military might? Global expansion? Or does his objective have more far-reaching consequences?

Gorbachev knows that in order to rule the world, he must control the minds of men. And now he has the ways and means to do it. Hitler didn't have network news or instant printouts, but Gorbachev has both and has made each an integral tool of his communicative process.

The desire to change the "inner man" has always been foremost in the mind of the Marxist, even preceding physical violence. For this reason, the Soviets have been forerunners in the field of psychology, para-psychology, behavioral sciences, and varying mind control techniques.[1] Psychology can be traced to roots of Eastern religions, which have been legitimized by mortal intellectualism and used effectively by the Soviets to accomplish their purposes.[2]

The apostle Paul exhorts us to "be transformed by the renewing of your mind" (Romans 12:2), for within the mind of man is the power of life and death over our spiritual existence. The doorway for such a struggle over who controls the spiritual destiny of man is the *mind*. How will that control be determined: by the Word of God for the Christian, or the self-gratifying ideology of the Marxist for the new age man? There can be no compromise.

That is the reason the Soviets' intervention in American affairs is so effective and widespread. Its extensive use of psychological misinformation and subliminal thought control techniques are broadly placed within established institutions of learning, communication facilities, and public institutions—including the established church.

Go and Change History

That is precisely why the Church is the key to the world's survival in the decade of the 1990s. Only the Church holds the treasure of the Truth. God seeks not to control men but to set us free through faith in His Son, Jesus Christ.

The Christian is under command to "Go into all the world and preach the good news to all creation" (Mark 16:15). We are obligated to demonstrate the love of God to a lost and dying world.

Christians of the Western world must take upon themselves the selfless burden of helping those suffering under governmental restrictions within the Soviet orbit of influence and domination. America has been singled out from among the nations of this world to be a leader and example of Christ-like love. We are to go abroad to those enslaved by barbed wire, armed guards, bureaucratic restrictions—or mind control.

No one knows what would happen if the Soviet Union had the same opportunity to hear the gospel of Christ as America has had. Because of the great spiritual famine that exists in the Soviet Union, the entire nation may repent if only a glimmer of spiritual light shines through the darkness.

Scripture assures us that "God does not show favoritism" (Acts 10:34). The outcome of total repentance for the Soviet Union could easily change the course of history! Repentance from the North would prevent World War III!

Amazingly enough, the army of God, not the army of the United States, is the determining factor that controls the destiny of the Soviets—and the world.

The Church is the only means through which Soviet people can be exposed to the gospel of Jesus Christ. Does the task set before the Church seem gigantic? Considering the power Christ bestowed to His Church, we have only lame excuses for not accomplishing the commandment to be witnesses "to the ends of the earth" (Acts 1:8).

> Now to him who is able to do immeasurably more than all we ask or imagine, according to his power that is at work within us—Ephesians 3:20.

> Then the sovereignty, power and greatness of the kingdoms under the whole heaven will be handed over to the saints, the people of the Most High. His kingdom shall be an everlasting kingdom, and all rulers will worship and obey him—Daniel 7:27.

> The weapons we fight with are not the weapons of the world. On the contrary, they have divine power to demolish strongholds—2 Corinthians 10:4.

The Church serves a mighty God and wins. The ending has already been written: "And I tell you that you are Peter, and on this rock I will build my church, and the gates of Hades will not overcome it" (Matthew 16:18). God will not allow His Church to be destroyed.

It's Not Too Late

Even now it is not too late. "Come now," the prophet Isaiah wrote, "let us reason together," says the Lord. "Though your sins are like scarlet, they shall be as white as snow; though they are red as crimson, they shall be like wool'' (Isaiah 1:18).

The Lord also said:

"If my people, who are called by my name, will humble themselves and pray and seek my face and turn from their wicked ways, then will I hear from heaven and will forgive their sin and will heal their land''—2 Chronicles 7:14.

"If at any time I announce that a nation or kingdom is to be uprooted, torn down and destroyed, and if that nation I warned repents of its evil, then I will relent and not inflict on it the disaster I had planned—Jeremiah 18:7,8.

Even though the sins of Sodom and Gomorrah were abominable before the Lord, God would have still spared those cities when Abraham interceded for them if only ten righteous people could have been found there. But among the population of those two wicked cities, the Lord could not find ten who could deter God's fiery judgment through their righteousness. So God destroyed Sodom and Gomorrah. (See Genesis 18:20-32.)

When the prophet Jonah was sent to the great city of Nineveh to preach repentance to its wicked citizens, he refused. Nevertheless, God in His infinite mercy brought Jonah to them in the belly of a great fish. When Jonah preached to that wicked city, the people repented. God spared the city in spite of the reluctant intercessor. The king of Nineveh himself proclaimed: "Let man and beast be covered with sackcloth. Let everyone call urgently on God. Let them give up their evil ways and their violence. Who knows? God may yet relent and with compassion turn from his fierce anger so that we will not perish'' (Jonah 3:8,9).

The sins of Nineveh were so great the sins of the owners of the animals were imputed to the animals, thus requiring them to be covered with sackcloth, and God forgave all and spared the land.

Finally, that God may be understood more intimately, read His words as recorded by the prophet Ezekiel:

> As surely as I live, declares the Sovereign Lord, I take no pleasure in the death of the wicked, but rather that they turn from their ways and live. Turn! Turn from your evil ways! Why will you die, O house of Israel?—Ezekiel 33:11.

God is even now waiting for an intercessor who will stand in the path of fiery judgment certain to follow if none repent. Are you that intercessor? Where is the intercessor for the Soviet Union; the United States?

The responsibility for the world's spiritual condition lies solely with the Church. In fact, the warning of God is upon us in these words:

> "When I say to a wicked man, 'You will surely die,' and you do not warn him or speak out to dissuade him from his evil ways in order to save his life, that wicked man will die for his sin, and I will hold you accountable for his blood"—Ezekiel 3:18.

Not only does God hold individual believers accountable, He also expects the Church—the Body of Christ—as a whole to have as our main objective the salvation of the world.

What Are You Waiting For?

When the resurrected Christ spoke with His disciples prior to His ascension, the disciples must have known that not everything promised in God's Word had taken place. Numerous Old Testament prophecies promised that God would establish justice on earth and that the whole world would be filled with the knowledge of God.

Yet standing on the Mount of Olives, they looked down over Jerusalem and saw a city occupied by Roman troops. No wonder the disciples asked Jesus if now was the time He was going to complete the coming of His kingdom.

Today's Church thinks like Christ's disciples. We see only the events around us and overlook Jesus' teaching about the kingdom of God and His specific instructions to carry on His ministry. That should be the priority of our lives until His return. But many fail to obey.

No wonder we misunderstand Scripture, are slow to believe, are surprised at God's intervention in our lives, and find it difficult to grasp God's whole plan and our place within it. Like the disciples, we stand around staring at one another, wondering what to do next.

Suddenly Jesus was gone, ascended into the heavens as His dumbfounded followers watched helplessly in amazement. God has an answer for this dilemma as well. Angels are dispatched with a simple message: Jesus will return.

> "Men of Galilee," they said, "why do you stand here looking into the sky? This same Jesus, who has been taken from you into heaven, will come back in the same way you have seen him go into heaven"—Acts 1:11.

Today, with entire civilizations separating us from the disillusioned disciples, we are reminded of only one thing: Jesus will return. The middle-time is simply that: a time between a particular day in the past when Jesus departed and a particular day in the future when He will come again.

For the Christian, each day that passes should reaffirm the hope of His coming through the reality of His presence in our lives. For the non-believer, every hour that remains provides one last chance for eternal salvation.

And no matter how far off, His return should be continually visible to all through the hope and anticipation evidenced today in the Church—a hope of eternity that is transforming our very lives, our families, our possessions, our sufferings, indeed our entire world.

22
It's Harvest Time

Recently, a well-educated young woman, who desired to commit her life to child evangelism in Eastern Europe, told me she was unable to raise any financial support from her local church. This church, a member of the largest Protestant denomination in the United States, spent huge sums of money on their beautiful facilities but could not afford to send a young missionary to an area desperate to hear the Word of God.

Reaching these "unreachable" people should be the priority of the church. Yet 90 percent of the church's missionary force and 99 percent of the church's funds are focused on the small minority of the world's population where traditional religious programs can be maintained.

Funds and efforts are mainly concentrated on buildings, domestic projects, and local mission efforts. These funds are spent on ourselves—the English speaking world—which numbers less than 10 percent of the world's population.

I've watched in embarrassment as Eastern European Christians, in the U.S. for the first time, viewed the extravagant facilities of American churches with their plush sanctuaries, well-equipped gymnasiums, and television studios. These men were deeply grieved by what they saw. "Brother," asked one Russian pastor who had struggled for years to survive in Soviet labor camps, "how can they be Christians and read the same New Testament I read and use their money in such a way?"[1]

This article from the French Communist paper *Paix et Liberte (Peace and Liberty)* should force those of us in America to answer that question. The author sends this message to Christians:

> The gospel is a much more powerful weapon for the renewal of society than is our Marxist philosophy. All the same, it is we who will finally beat you. We are only a handful, and you Christians are numbered by the millions. But if you remember the story of Gideon and his three hundred companions, you will understand why I am right.
>
> We communists do not play with words. We are realists, and seeing that we are determined to achieve our object, we know how to obtain the means. Of our salaries and wages, we keep only what is strictly necessary and give the rest for propaganda purposes. To this propaganda, we also consecrate all our free time and part of our holidays. You, however, give only a little time and hardly any money for the spreading of the gospel of Christ.
>
> How can anyone believe in the supreme value of this gospel if you do not practice it, if you do not spread it, and if you sacrifice neither time nor money for it? Believe me, it is we who will win, for we believe in our communist message and are ready to sacrifice everything, even our lives, in order that social justice shall triumph. But you people are afraid to soil your hands.[2]

Oblivious to what is going on around the world, the North American church has failed to recognize the urgency of the times. We continue in our selfish ways, with little or no concern for our lost and dying world.

Our mission, as described in the New Testament, is to reach the world and bring the lost into the Body of Christ. That has always been the mission of the Church, and it has not changed. If we sit back and wait for the world to suddenly awake to revival, we will totally miss God's plan for today.

Eighty-three percent of the non-Christian population of the world resides in countries that partially or completely restrict traditional missionary approaches. In fact, one-sixth of the world's population lies within the boundaries of the Soviet Union.

But has the church in North America changed its approach since March 1985, the last date of change in Soviet administrations? Could glasnost be God's vehicle to evangelize the entire Soviet Union? Could the desperate hope for spiritual truth of three generations of legal atheists be fulfilled in our lifetime? If so, are we taking advantage of this period of glasnost and reaching the communist countries with the gospel?

A New Exodus

Since the mid-1970s, prophetic words coming out of the Soviet Pentecostal churches have consistently spoken of:

1. Increased religious freedoms
2. Mass immigration of believers from the Soviet Union
3. Subsequent severe persecution

Few Soviet Christians outside the Pentecostal communities believed such prophecies to be true. But thousands of Soviet Pentecostals began to act on what they had heard and petitioned the Soviet government for exit visas.

By 1980, thirty thousand men, women, and children relinquished their Soviet citizenship, expecting immediate deliverance from the extreme atheistic harassment they were experiencing. But neither relief nor exit ever came. Actually, the persecution increased in Brezhnev's last years and continued under Andropov (a former KGB head) and Chernenko. Those who had applied for exit visas were especially sought out by the KGB.

Such prophecies had almost been forgotten when Mikhail Gorbachev came to power in March 1985. Then, things began to change. The release of most religious prisoners was finalized and police harassment was relaxed. Many within the church recognized that this was the time of religious freedom that had been prophesied.

Suddenly, with no explanation and without any prompting from the West, hundreds of believers (99 percent Pentecostal) began to receive exit visas from Soviet authorities.

The exodus began slowly with some 100 refugees arriving in Vienna, Austria, in June of 1988. By November of that year, 500 a month were being processed.

Why are Soviet believers leaving? They say, for three reasons:

1. No significant government help is being given to Pentecostals, resulting in a total lack of tangible physical support.
2. Prophecies confirm the propriety of the exodus.
3. A sense of hopelessness pervades the lives of all Soviets.

"The real concern for the Pentecostals," said recent Soviet Pentecostal emigre Boris Perchatkin now living in West Springfield, Massachusetts, "was—What is going to happen to us tomorrow?"

Exiting hastily under Israeli permits, 150 Soviet immigrants per week are received into refugee camps in

Rome en route to the West. An estimated 50,000 Pentecostals remain, wanting to leave.

U.S. Immigration officers anticipate 6,000 Soviet Pentecostals will be processed in 1989. As a result of this mass exodus, Western Pentecostal denominations and churches have been caught completely off guard. While Jewish people around the world have established a sophisticated network to take care of immigrating Soviet Jews, churches in the West are unprepared to help fellow believers.

Why is the church in the West so apathetic and unconcerned? Dr. Mark Elliott, Director of the Institute for the Study of Christianity and Marxism provides a possible answer:

> The Jewish community is totally united on their helping Soviet Jews. Yet U.S. Christians cannot even agree that Christians within the Soviet Union need help. This partially explains why the U.S. Church is so unprepared now to help these refugees.

The Third Wave of the Holy Spirit

Not only is the North American church unfamiliar with *current* events dominating the world scene today, it is just as unknowledgeable of *spiritual* events happening around us.

C. Peter Wagner, a missiologist of the Fuller School of World Missions, in his book *The Third Wave of the Holy Spirit,* describes today's events as a dramatic follow-up of a massive intervention of God's power. Beginning with Azusa Street in Los Angeles in 1906, and continuing through the Jesus movement of the early 1960s and the charismatic explosion of the 1970s, a third wave of the Holy Spirit is now being felt literally all over the world.

The latest move began in the late 1960s in Guatemala. This traditionally Roman Catholic country suddenly experienced massive revival culminating at the highest levels of authority within the country.

China has also seen outstanding church growth. In the early 1970s, when President Nixon began making overtures toward China, no one knew if the church within the People's Republic of China even existed. Today, estimates in China say 5 percent of the total population of the country is evangelical. When the communists swept into power in 1949, evangelicals numbered only about 1.3 million. Since then, the church has grown 3,000 to 4,000 percent.

Without western intervention, worldwide church growth within the past decade has been phenomenal. Stories of miracles and healings abound. Professor Wagner described today's church as pentecostal or charismatic rather than protestant or catholic.

"[China has] a quarter of the world's population, and one of the highest rates of Christian growth that has ever been seen," Wagner said.[3] One former missionary to China estimates that in the three years following 1980, as many as 27,000 people per day may have become Christians.

Donald McGavran, founder of Fuller School of World Missions in Pasadena, California, asserts the church is growing even faster in many African countries. Sub-Saharan Africa, McGavran said, is "becoming a Christian land mass," just as Europe did between the years 200 and 1000 A.D.

Countries like Nigeria, Uganda, Ethiopia, and the Ivory Coast are seeing explosive church growth. Some 67 to 72 percent of the population of Kenya profess to be Christian. The greatest growth in Africa is among Pentecostal churches, mainline charismatic churches, and churches that emphasize missions, according to the General Secretary of the Association of Evangelicals of Africa and Madagascar.

Worldwide Opportunities

What triggered the abrupt change from the "God is dead" ideology prevalent in the world only two decades ago?

"Wars, earthquakes, strife, refugees, famines—all can make people more responsive to the gospel," said Jim Montgomery, president of Dawn Ministries.[4] Optimum openness to the gospel centers around trauma, crisis, and disruption.

Churches in Mexico City found greater opportunities for ministry subsequent to the earthquake of 1985. Columbians in volcano-stricken areas have been more open since that disaster. Cambodian refugee camps in Thailand and Afghan Muslim refugees in Pakistan are current examples of opportunism.

In Argentina, the evangelical church is growing at an annual rate of 12.5 percent. "The Falkland Islands crisis changed the whole national social psychology of the Argentines and opened them to the gospel like never before," said Dr. Wagner.[5]

Even materialistic Japan, less than 1 per cent Christian, is opening up to the gospel for the first time since World War II. Annual evangelical growth there is a hefty 7.2 percent, according to figures released by the Global Mapping Project, Inc.

"Anything that disrupts society tends to open people to the gospel—when people get the feeling that society isn't working; that there are no answers for their problems," Montgomery said.[6]

Obviously, throughout the world, countries and people are in crises. Natural disasters, warfare, rocky economies, failed socialism, rapid changes in society—all contribute to increased instability in today's world.

Is There Really a God?

"The collapse of religion that was foreseen twenty years ago is just not taking place," said Rev. David B. Barrett, a leading authority on religious statistics. The secularism, agnosticism, and atheism of the 1960s have failed.

"What hadn't been realized," Barrett said, "is that these 'isms' have no idealism to offer. The young are not satisfied with this kind of substitute. They don't want it."

The turnabout has been particularly embarrassing to the Soviets "and a shock to them as well," Barrett concluded. "In the Soviet Union, there is a very significant, mostly Christian revival in the cities, especially among the young."[7]

"What is going to happen to us tomorrow?" is a unanimous plea from every household within the Soviet Union. For many it is simply a plea for subsistence, security, and sanctuary.

For literally millions of Soviet citizens it is a desperate attempt to express questions of doubt placed within their spirits by atheistic kindergarten teachers decades previously: Is there really a God? Is there really life after death? Is there really a heaven and a hell? Is the Bible a book of myths?

Teaching services in Soviet churches are now diverted to the presentation of simple evangelistic messages in deference to the masses of unbelievers (most first-time attendees) flooding the meetings. Invited by friends or attracted by a printed invitation, many Soviet people come to churches seeking an answer to their great spiritual hunger.

Evangelical churches in the Soviet Union are filled with new inquirers, and many newcomers are converted to Christ. Most have dramatic and emotional salvation experiences—all are life-changing.

Imagine the thrill of hearing someone honestly and simply say, "I want to know God. How can I? Will you help me?" Excitement permeates Soviet churches as pastors and laymen have the joy of leading unbelievers—people who have never prayed before in their lives—in the sinner's prayer.

Harvest Time in Eastern Europe

For the past two decades, God has been busy bringing people around the world to Himself. North America, Central

America, South America, Asia, Africa—the list continues across time zones, date lines, literally spanning eternity.

The obvious omission? The Muslim world and Eastern Europe where the church has experienced little growth during the decades since World War II. The church in the Soviet Union has waited even longer for significant change. Yet revival for the Soviet Union is on the horizon.

Two-thirds of all European Baptists now reside in *Eastern* Europe. In addition, over *two-thirds* of all European Pentecostals are behind the "Iron Curtain."

One Iron Curtain pastor remarked to me:

> It's our only hope in this country. I work night and day knowing this might be our last chance to have an impact on this country. No one knows how long it will last.

As Soviet Christians see the need for massive evangelization efforts, they are boldly approaching the government for more liberty. In addition, churches are establishing methods of communication among themselves and cooperating in unprecedented ways by sharing literature and evangelistic opportunities.

A Soviet pastor said,

> We have seen how well the Lord has opened doors in our country—tremendous avenues for preaching the gospel in the Soviet Union. These doors have not opened by themselves. They have been opened by the fervent prayers of men—prayers of the church in the western world.

Without a doubt, strange, unforeseen events are taking place within the Soviet Union. In October 1988, city-wide evangelism meetings were held in Riga, Latvia. Over 14,000 people attended the two services held in a rented ice hockey coliseum. Over 670 people made professions of faith with dozens more receiving special prayer.

Such an event was possible for the first time since the 1940 takeover of Latvia by the Soviets. Other conferences are scheduled for 1989. Video tape available in the West confirms hundreds of new believers experiencing baptism in rivers and lakes throughout the summer of 1988, observed by tens of thousands of onlookers.

Soviet citizens are showing renewed interest in the church—particularly the evangelical church rather than the Russian Orthodox Church. In Estonia, recent developments seem to permit the teaching of children for the first time, some limited charitable activities by church members (hospital visits, etc.) and some person-to-person evangelism.

This plea from a pastor of a congregation of over 2000 believers should challenge every western Christian to earnest repentance: "Brother," he told me on one occasion, "I don't know how long I have; one week, six weeks, a year. My life is completely in the control of other people. But, if you will get us the help we need in providing Scriptures, literature, and training resources, we'll turn this country upside down for Jesus Christ."[8]

Jesus challenged His disciples to have eyes of opportunity.

> "Do you not say, 'Four months more and then the harvest'? I tell you, open your eyes and look at the fields! They are ripe for harvest"—John 4:35.

There are harvest opportunities in the Soviet Union and Eastern Europe today that did not exist six months ago. It's harvest time!

Now is the Time!

But where will the Church be ten years from now? Still reclining in velour-covered pews while the world plunges into a fiery hell?

The truth is—the future of the Church and the world is being decided today. Now is the time for the Church to act. If we fail to "go into all the world and preach the gospel" today, tomorrow may be too late. The forces of darkness may be too powerful; the political barriers may be inpenetrable; the minds of men completely dominated by New Age thinking, Islam, Marxist ideology, humanism, or some other satanic deception. What will the Church do then?

If we are reluctant to act today when doors are opening to the message of the gospel around the world, what will we do when "the night comes and no man can work"? Will we wring our hands and wait to be whisked away into heavenly bliss?

God has opened the gates today. Now is the time. Let us go forth with the only message that can save our "wicked and perverse generation" from destruction.

If we are to be effective, however, the Church must proclaim the gospel in ways that are relevant to current events and world situations. Otherwise, the Church will be overrun by pagan, atheistic forces that will devastate God's plan to use the Church in bringing the world to Himself. If the Soviet Union and Islamic forces unite together and attack Israel, World War III could be Satan's tool to crush the Church and the nation of Israel—thus effectively preventing the Church's evangelization of the world.

If that happens, however, God will be forced to intervene physically and directly, responding to military aggression that will initiate World War III then Armageddon and spiritual judgment.

God's People—the Church

Theologians today read the thirty-eighth and thirty-ninth chapters of Ezekiel to predict a foreign enemies' invasion of Israel and God's physical intervention to save His chosen nation. Although such a happening is to be taken literally, the emphasis of this passage is really God's people—the Church—and His relationship with them.

No foreign enemy will ever prevail against the people with whom God has established His everlasting covenant. While conveyed through an old covenant with Abraham, these spiritual principles were renewed through a new covenant of which you and I are a part today.

In these passages from Ezekiel, God established one of the most important principles in Scripture. By refusing to allow the building of the temple that the Jews demanded, God was making it clear that the future Church would be *people* not *buildings*. God's priority has been, and always will be, His people.

This principle set forth 2500 years ago and confirmed throughout the New Testament powerfully proclaims that the gates of hell will never prevail against God's people— His Church. Jesus told us that in this world we would have tribulation, but God will never allow any outside oppression to overpower the Church. If spiritual or physical forces threaten to destroy the Body of Christ, God will intervene. The Bride of God's Son is the Church, and God will protect her as promised in His Word.

At the same time God's heart bleeds for a lost and dying world. "God so loved the world," and He desires that no one perish but that all be brought into a right relationship with Him through His Son Jesus Christ. This forms the basis for New Testament evangelism and world missions outreach—to bring the lost into the Body of Christ—the Church.

Such is the predicament the Church finds itself in today and why the key to God's intervention lies within the Church. That is why Jesus Himself does not know the timing of such intervention. God is waiting, watching, agonizing over souls lost for an eternity. Perhaps God Himself is putting events into motion to give the Church its last chance to impact the world for Jesus Christ.

That is why it is so important for us today in the Church to acknowledge our ineffectiveness over the past seventy years in the Soviet Union, the Islamic world, and Asia. That is why we must reach the unreached before it's too late.

God's End-Time Strategy

Throughout the ages, just when the opposition seemed too formidable—when all seemed hopeless—God stepped in. God has "stepped in" in the Soviet Union. Most of these current opportunities available to evangelize the Soviet Union have not been prevalent in our lifetime.

God is still on the throne with a priority of bringing the world to a saving knowledge of Himself. To that end, physical circumstances are simply spiritual tools. God's consistency throughout Scripture—the Exodus, the wilderness wanderings of Israel, the tabernacle, Solomon's temple, the New Testament covenant, the priesthood of the believer— all point to an unending thread of unbroken commitment to bring hurting people to Himself.

That is why the mentality of today's world cannot be measured by economists, political strategists, militarists, or social scientists. They are incapable of predicting what is ahead or when events will happen.

Only Scripture provides the answer, and that key is being extended to the Church alone. Only through the inspiration of the Holy Spirit can the Church receive the wisdom to understand its role today in what is happening in the Soviet Union.

Anyone involved in a spiritual relationship with Almighty God realizes that His ways are not man's ways. Thus, out of the ineptness and ineffectiveness of past traditions and methodologies tried by the Church to evangelize the world, we must consider that God has a strategy—a superior strategy to accomplish His purposes.

God's strategy, outlined in John 4:38 depends on you and me!

> "I sent you to reap what you have not worked for.
> Others have done the hard work, and you have
> reaped the benefits of their labor"—John 4:38.

God is helpless, He says, to bring in the harvest using only those who have planted the seed or tilled the ground. God is waiting on you and me to begin reaping. You and I are allowed the benefit and reward of the hard labor others have performed.

God has a strategy for evangelizing the Soviet Union and ultimately the world. And the battle lines are drawn—not behind the Iron Curtain, but in our own churches in the West. The trenches are within our own church pews, in mission conference rooms, and in our individual prayer closets.

God's plan of operation still involves sending people. Gideon was told to "Go in the strength you have and save Israel out of Midian's hand" (Judges 6:14). God chose to prove Himself strong with Gideon who apologized, "My clan is the weakest in Manasseh, and I am the least in my family" (Judges 6:15).

The amazing phenomenon of the Christian faith is that God chooses people—superior people—to go on His behalf. Not superior in the eyes of the world; nor necessarily more spiritual than others serving elsewhere; but certainly "set apart" to allow themselves to be uniquely equipped by the Holy Spirit to complete the task for which few are chosen.

23
Revival Now!

On a windy day near the Swedish coastal city of Helsing-
borg, a woman was taking an afternoon stroll along a wind-
swept shore. Suddenly, she stumbled upon a bottle that had
been washed up on the sand. Something about the bottle
caught her attention, and she noticed there was a slip of
paper inside with writing on it.

The woman carefully uncorked the bottle but found to
her dismay that she could not read the note. One of her
friends suggested that it might be written in Russian. Translation revealed that it was a message from the Soviet Union
addressed to a popular Russian language Christian radio
evangelist in Stockholm.

"Please send me a New Testament or a Bible," was the
plea.

The message had come from a radio listener near Kiev
in the Ukraine—hundreds of miles from the ocean that had
carried the request to the western coast of Sweden.

Unusual? This bottled message echoes the hungry cry of
millions of imprisoned souls in the Soviet Union.[1]

Despite the obvious lack of desire on the part of the 20th
century church to evangelize the Soviet Union, this field has

been prepared for revival by the Holy Spirit Himself. The only question remaining is whether or not you and your church will participate.

The prophet Zephaniah talked of a day for "the church" when the Lord would "deal with all who oppressed you; I will rescue the lame. . . . I will give you honor and praise among all the peoples of the earth when I restore your fortunes [bring back your captives] before your very eyes" (Zephaniah 3:19,20).

Right before our eyes God is "turning back the captivity" of the church within the Soviet Union. Now you can go, send others, or provide resources for this captive church. Using a new strategy through which only God will receive glory, you will receive rewards for all eternity. (See John 4:38.)

Send Us Bibles

Allow me to remind you that 98 percent of the Soviet Union's population has never had access to any portion of Scripture since World War II. Of 283 million people there is only one piece of Scripture for every 133 Soviet citizens.

Of the Christians who make up 34.5 percent of the Soviet population, most are unregistered, non-affiliated worshipers who have no access to structured religious programs. These people seldom see Scripture in any form, despite the claim by Soviet authorities that 1.2 million pieces were distributed in 1988.

If there is little Scripture, there are fewer hymnals, teaching books, liturgical helps, study aids, Christian literature, and children's materials. On one trip behind the Iron Curtain, a Soviet brother told me:

> We need money, food, many physical helps but send us Bibles. All the other things we can manage ourselves, but we have no means of getting Bibles.[2]

With a few exceptions, Soviet pastors and church leaders represent the third generation of leadership who have had no access to a Bible school, Christian college, or seminary. In addition to the need for teaching material, literature, and Bible study aids, the most desperate need is to train church leaders. Without trained leadership, the Soviet church is unable to equip their people for ministry.

Despite some recent changes in government policy, children are legally not permitted in worship services. Soviet law prohibits anyone under the age of eighteen from being baptized. "Sunday schools," as we understand that term in the West, are non-existent.

In certain areas, however, teaching possibilities loom on the horizon as imminent. Yet, there are no trained children's workers, no children's materials, literature, or visual aid programs available to help reach the children with the gospel message of Jesus Christ. As one church leader said recently:

> I appreciate so much the nice gifts you have brought us; the food, the clothes, the personal items we desperately need; but please bring my children more Christian literature. We're starved for Christian reading materials for our children.[3]

Requests like this one led us to found Mission Possible Foundation. God gave us the burden to reach out to our brothers and sisters in the Soviet Union who were struggling to grow in their Christian walk.

For seventy years, we in the West have allowed the church in the Soviet Union to grope in darkness. Now these faithful believers find themselves totally unprepared to evangelize their own people much less other nations.

How You Can Help

Through the trained staff of Mission Possible Foundation and its extensive, long-term involvement within the Soviet

Union, we can directly link church to church, or individual to individual. Outreaches not previously possible are now open.

Here are several ways you or your church can help provide literature to your brothers and sisters in the Soviet Union:

Form Western-Soviet Denominational or Group Alliances. Authorization is now possible to send direct gifts of Scripture to churches or denominations of your choice. The majority of exposure is with registered churches or denominations.

Adopt a Church. A Western church can currently adopt a Soviet church and mail up to five pieces of literature and Bibles per person to the believers in that church. This requires an official district document that can be obtained by Mission Possible personnel. This mailing can encompass registered or unregistered churches.

Link Individuals to Individuals. When individuals in your group want to do more, they may obtain names and addresses of Soviet Christians and facilitate mailing packages of Scripture/literature. Then you can continue to communicate with them on an ongoing basis.

Authorize Printing. Participate in printing operations that are officially authorized within the Soviet Union. These are currently directed 90 percent toward Orthodox and 10 percent toward Protestants.

Print Covertly. Mission Possible has several years' experience of printing Scripture/literature in the Soviet Union. This is directed exclusively to unregistered evangelical churches. Places in the Soviet Union are ready to begin such operations if a sponsor can be located.

Visit the Soviet Union. Travel restrictions have been eased significantly for westerners. You can visit Soviet churches bringing a much needed "greeting" and encouragement from the West.

Establish a Soviet Union Missions Minister or Director. Mission Possible has a staff person who can assist in educating, training, and motivating a person from your church in how to lead a group to the Soviet Union for ministry.

Write Letters. Names of Soviet Christians are available who desire encouragement from western Christians. There are many pastors and lay leaders still in Soviet prisons today. Letters to them are such an encouragement. Mission Possible can provide all the information you will need.

Pray. Join Mission Possible's intercessory prayer warriors. Learn how to "stand in the gap" for these brothers and sisters in the Lord. Pray that this "window of opportunity" will stay open and will spread to other communist lands.

Church Leadership Training Programs

If you or your church desire to help train Soviet pastors and Christian leaders through Mission Possible's four-year curriculum, you can:

Sponsor Pastor Training. With little or no formal training having been available in the past, many pastors are eager to embark on a long-term training regimen. This, so far, is being conducted one-on-one through correspondence.

Sponsor Seminar Training. Your group can sponsor a Mission Possible teaching team to go to specific Soviet districts to train key leaders within a church or denomination for one or two days. The topics could range from child evangelism to church planting.

Provide Translation Assistance (Writing/Editing). At present, portions of the leadership training curriculum need to be written, edited, and translated into the Russian language. The first year needs to be translated into additional Soviet languages. Personal assistance is required.

Assist with New Course Material and Books. Theological, practical teaching helps/programs may be suggested/developed for Soviet application.

Children's Ministry

No ministry to the captive Soviet Church would be complete without help for the children.

At the heart of Mission Possible's Children's Ministry is the gift to a Soviet church of a complete felt set unit. These are 12-inch flannel figures depicting classic children's Bible stories. A complete set includes six backgrounds and six hundred accompanying characters, animals, and figures. All instructions are translated into the primary language.

With your help Mission Possible can evangelize Soviet children through:

Denominational/Group Alliance. One Soviet evangelical group has asked for five hundred felt sets. Numerous groups have requested one to two hundred. Your church denomination or group can be this valuable source.

Linking Your Church to a Soviet Church. One or two felt sets can be shipped via the mail to a Soviet church upon request from within the Soviet Union.

Individuals Sponsoring Felt Sets. An individual may sponsor one or more felt sets on any given trip made by Mission Possible staff to individual Christian families within the Soviet Union.

Seminar Training. Mission Possible sends in teaching teams for one or two day seminars showing the Soviet teachers how to use the children's materials effectively. Sponsors are needed for these teams.

Translation Assistance (Writing/Editing). Writing out one or more of the Bible stories for the Soviet teachers helps them to "draw out" the story and show it effectively on the felt set. Ultimately, supplemental materials and children's songs will need to follow the felt sets.

Production/Purchase/Transportation of video cassettes, video recorders/players for teaching children and child evangelism application. Music videos for youth are desperately needed for those too old for felt set emphasis.

All the tools are in place and ready for workers to begin immediate reaping. God has uniquely ordained people, places, and resources for effective usefulness within the Body of Christ for His work in the Soviet Union. God has faithfully honored the years of extreme sacrifice and hard labor of thousands, perhaps millions of His children who have never bowed the knee to Marx and Lenin.

Gateway to World Revival

God has heard the intercession of millions in the West who have prayed unceasingly for revival in the Soviet Union; He has honored the faith of those who have gone or sent loved ones behind the Iron Curtain. Yet the key to the immediate evangelization of the Soviet Union lies with the believer who has seldom prayed for this massive land and the pastor who has yet to commit his church's resources to the needs of the Soviet people.

The Soviet cry for help, heard by the western church today, is similar to the one the apostle Paul heard in the first century. Only the areas of need have changed. Instead of Macedonia (Europe), it is now Estonia (the Soviet Union). Thank God that the same resource of assistance available then to meet the deep emotional, spiritual, and moral scars embedded by generations of abuse, bitterness, and hopelessness are available now.

Approximately seventy years elapsed from Jesus' birth until Paul received God's vision for Europe. Ironically, the Soviet Union has been "closed" to the church for seventy years of this century.

What will be our response? Thousands of Soviet Christians are risking their lives now in an effort to leave their country before the inevitable fulfillment of a third prophecy promising intense persecution.

Will the door shut next week? In six months? A year? Just as important, how would revival in the Soviet Union affect the world? Over 120 language groups within the country are now without the gospel. If they should suddenly come under spiritual conviction and revival should break out, would we be prepared?

If that happens, revival could extend quickly to the other communist bloc countries, to China, to the Muslim world through the 50 million Soviet Muslims and the Soviets' Arab alliances. India would be affected, South East Asia, even North Korea.

Every national stronghold of the devil known today would come under intense influence of Soviet revival—and almost immediately. Suddenly, within months, rather than generations, the light of the gospel message could permeate darkness impenetrable by the western church in this century.

The Gates are Open

No one overlooks the U.S.S.R. today. Economists don't; diplomats can't afford to; militarists dare not; even ecologists train a constant eye on this huge source of world influence. Neither does God overlook what has happened in the course of history within the boundaries of the Soviet Union nor what we've failed to accomplish as a church over the past century.

Now a predominance of historical fact, Scriptural reference, and physical evidence points to one conclusion: The next decade turns completely on what happens within the Soviet Union.

Regardless of what you think of Gorbachev and where his reform policies will take the Soviet Union, one fact remains: The only hope for world survival centers on an immediate and massive spiritual repentance among the Soviet people. This is the only possibility that could develop a grass roots movement strong enough to effect change in political direction.

Our alternatives for survival in America, as a nation and a church, are simple. If we look to any source, the United

Nations, NATO, or any alignment of nations to influence and alter Soviet direction other than the Church, we look in vain. Such actions, timely initiated, might delay or postpone Soviet intentions but not change them.

As a New Testament Church, our desire, our passion should not be merely to survive, but to conquer—to emerge victorious—to be an active part of God's plan to bring the world to Himself prior to the physical return of Jesus Christ.

How much better to share the love of Jesus and see genuine repentance than to see the judgment of God expressed through war and destruction! But are we willing to pay the price to evangelize the people of the Soviet Union?

Perhaps glasnost is not so much for the Soviets as it is for the church in the West—our last opportunity to offer Jesus Christ to every Soviet man, woman, and child. Our last opportunity to alter God's timetable in bringing the world to Himself.

> Open up, O ancient gates, and let the King of Glory in. Who is this King of Glory? The Lord, strong and mighty, invincible in battle. Yes, open wide the gates and let the King of Glory in—Psalm 24:7-9, *The Living Bible.*

Glasnost *is* the gateway to world revival.

Many Christians meet outdoors for worship, conducting services without the aid of Bibles or hymnals.

Throughout the Soviet Union, believers, and many interested unbelievers, consistently pack small churches like this one.

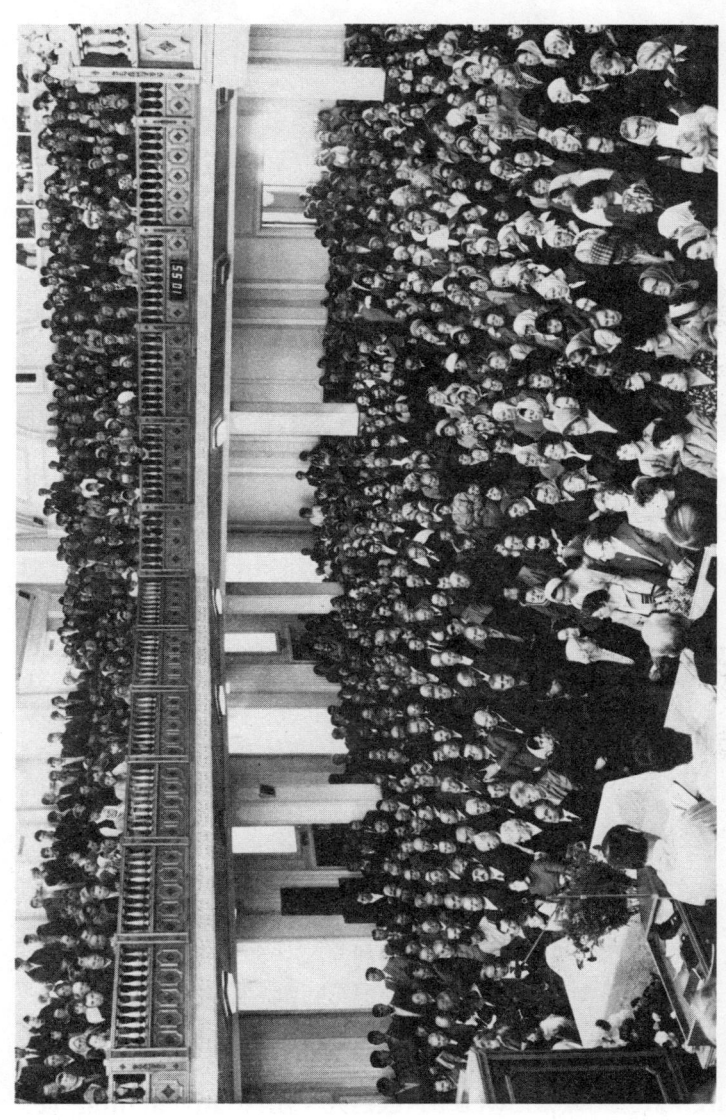

This Moldavian registered Baptist church is always full and regularly attracts many new inquirers.

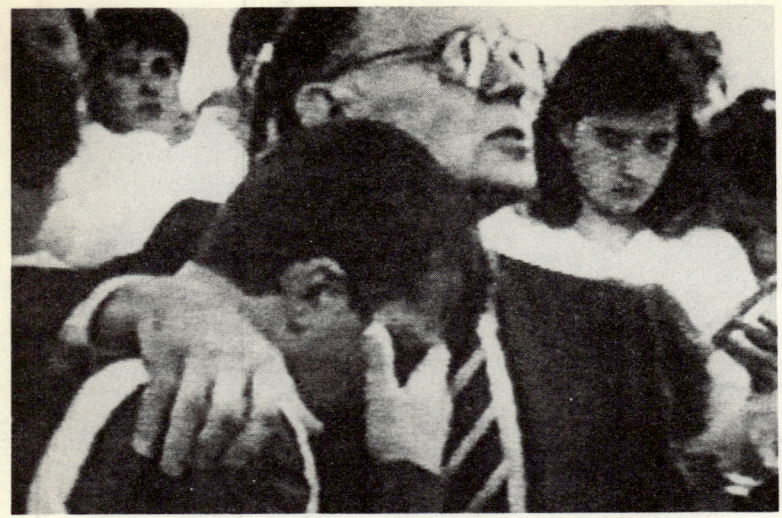

An evangelist counsels a young convert at a Soviet church service that attracted hundreds of young people.

Children are now allowed to receive Christian teaching, yet there are few trained children's workers and little material.

Water baptism of new converts publicly proclaiming their faith often draws hundreds of curious onlookers.

Evangelism Conference of October 16, 1988 in Riga, Latvia, U.S.S.R. resulted in 670 registered decisions for Christ.

Soviets Search for God

NEW VIDEO!

35 minutes of current video footage
from the Soviet Union.

See thousands of Soviets respond to
increased opportunities to hear the gospel!

Available for $15.00

U.S. currency only. Price subject to change. VHS.

---

*To order or for information on how you
or your church can be involved write:*

Mission Possible
P.O. Box 2014
Denton, Texas 76202
817-382-1508

Notes

Chapter 2

1. Mikhail Gorbachev, *Perestroika: New Thinking for Our Country and the World* (New York: Harper & Row, 1987), p. 150.
2. Mikhail Gorbachev, *Perestroika,* op. cit. as quoted in *Time,* January 4, 1988, p. 30.
3. Frederick Engels, *Manifesto of the Communist Party* (Moscow: Progress Publishers), p. 68.
4. Translated and reprinted from "Russkaya Mysl," *La Pensee Russe,* August 28, 1987, Paris, France.
5. Associated Press, *Tribune Review,* February 5, 1989.
6. *Christian Science Monitor,* June 16, 1987, p. 40.
7. Ibid., p. 1.
8. *Denton Record-Chronicle,* December 23, 1987, A-2.
9. *The World Book Encyclopedia* (Chicago: Field Enterprises Educational Corporation, 1974) Vol. 21, p. 411.
10. *Christian Science Monitor,* op. cit., p. 40.
11. Ibid.
12. *Christian Anti-Communism Crusade,* January 15, 1988, p. 6.
13. *Christian Science Monitor,* op. cit., p. 40.
14. *Denton Record-Chronicle,* op. cit., 2-A.
15. *Dallas Times Herald,* November 9, 1987, A-11.
16. *The Guardian,* November 18, 1987.
17. *Dallas Times Herald,* March 1, 1988, A-9.
18. *Dallas Times Herald,* November 9, 1987, A-11.
19. *The Guardian,* op. cit.

20. J. Edgar Hoover, *Masters of Deceit* (New York: Henry Holt & Co., 1958), p. 35.
21. *Dallas Times Herald,* March 9, 1989, A-3.

Chapter 3

1. *Dallas Times Herald,* July 18, 1988, A-11.
2. *Time,* January 4, 1988, p. 20.
3. Gorbachev, *Perestroika, op. cit.* as quoted in *Time,* op. cit., p. 21.
4. Ibid., p. 22.
5. *Dallas Times Herald,* January 24, 1988, A-4.
6. *Dallas Times Herald,* June 29, 1988, A-1.
7. *Denton Record-Chronicle,* June 23, 1988, A-2.
8. *Dallas Times Herald,* June 28, 1988, A-13.
9. *Dallas Times Herald,* January 24, 1988, A-4.
10. *Denton Record-Chronicle,* June 26, 1988, A-2.
11. *Denton Record-Chronicle,* July 29, 1988, A-2.
12. Ibid.
13. *Dallas Times Herald,* July 30, 1988, A-10.
14. *Dallas Times Herald,* July 3, 1988, A-12.
15. *Houston Post,* November 25, 1987, E-2.
16. *Wall Street Journal,* October 13, 1987, p. 30.
17. Ibid.
18. *Dallas Times Herald,* June 5, 1988, A-6.
19. *Dallas Times Herald,* September 29, 1988, A-1.
20. *Dallas Times Herald,* September 30, 1988, A-8.
21. *Dallas Times Herald,* October 3, 1988, A-1.
22. *Dallas Times Herald,* October 1, 1988, A-14.
23. Ibid., A-1.
24. *Denton Record Chronicle,* October 2, 1988, A-2.
25. *Dallas Times Herald,* October 2, 1988, A-1.
26. Ibid., A-22.
27. *Dallas Times Herald,* October 3, 1988, A-6.
28. *Dallas Times Herald,* October 2, 1988, A-22.
29. *Dallas Times Herald,* October 11, 1988, A-11.
30. *The Atlanta Journal and Constitution,* November 2, 1988, 1-A.

Chapter 4

1. *Dallas Times Herald,* December 14, 1987.
2. *Dallas Times Herald,* December 19, 1987, A-27.

3. *Dallas Times Herald,* December 13, 1987, A-31.
4. *Dallas Times Herald,* December 19, 1987, A-27.
5. Ibid.
6. *Dallas Times Herald,* December 7, 1987, A-9.
7. Ibid.
8. *Dallas Times Herald,* December 26, 1987, E-11.
9. Gorbachev, *Perestroika,* op. cit. as quoted in *Time,* op. cit., p. 25.
10. *Dallas Times Herald,* June 1, 1988, A-8.
11. *The New York Times,* reprinted in *Denton Record-Chronicle,* June 3, 1988, A-10.
12. *The Houston Post,* June 3, 1988, A-3.
13. *Dallas Times Herald,* May 22, 1988, A-19.
14. *Dallas Times Herald,* December 8, 1987, A-16.
15. *Denton Record-Chronicle,* May 29, 1988, A-10.
16. *Dallas Times Herald,* January 23, 1988, A-2.
17. *Denton Record-Chronicle,* June 21, 1988, A-6.
18. *Christian Awareness Ministries Newsletter,* Summer 1988, p. 1.
19. Mission Statements from the Soviet-American Citizens' Summit, p. 3, as quoted in *Christian Awareness Ministries Newsletter,* op. cit., p. 2.
20. Ibid.
21. *Dallas Times Herald,* July 24, 1988, A-20.
22. John A. Stormer, *None Dare Call It Treason* (Florissant, MO:Liberty Bell Press), p. 88.
23. *Denton Record-Chronicle,* February 28, 1989, A-9.
24. Marilyn Ferguson, *The Aquarian Conspiracy: Personal & Social Transformation in the 1980s* (Los Angeles, 1980), p. 23.
25. Gorbachev, *Perestroika,* op. cit., p. 30.
26. *Time,* January 4, 1988, p. 16.
27. Columnist Charles Krauthammer, *Dallas Times Herald,* December 9, 1988, A-21.
28. *Dallas Times Herald,* January 1, 1989, A-10.
29. Ibid., A-11.
30. *Dallas Times Herald,* June 5, 1988, A-7.

Chapter 5

1. *Dallas Times Herald,* October 15, 1988, A-3.
2. David Barrett, *World Christian Encyclopedia* (New York: Oxford University Press, 1982), p. 696.

3. Quoted in *World Press Review,* June 1988, p. 11.
4. *International Herald Tribune,* August 24, 1987, p. 1.
5. *Dallas Times Herald,* November 18, 1988, A-1.
6. *New York Times,* February 5, 1988, p. 26.
7. *International Herald Tribune,* July 4,5, 1987.
8. Ibid.
9. *Dallas Times Herald,* September 20, 1988, A-7.
10. *Dallas Times Herald,* March 22, 1988, A-14.
11. *Pulse,* January 24, 1988, p. 4.
12. *Light In The East Newsletter,* undated, on file with author.
13. *The Europa Yearbook 1987,* (London), Statistical Survey, U.S.S.R., 2755ff.
14. Associated Press, February 11, 1989.
15. *Time,* November 9, 1987, p. 74.
16. *National & International Religion Report,* January 18, 1988, p. 6.
17. "Soviets Give Jewish Emigration Tally." *Chicago Tribune,* July 10, 1987.
18. *Time,* December 14, 1987, p. 33.
19. *National & International Religion Report,* op. cit.
20. *Time,* November 9, 1987, p. 74.
21. *National & International Religion Report,* January 16, 1989, p. 6.
22. *Time,* November 9, 1987, p. 74.
23. "Refuseniks Given OK to Emigrate,"*Dallas Times Herald,* (article on file with author, undated).
24. *Dallas Times Herald,* December 26, 1987, A-23.
25. Associated Press, February 11, 1989.
26. Yaroslov Bilinsky, *The Second Soviet Republic: The Ukraine After World War II* (New Jersey: Rutgers University Press, 1964), p. 288.
27. Ayshe Seymiratova, "Mustafa Dzhemilev: Active Participant in the National Movement of the Crimean Tatars and the Human Rights Movement in the U.S.S.R.," as quoted in *A Brief History of the Crimean Tatars & Their Struggle For Civil Rights in the Soviet Union,* an unpublished thesis by Douglas Mann, on file with the author, April 24, 1987, p. 11.

Chapter 6

1. *Pulse,* October 9, 1987, p. 1.
2. The estimates of Aleksandr Solzhenitsyn, taken from *Eternity,* November 1987, p. 16.
3. David Barrett, *World Christian Encyclopedia* (New York: Oxford University Press, 1982) p. 695.
4. Ibid., p. 697.
5. *The Samizdat Bulletin,* September 1987, p. 12.
6. Barrett, p. 697.
7. Ibid., p. 694.
8. Ibid.
9. Ibid., p. 690.
10. Ibid.
11. *The Right To Believe,* (Issue 2/3 for 1987), p. 2.
12. *Keston News Service,* October 6, 1988.
13. Barrett, p. 697.
14. *Tulsa Tribune,* April 2, 1988, B-26.
15. Ibid.
16. *Radio Liberty Research,* December 3, 1987, p. 4.
17. *Tulsa Tribune,* op. cit.
18. *Keston News Service,* June 25, 1987.
19. *Breakthrough,* January/February, 1988, p. 2.
20. *Dallas Times Herald,* November 4, 1988, A-5.
21. *E P News Service,* January 29, 1988, p. 1.
22. *Moody,* December 1987, p. 80.
23. Ibid.
24. Ibid.
25. *Denton Record-Chronicle,* September 1, 1987, p. A-2.
26. *Open Doors News Service,* February 10, 1988, p. 4.
27. Ibid., p. 5
28. Ibid.
29. *E P News Service,* June 17, 1988, p. 4.

Chapter 7

1. *Book News,* December 15, 1987, p. 3,4.
2. *Dallas Times Herald,* November 14, 1987, F-11.
3. *Eternity,* March 1987, p. 16,17.
4. Ibid., p. 17.
5. Ibid.
6. Ibid.

7. *Keston News Service,* September 10, 1987, p. 21.
8. Ibid., p. 22.
9. *The Sacramento Bee,* April 16, 1988.
10. Ibid.
11. Ibid.
12. *Eternity,* op. cit., p. 18.
13. *Forerunner,* January-February 1988, p. 5.
14. Karl Marx and Friedrich Engels, *Historisch-kutisch Gesan-tausgabe, Werke, Schriften, Briefe,* (Complete historical critical edition: Works, Writings, Letters), on behalf of the Marx-EngelsInstitute, Moscow, published by David Rjazanov (Frankfurt-am-Main, 1927).
15. Vladimir Ilyich Lenin, in a personal letter to the Russian author, Gorki in 1913.
16. *New York Times,* August 23, 1987, Section 4, p. 1.
17. *Keston News Service,* June 25, 1987, p. 21.
18. *Newsweek,* June 22, 1987, p. 39.
19. *International Herald Tribune,* May 2, 1988, p. 2.
20. *Evangelical Missions Quarterly,* July 1988.
21. *Idea,* Information Service of the German Evangelical Alliance, June 5, 1987, p. 11.
22. *International Russian Radio Letter,* undated, on file with author.
23. *Evangelical Missions Quarterly,* July 1988, p. 252.
24. *National & International Religion Report,* August 15, 1988, p. 4.
25. Confidential resource documents on file with the author.
26. *Keston News Service,* March 31, 1988, p. 9.
27. *CSCE Digest,* May 1987, p. 8.
28. *The Right To Believe,* (Issue 2/3 for 1987), p. 1.
29. *Moody,* December 1987, p. 80.
30. *Christianity Today,* December 13, 1986, p. 30.
31. *Christianity Today,* June 12, 1987.
32. *Christianity Today,* December 13, 1986, p. 29.
33. *Christianity Today,* December 13, 1986.

Chapter 8

1. *U.S.News & World Report,* September 26, 1988, p. 10.
2. *Dallas Times Herald,* January 30, 1988, A-13.
3. *Dallas Times Herald,* September 24, 1987, A-19.
4. Ibid.
5. *Time,* September 7, 1987, p. 54.

6. *International Herald Tribune,* September 9, 1987, p. 27.
7. Ibid.
8. *Dallas Times Herald,* August 17, 1988, A-24.
9. *Dallas Times Herald,* August 17, 1988, A-24.
10. Ibid.
11. *International Herald Tribune,* August 18, 1987, p. 1.
12. *International Herald Tribune,* September 15, 1987.
13. *Dallas Times Herald,* October 27, 1988, A-12.
14. *Dallas Times Herald,* November 27, 1988, A-11.
15. *Keston: The Right to Believe,* (Keston College, England, 1987), Issue 213, p. 1.
16. *Dallas Times Herald,* February 11, 1988, A-10.
17. *New York Times,* October 27, 1987, p. 5.
18. Ibid.

Chapter 9

1. *Time,* January 4, 1988, p. 16.
2. Gorbachev, *Perestroika,* op. cit., p. 10.
3. Gorbachev, op. cit., p. 17.
4. Conference paper presented at Sakharov Conference, 1985, London, England, notes on file with author.
5. Gorbachev, *Perestroika,* op. cit., p. 24.
6. *International Herald Tribune,* August 17, 1987, p. 42.
7. *Denton Record-Chronicle,* January 22, 1988, A-2.
8. *Dallas Times Herald,* October 13, 1988, A-1.
9. *Dallas Times Herald,* October 17, 1987, F-1.
10. Ibid.
11. Ibid.
12. *Perspective,* March 1988, Pat Robertson.
13. Hedrick Smith, *The Russians* (Ballantine Books, 1976) quoted in Ralph Mann, *Red November* (Orange, CA: Promise Publishing Company, 1988), p. 55.
14. Smith, quoted in Mann, p. 55,56.
15. *Houston Chronicle,* January 17, 1988, Section 1, p. 24.
16. *Dallas Times Herald,* January 30, 1988, A-13.

Chapter 10

1. Dave Hunt, *Peace, Prosperity, and the Coming Holocaust* (Eugene, OR: Harvest House, 1983) p. 227,228.
2. *Time,* June 6, 1988, p. 29.

3. *The Guardian,* reprinted in *World Press Review* October 1987, p. 26.
4. *U.S.News & World Report,* December 14, 1987, p. 10.
5. *The Soviet Observer,* January 15, 1988, p. 1 quoting Soviet weekly *Ogonek,* No. 41, 1987.
6. Ibid., p. 2.
7. Ibid., p. 3.
8. Conference paper presented at Sakharov Conference, 1985, London, England. Notes on file with author.
9. *The Guardian,* op. cit. p. 25.
10. Sakharov Conference, op. cit.
11. *The New York Times,* December 26, 1987, p. 4.
12. Associated Press, January 1989.
13. *Time,* June 6, 1988, p. 37.
14. Associated Press, January 1989.
15. *The Guardian,* op. cit. p. 25.
16. Ibid.
17. Ibid.
18. *The Guardian,* op. cit., p. 24.
19. *Time,* January 4, 1988, p. 29.
20. *U.S.News & World Report,* February 22, 1988, p. 59.
21. Ibid.
22. *Dallas Times Herald,* February 8, 1988, A-16.
23. Agency for International Development, Office of U.S. Foreign Disaster Assistance, Situation Report No. 15, December 30, 1988.
24. *Dallas Times Herald,* February 16, 1989, A-12.
25. *New York Times,* December 25, 1987, p. 1.
26. Ibid.
27. Ibid.
28. *Dallas Times Herald,* February 14, 1988, A-12.

Chapter 11

1. *Denton Record-Chronicle,* June 8, 1988, A-8.
2. *Christian Science Monitor,* June 30, 1987, p. 11.
3. *New York Times Sunday Magazine,* July 19, 1987, p. 28.
4. *International Herald Tribune,* July 4-5, 1987.
5. *Dallas Times Herald,* May 11, 1988, A-9.
6. *Dallas Times Herald,* January 24, 1988, A-4.
7. *Denton Record-Chronicle,* November 15, 1987, A-17.
8. *Denton Record-Chronicle,* May 1, 1988, A-4.
9. *U.S.News & World Report,* December 14, 1987, p. 57.

10. *Orlando Sentinel,* September 11, 1988, p. 20.
11. *Wall Street Journal,* May 19, 1987, p. 52.
12. *Wall Street Journal,* December 7, 1987, p. 22.
13. *International Herald Tribune,* April 22, 1988, p. 42.
14. *New York Times,* October 15, 1987, p. 27.
15. *New York Times,* December 3, 1987, p. 1.
16. *Wall Street Journal,* December 7, 1987, op. cit.
17. Ibid.
18. *New York Times,* October 15, 1987, op. cit.
19. *Wall Street Journal,* January 15, 1988, p. 18.
20. *Dallas Times Herald,* May 10, 1988, A-4.
21. *U.S. News & World Report,* December 19, 1988, p. 20.
22. *New York Times,* February 1, 1988, p. 30.
23. *New York Times,* January 21, 1988, p. 27.

Chapter 12

1. *Dallas Times Herald,* January 24, 1988, A-4.
2. *International Herald Tribune,* August 10, 1987.
3. Ibid.
4. *Denton Record-Chronicle,* December 8, 1988, A-17.
5. *Business Week,* December 7, 1987, p. 88.
6. *Wall Street Journal,* July 17, 1987, p. 1.
7. Ibid.
8. Ibid.
9. *The Soviet Observer,* January 1-15, 1988, p. 7.
10. *U.S. News & World Report,* April 4, 1988, p. 53.
11. *Chicago Tribune,* September 18, 1986, Section 1, p. 14.
12. *Radio Liberty Research,* March 27, 1987, p. 87.
13. *Chicago Tribune,* op. cit.
14. *International Herald Tribune,* April 26, 1988, p. 15.
15. *Chicago Tribune,* op. cit.
16. Ibid.
17. *New York Times,* October 28, 1987, p. 6.
18. *New York Times,* February 16, 1988, p. 20.
19. *International Herald Tribune,* September 10, 1987.
20. *Christian Science Monitor,* April 7, 1987, p. 40.
21. Ibid.
22. *New York Times,* December 14, 1987, p. 32.
23. *New York Times,* November 29, 1987.
24. James Finnerty, *Surrendering America—A Decade of Unilateral Disarmament* (Great Barrington, MA: American Institute for Economic Research, 1978), p. 22.

Chapter 13

1. *Chicago Tribune,* September 18, 1986, Section 1, p. 14.
2. *Dallas Times Herald,* October 10, 1988, A-12.
3. *International Herald Tribune,* September 3, 1987.
4. *Denton Record-Chronicle,* January 27, 1988, A-8.
5. Ibid.
6. *Dallas Times Herald,* December 12, 1987, A-27.
7. Personal notes of author from interviews with resident Europeans.
8. "Exiles Are Flocking to West Germany," *Insight,* November 14, 1988, p. 41.
9. Gorbachev, *Perestroika,* op. cit., p. 191.
10. *Denton Record-Chronicle,* October 12, 1988, A-2.
11. *Europeo Magazine,* July/August 1988, p. 38.
12. Ibid.
13. Ibid., p. 39.
14. *Christian Science Monitor,* September 11, 1987, p. 10.
15. Ibid.
16. *Dallas Times Herald,* May 17, 1988, A-13.

Chapter 14

1. *Dallas Times Herald,* April 14, 1988, A-27.
2. *International Herald Tribune,* May 2, 1988, p. 4.
3. Ibid.
4. *International Herald Tribune,* April 23, 1988, p. 9.
5. Ibid., p. 13.
6. *Le Monde,* quoted in *World Press Review,* August 1988, p. 42.
7. *Dallas Times Herald,* May 19, 1988, A-7.
8. *Dallas Times Herald,* October 6, 1988, A-1.
9. "Iranian-Soviet Ties to Expand Remarkably," *Insight,* January 16, 1989, p. 30.
10. *Europeo Magazine,* reprinted in *World Press Review,* January 1988, p. 51.
11. *Klassekampen,* reprinted in *World Press Review,* January 1988, p. 52.
12. *Dallas Times Herald,* July 26, 1988, C-1.
13. *Dallas Times Herald,* March 5, 1989, 1-19.
14. *Europeo Magazine,* op. cit.
15. *Dallas Times Herald,* January 21, 1988, C-2.
16. *Dallas Times Herald,* January 29, 1988, C-2.

17. *Dallas Times Herald*, January 21, 1988, A-16.
18. *Dallas Times Herald*, December 11, 1987, C-1.
19. *Dallas Times Herald*, December 13, 1987, J-5.
20. *New York Times*, November 13, 1987, p. 30.

Chapter 15

1. Gorbachev, *Perestroika*, op. cit., p. 254.
2. Etsu Kuwata, "What Will The Removal of INS Bring On The West European Strategy By Means of Conventional Weapons?" Translated from *Japan Military Review*, February 1988.
3. *Dallas Times Herald*, February 28, 1988, K-1.
4. *U.S.News & World Report*, January 25, 1988, p. 45.
5. Etsu Kuwata, op. cit.
6. *U.S.News & World Report*, March 7, 1988, p. 42.
7. *Dallas Times Herald*, January 19, 1989, A-5.
8. *The Guardian of London*, reprinted in *World Press Review*, December 1988, p. 22.
9. *Time*, December 14, 1987, p. 20.
10. Ibid., p. 21.
11. Ibid.
12. *Dallas Times Herald*, April 30, 1988, A-9.
13. *Dallas Times Herald*, December 15, 1987, A-11.
14. *International Herald Tribune*, May 2, 1988, p. 6.
15. *Denton Record-Chronicle*, January 12, 1988, A-11.
16. *Dallas Times Herald*, October 2, 1988, A-5.
17. *U.S. News & World Report*, January 16, 1989, p. 19.
18. Ibid.

Chapter 16

1. *U.S.News & World Report*, January 23, 1989, p. 24.
2. *Dallas Times Herald*, February 28, 1988, K-1.
3. Ibid.
4. *U.S.News & World Report*, December 14, 1987, p. 31.
5. *Dallas Times Herald*, January 19, 1988, A-9.
6. *World Press Review*, January 1988, p. 40.
7. *Denton Record-Chronicle*, May 17, 1988, A-11.
8. *Dallas Times Herald*, January 21, 1989, A-12.
9. *Denton Record-Chronicle*, March 6, 1989, A-10.

Chapter 17

1. *Dallas Times Herald,* December 16, 1987, A-27.
2. *Dallas Times Herald,* March 10, 1989, A-5.
3. *International Herald Tribune,* April 22, 1988.
4. *U.S.News & World Report,* May 9, 1988, p. 31.
5. Ibid.
6. *Dallas Times Herald,* April 28, 1988, A-3.
7. Thomas E. Beardon, ''Soviet Phase Conjugate Weapons,'' *Committee To Restore The Constitution Bulletin,* January 1988.
8. *Boston Globe,* February 11, 1975, p. 1.
9. Beardon, op. cit.
10. Letters to the author on file.
11. Beardon, op. cit.
12. *Dallas Times Herald,* July 23, 1988, A-6.
13. Beardon, op. cit.
14. Ibid.
15. Ibid.
16. Ibid.
17. *Aviation Week & Space Technology,* February 29, 1988, p. 55.
18. Beardon, op. cit.

Chapter 18

1. *Dallas Times Herald,* April 30, 1988, A-1.
2. *Dallas Times Herald,* September 13, 1988, A-8.
3. *International Herald Tribune,* November 2, 1986, p. 8.
4. *U.S. News & World Report,* January 23, 1989, p. 12.
5. Gorbachev, *Perestroika,* p. 155.
6. Ibid., p. 157.
7. *The New York Times Magazine,* September 7, 1986, p. 26.
8. Ibid.
9. *Dallas Times Herald,* January 19, 1988.
10. *The New York Times Magazine,* September 7, 1986, p. 105.
11. *Denton Record-Chronicle,* February 11, 1988, A-9.
12. *Wall Street Journal,* European Edition, May 2, 1988, p. 22.
13. Ibid.
14. *Dallas Times Herald,* March 17, 1988, A-7.

15. *U.S.News & World Report,* January 25, 1988, p. 47.
16. Timothy Ashby, *The Bear In The Back Yard* (Lexington, MA: D.C. Heath & Company, 1987), p. 72.
17. *Dallas Times Herald,* July 30, 1988, A-10.
18. Ashby, p. 77.
19. Ibid., p. 76.
20. Anatoly A. Gromyko and A. Kokoshin, "U.S. Foreign Strategy for the 1970s," *International Affairs,* October 1973, p. 71.
21. *Dallas Times Herald,* February 28, 1989, A-5.

Chapter 19

1. Quoted in Mission Possible letter dated April 1980, p. 1.
2. *Dallas Times Herald,* December 26, 1987, A-18.
3. Ibid.
4. *U.S.News & World Report,* April 4, 1988, p. 42.
5. *L'Express* as reprinted in *World Press Review,* March 1989, p. 17.
6. *Dallas Times Herald,* January 30, 1988, A-19.
7. *Dallas Times Herald,* July 14, 1988, A-9.
8. *Dallas Times Herald,* July 22, 1988, A-13.
9. *World Press Review,* April 1988, p. 28.
10. Ibid.
11. *Houston Post,* November 24, 1979.
12. Dave Hunt, *Peace, Prosperity and the Coming Holocaust,* op. cit., p. 227-228.
13. Quoted in *NAE Action,* May, 1972.
14. An estimate of Aleksandr Solzhenitsyn, quoted in *Eternity,* November 1987, p. 16.
15. *Keston News Service,* July 7, 1988, p. 7.
16. Ibid., p. 8.
17. Ibid., p. 7.
18. Hunt, p. 227-228.
19. *Dallas Times Herald,* June 26, 1988, A-27.
20. *Dallas Times Herald,* February 24, 1989, A-5.

Chapter 20

1. Floyd Hamilton, *The Basis of Christian Faith* (New York: Harper and Row, 1964), p. 160.

2. Thomas Scott, Rector of Aston Sandford, *The Holy Bible with Explanatory Notes, Practical Observations, and Copious Marginal References* (London, 1828), explanation of Ezekiel 38.
3. *Christ for the Nations,* February 1980, p. 3.
4. Thomas Scott, op. cit.
5. Ibid.
6. Grant McClung, Jr., Editor, *Azusa Street and Beyond* (South Plainfield, NJ: Bridge Publications, 1986), p. 98.
7. Statement to Constitutional Convention, 1787, New York City, New York.
8. Personal letter to Moses Robinson, March 23, 1801.
9. Farewell address of George Washington, September 17, 1796, New York City, New York.

Chapter 21

1. Dave Hunt, *Peace, Prosperity, and the Coming Holocaust* (Eugene, OR: Harvest House, 1983), p. 157.
2. Ibid., p. 166.

Chapter 22

1. Ralph Mann, *Red November* (Orange, CA: Promise Publishing Company, 1988), p. 96.
2. *Paix et Liberte,* quoted in Mann, p. 173.
3. Mann, p. 169.
4. Ibid., p. 170.
5. Ibid.
6. Ibid.
7. Ibid., p. 170,171.
8. Ibid., p. 63,64.

Chapter 23

1. Ralph Mann, *Red November* (Orange, CA: Promise Publishing Company, 1988), p. 37,38.
2. Ibid., p. 36.
3. Ibid.

To contact Ralph Mann
or to purchase a copy of his first book, *Red November,*
write or call:

Mission Possible
P.O. Box 2014
Denton, Texas 76202
817-382-1508